The
Elements
of Choice

The
Elements
of Choice

Why the Way We Decide Matters

Eric J. Johnson

RIVERHEAD BOOKS   NEW YORK   2021

RIVERHEAD BOOKS
An imprint of Penguin Random House LLC
penguinrandomhouse.com

Copyright © 2021 by Eric J. Johnson

Library of Congress Cataloging-in-Publication Data

Names: Johnson, Eric J., author.
Title: The elements of choice:
why the way we decide matters / Eric J. Johnson.
Description: New York : Riverhead Books, an imprint
of Penguin Random House LLC, 2021. |
Includes bibliographical references and index.
Identifiers: LCCN 2021015312 (print) | LCCN 2021015313 (ebook) |
ISBN 9780593084434 (hardcover) | ISBN 9780593084458 (ebook)
Subjects: LCSH: Decision making.
Classification: LCC BF448 .J638 2021 (print) |
LCC BF448 (ebook) | DDC 153.8/3–dc23
LC record available at https://lccn.loc.gov/2021015312
LC ebook record available at https://lccn.loc.gov/2021015313

International edition ISBN: 9780593421215

Printed in the United States of America
ScoutAutomatedPrintCode

Book design by Alexis Farabaugh

To Elke Weber, my family,
and all designers, now and in the future

Contents

The
Elements
of Choice

Shaping Choices

It is an illusion, really, that we alone determine what we choose. You walk into a restaurant and order a sandwich. Your spouse asks you what movie you want to see. Your doctor asks if you want to try a new drug to control your cholesterol. You search for a flight home for the holidays. You select an investment fund from your employer's retirement plan. You may not realize it, but in each choice, you have a hidden partner.

You choose something, but the restaurant, your spouse, the doctor, the airline's website, and your employer have all made decisions about how to pose those choices to you. *Their* design decisions will influence, intentionally or not, what you choose. The restaurant organized the sandwich options you saw, maybe with vegetarian on the right, meat on the left. Your spouse suggested some possible movies, but left others out. The doctor decided how to describe the consequences, side effects, and benefits of the drugs you could take to control your cholesterol. The website decided how to sort the flights and whether to present certain pieces of information, like the on-time performance of the flights and the baggage fees. And finally, your employer had a fund it would use for your retirement account if you did not make a choice.

We might vaguely agree that external factors influence our choices, but we don't appreciate that there are large and systematic ways in which presentation can change what we choose. Years of research have shown again and again that the way choices are posed affects our actions. We're much more likely to choose a retirement fund if the employer's website preselects that option for us. We make different choices if our doctor says that serious side effects occur in 1 percent of cases, as opposed to saying there are no side effects in 99 percent of cases. And while you might be convinced that you are picking the sandwich, many things about the menu, like the order of items and the headings of the categories, helped you make that choice.

All these details are part of something called *choice architecture,* the many aspects of how a choice is posed that can be manipulated, intentionally or inadvertently, to influence the decisions we make. The options may be the same, but the presentation can change your choice.

Before you make a decision, someone has molded many of the characteristics of that choice for you, and these design decisions will in some way affect what you choose. This book takes a close look at exactly how the way choices are presented can change the decision-making process. Whether they realize it or not, the people who present those choices—the restaurant owner, your spouse, your doctor, your employer— are *choice architects*. Stated more simply, choice architects are the designers of the decisions you make, just as you are the designer of countless choices for others and for yourself. To keep things simple, I will call the choice architects *designers* and the people making decisions *choosers*.

Choice architecture can be harnessed in surprising and surprisingly powerful ways, with positive results for both the designer and the chooser. But to do so, we must look closely at every detail of a choice's design, including elements we don't normally notice. After all, when we encounter a choice, we are too busy making the choice to contemplate how the presentation of options affects us. But get those details right, and better decisions can emerge.

I became interested in decision-making and decision design as I contemplated college. Coming from a working-class, Levittown-like suburb in New Jersey, it struck me that many of my friends from high school were considering very different options for their lives. In my high school, there were many academically talented students, but some were delighted to go to the local community college, and others, equally qualified, were applying to Ivy League schools. What made them consider different options? I saw, in the years that followed, that the choice of what to consider in large part determined their future.

Being lucky (and foolish) enough to talk my way into places where pathbreaking work in decision-making was done, I found myself in graduate school at Carnegie Mellon, and a postdoc at Stanford, places central to the beginning of a revolution in decision research and behavioral economics. This revolution was based on the idea that people use simplified rules of thumb, or heuristics, to make decisions. The classic demonstration involved people making inconsistent choices, caused by things that should not matter. Describing the same options as gains or losses can change choices. Telling people about irrelevant numbers can change how much they are willing to pay. People are much more willing to pay for insurance against a vivid risk, like cancer, than they are willing to pay for insurance that covers all diseases. There was soon a list of these effects, which was sometimes called "stupid human tricks," after David Letterman's comedy bits.

These results were usually cast as showing how people are irrational and generally bad at making decisions. I had always been interested in public policy and improving decisions, and I realized that we could flip that framing for positive ends: instead of exposing people as bad decision-makers by showing they were inconsistent, maybe we could make them better decision-makers by exploiting these inconsistencies. By changing how their choices were posed, we might help them make better decisions.

About this time, I was at the Wharton School of the University of Pennsylvania, organizing a team studying insurance decisions. We noticed that Pennsylvania and New Jersey were about to introduce new, less expensive types of auto insurance. Each state required insurance firms to use a different choice architecture to present the auto insurance choices. We predicted, correctly, that because of the way the choices were presented, the new policy would be more popular in New Jersey than in Pennsylvania. We wrote the governors and insurance commissioners of both states and even wrote an op-ed in a Philadelphia newspaper. Everyone ignored us, but the impact of the choice architecture was massive. The new policy was three times more popular in New Jersey. Because of their choices, Pennsylvanians paid billions of dollars more for auto insurance. Years later, my friend Dan Goldstein and I used the same idea to show that choice architecture made a big difference in whether people agreed to be organ donors.

A few years after that, I was working with a German auto manufacturer, consulting on the choice architecture of its website. On the site, people could pick engines, interiors, colors, and many other options when buying a car. But the automaker was presenting those options to buyers in a way that was detrimental to everyone involved: the automaker was losing potential revenue by guiding buyers to the cheaper options, and those options didn't really meet the buyers' needs or desires. With a few simple changes, we were able to increase the company's profit and improve customers' satisfaction with the vehicles they ultimately purchased.

More recently, I was a senior visiting scholar at the newly formed Consumer Financial Protection Bureau, consulting on many issues related to choice architecture. How do you write disclosures for loans and mortgages? How can you display information about a complex product, such as a prepaid credit card that has many different fees, given that the card has to fit in a wallet? How can you encourage people to comparison shop? And my favorite: How can you make sure people know what they're signing up for with overdraft protection, a banking service that pays your bill when you overdraw from your checking account? The bank will often charge something like $35 for each overdraft. Some people want this coverage, but others are incensed when a cup of coffee ends up costing $38 because of an overdraft. How can you make sure that everyone who has the product has made a good and informed decision?

Choice architecture is not just about how websites are designed or how policies are implemented. It is not just about professionals and researchers. We are all designers every day, posing choices to our friends, colleagues, and families. My friend is also a decision designer when, instead of asking his three-year-old whether she is ready to go to bed, he asks if she prefers to fly into bed or bounce into bed. He reported that bedtime became much less stressful for everyone involved when he started presenting options instead of a yes-or-no choice.

Choice architecture has a lot in common with actual architecture. Winston Churchill knew this, saying, "We shape our buildings and afterwards our buildings shape us." He was talking about the British House of Commons, which had recently been destroyed by German incendiary bombs during the last raids of the Blitz.

The building had been an oblong rectangle, modeled on the design of St. Stephen's Chapel, the site where the House of Commons previously met. Members were seated on opposing sides of the chamber. Some members of Parliament favored switching to a semicircular arrangement, like the amphitheaters used in both the U.S. Senate and House of Representatives. Others pointed out that the old chambers didn't actually have enough seats for everyone.

Churchill, Britain's prime minister at the time, would have none of it. In one of his better speeches, he argued to preserve "all the essential features of the old building." While politically conservative, he was not being sentimental or a traditionalist. He believed strongly that the shape of the building influenced its inhabitants, and that the nature of political discourse depended on two essential features of the old Commons.

The first was the oblong design, dividing the Commons into two halves, one for the ruling party, the other for the opposition, with the two parties directly opposite each other. Churchill argued that this was essential to the two-party system that dominated British politics. Looking directly at the opposition facilitated debate, concentrated attention on the other side, and took away attention from any shifting alliances within one's own party. Your side viewed the common enemy. The distance between the two halves was, by tradition, two sword-lengths apart. Churchill compared this to a semicircle where the speaker is at the front, addressing the entire chamber, looking as much at their supporters as at the opposition.

The second was the size of the building, which was too small to hold all 650 members of the House of Commons. This facilitated a conversational style of debate, and a packed house gave the proceedings a sense of importance and urgency.

Churchill prevailed, and anyone can witness the impact of

architecture by watching Prime Minister's Questions a famously confrontational affair that occurs every Wednesday at noon when Parliament is in session. The questions, often thinly disguised attacks, are posed to the prime minister and supported by quips and guffaws from the opposition. It is quintessential politics as theater.[1]

Just as the Commons' oblong shape focuses attention on the opposition and causes members to think about their reactions and comebacks, choice architecture focuses our attention and thought on particular options while neglecting others. Physical architecture and choice architecture are always present and always have an influence, even when we are unaware of them. While a building may lack an architect, it does have windows and doors. Someone decided the placement of the doors, and that determines where we enter and exit. Similarly, intentionally or not, choice architects present choices that will make a difference in what information we examine and what we ignore. Not knowing about choice architecture can result in designs that steer choosers in ways neither we nor they imagine.

D octors are busy decision-makers. In the examination room they complete, on average, ten different tasks per hour, including taking a patient's history, discussing symptoms, and performing a physical exam. But doctors have a new companion: an electronic health record system (EHR). Every encounter with a patient involves using the system to record facts like a patient's blood pressure, diagnoses, and treatment decisions. When researchers look at how doctors spend their time, they see that the EHR is the second most important thing in the room. Half a doctor's time is spent communicating with and examining the patient, but a whopping 37 percent is spent working with the EHR. The old physician's prescription pad and pen have been replaced by a screen, keyboard, and mouse. This may improve record keeping, but an EHR is a choice architecture that can affect how doctors treat their patients.

Generic medicines are chemically equivalent to brand-name medicines but much less expensive. A brand-name drug, such as the antihistamine Allegra, can cost five times more than its generic equivalent, fexofenadine hydrochloride. Generics are not just cheaper but can also result in healthier patients. When medicines cost less, patients take them more faithfully precisely because they are more affordable.

Hospitals have tried many ways to encourage doctors to prescribe generics, barraging them with emails, holding seminars, and making other interventions that prove equally ineffective. EHRs often have pop-ups encouraging doctors to prescribe generics. They are quickly dismissed and ignored. The overuse of pop-ups results in doctors quickly dismissing all alerts without reading them, something called *alert fatigue*. One study even tried paying physicians to prescribe generics, but that too failed. Changing physician behavior is so hard that some states simply allow pharmacists to substitute generics for the brand-name drugs doctors prescribe.[2]

Paying doctors to prescribe generics does not work because it addresses the wrong problem. A simple change in the interface, developed by researchers at the Weill Cornell Medical College, has proven much more effective. It is based on how physicians remember drugs. Doctors simply have an easier time recalling brand-name medicines. After all, *Allegra* comes to mind much more readily than *fexofenadine hydrochloride*. Brand-name drugs are also heavily advertised. When pharmaceutical companies give doctors free samples as well as notepads and pens with the drug's name on them, it cements that name in their minds.

This leads busy physicians to get into a habit. When they need to prescribe an antihistamine, they start typing "All" into the EHR and the system helpfully auto-completes the field with "Allegra." The designers thought they were aiding the doctors with this function, and these keystrokes become habitual.

The Weill Cornell team changed the interface so that the EHR automatically substituted the name of the generic drug when a doctor started typing the name of the brand. For example, when someone typed "All" the system would immediately offer "fexofenadine hydrochloride." Doctors could go back to the brand-name drug by checking a box that said "Dispense as written." But they seldom did. Doctors left the generic option in place almost all of the time. The EHR substituted its perfect knowledge of the generic equivalent for the doctors' imperfect or nonexistent recall.[3]

This more than doubled the proportion of prescriptions for generics, and since generics are, on average, 80 percent less expensive than brand-name drugs, this produced large cost savings both for the hospital and patients.

How exactly did the EHR change the doctors' choices? Doctors, like all choosers, are sensitive to the amount of effort required to make a choice. Small changes, like auto-correcting the name of the brand-name drug to the generic, affect their decisions. They could easily have prescribed the brand-name drug, like before, but having to make a single mouse click changed what they did. They chose the most *plausible path*, a way of navigating the information in front of them. A chooser's plausible path will determine what information they look at and what they ignore. And like all choosers, doctors depend on their memory. They don't always remember everything they might about options; instead, they use *assembled preferences* based on the subset of things they recall. For the doctors, it was easier to remember the brand name, but harder, if not impossible, to remember the generic. Changing what people call to mind most easily is another important way that designers can change choice.

The term *choice architecture* was coined by my friends Richard Thaler and Cass Sunstein in their book *Nudge*. The field has had that name for only a little over a decade, but the idea of choice architecture has been around for a while. In earliest antiquity, traders must have made deliberate decisions about how to present their goods at the market and tweaked them based on trial and error. What did they put at the front of their blankets? Did they arrange goods from best to worst, or from most expensive to cheapest? In the last thirty or so years, academics have become obsessed with demonstrating that changing the presentation of options affects choice, in part because these demonstrations are so inconsistent with traditional economics.

The New York City Taxi and Limousine Commission un-intentionally demonstrated this when they accidentally ran a choice-architecture experiment. The commission was trying to modernize the famous yellow cab fleet in the city, adding a video screen, GPS, and credit-card readers to existing cabs. The two companies who did the work each chose a different way of showing riders how they could tip. One gave the choices of 15, 20, and 25 percent; the other gave the choices of 20, 25, and 30 percent. With either credit-card reader, the rider could press an "Other" button and enter any amount they wanted. In standard economics, people should simply type in the amount that they want to tip, independent of the categories provided; but here the different set of choices resulted in different tipping. People were about six times more likely to tip 15 percent when that was an option. Overall, cabbies made 5 percent more when they drove cabs with the higher tip suggestions. An accidental change in the choice architecture made cabbies better off.[4]

This book goes well beyond the simple idea that defaults and other choice-architecture tools can nudge people into desired behaviors. It's much more important to understand *how* choice architecture changes choices. By understanding the reasons that defaults changed the tipping habits of cab riders, you can use choice architecture more effectively and responsibly. You'll understand when it will work well, and when it might backfire.

I should also mention another revolution that's taken place in the behavioral sciences over the last ten years. A number of notable failures to replicate famous studies have brought intense focus to the importance of reproducibility. A finding from one study doesn't mean much until other scientists are able to show the same results. While I will sometimes talk about one particular study, for the most part I will be using individual findings to summarize a larger body of research. Meta-analysis has become a key tool for drawing significant results from a large number of studies, and we'll examine this method in detail in chapter 5. Understanding the significance of individual studies and the ways that scientists can assess large bodies of research can make you a better consumer of what you read, here and elsewhere.

D efaults may be the best-known element of choice architecture, but they have plenty of company in the decision-design tool kit. To illustrate this, imagine you have a new job, where you have been asked to lead a team constructing a new website that allows people to choose health insurance plans.

Picture yourself standing in front of an expansive whiteboard, drawing a picture of what the first screen of the website might look like. In the language of web design, this mock-up is called a *wireframe*. It is a first step in website design.

You, the designer, ponder the questions that face you and your team:

- How many insurance plans should you present on the webpage?[5]

- If you present only some plans, how do you select the ones to present?

- How do you order the plans? Alphabetically? If you do this, does it give the alphabetically early plans an unfair advantage?

- How do you describe the plans? Even saying how much they cost is complicated. There are monthly premiums, copayments, and deductibles. You are not even sure people understand these terms.

You step back and look at what you and your team have written on the whiteboard. You get the uneasy feeling that your selections will affect what insurance people will choose, but you aren't sure how.

You can see that the designer's job is daunting. A health care website is not a random example, of course. Starting in October 2013, 8 million Americans chose health insurance for the first time as part of the Patient Protection and Affordable Care Act, also known as Obamacare. Ignore, if you can, the fact that the rollout was a technological disaster or that the topic remains politically fraught. I led a team that did research looking at what, for me, was the real challenge: presenting policies to people in a way that would let them buy insurance that met their needs at the best possible price. We met with officials at the Department of Health and Human Services, leaders of different state exchanges, and insurers. To say they were initially skeptical of choice architecture would be generous, but as you will see later in the book, our work did have an effect.

A designer has to select what I will call *choice-architecture tools,* or *tools* for short. For health exchanges, one tool is selecting the right number of options. A second is deciding what will be the default option if people don't make a choice. These tools will probably influence each other: having more options might make choosing the default more attractive.

There are other tools. The designer will need to decide what attributes to present, and how to present them. Prices may be obvious, but other attributes less so. Do we use numbers, letter grades, or stars when we talk about patient satisfaction? How do we describe the size of the network of doctors?

Finally, since this is a website, we can use the interactive nature of the web to customize the tools, to do calculations, and even to help people better comprehend health insurance. I call these potentially powerful interactive environments *choice engines.* Just as a search engine helps you find information, a choice engine helps you make a choice.

I've talked about designers mistakenly selecting tools that might lead to bad decisions, as with the German automaker's website and the EHR's auto-complete function for brand-name drugs. But not all bad choice architecture happens by accident. Designers often have their own best interests, and not those of the chooser, front and center. There are many ways that a designer can behave maliciously. They might pick defaults that increase their profit without meeting the customer's needs, or they may use order to increase the consumption of food that is lower cost to produce but less healthy for the chooser.

When Apple introduced a new version of its operating system for the iPhone, iOS 6, in September 2012, it included a new technology for tracking users, the "advertising identifier." The tracker, according to Apple, was "a non-permanent, non-personal, device identifier, that advertising networks will use to give you more control over advertisers' ability to use tracking methods. If you choose to limit ad tracking, advertising networks using the advertising identifier may no longer gather information to serve you targeted ads."[6]

That sounds fair enough, if you can understand it. You have the choice to not have your online behavior tracked by advertisers. But, as the British cognitive scientist Harry Brignull points out, it is not that easy to exercise that choice.

First, the default setting—what happens if you don't make an active choice—was for tracking to be on. Is that what most people wanted? If you didn't, you were in for a game of click and seek to change the setting. You might have started looking under "Privacy," but it wasn't there. Instead, you had to select the unhelpfully labeled menu "General," then the equally vague "About." If you scrolled down to the sixth item on that submenu, you would find another menu, "Advertising." Under that, you finally found the right place and a switch labeled "Limit ad tracking," set to "Off." But does that mean that limiting ad tracking is on or off? Remembering that double negatives mean a positive, you'd ideally realize that "Off" in this case meant ad tracking was on. Apple eventually moved the setting to where you might expect it, under "Privacy," but the confusing wording remains.

Does this choice architecture mislead or confuse people? About 30 percent of those respondents who think they have limited tracking actually do not when you look at their phone.[7]

It goes beyond ad tracking. People do not seem to understand much about what privacy decisions they make, and 59 percent say they understand very little or nothing about what companies do with the data that they collect. Only one in five Americans often or always read privacy policies when asked. The rest say that they seldom or never read them. It is hard to make an informed decision when you don't read what is at stake.[8]

Yet decisions about your phone greatly affect how firms make money. In addition to selling you the phone, Apple gets sizable payments from Google to ensure that its search engine is preinstalled on your iPhone. Initially, in 2014, the payments were $1 billion, but it's believed that by 2020 they increased to $12 billion.[9] This is huge. Google's U.S. search advertising revenue is $40 billion total. For Apple, the payments from Google represent 14 to 21 percent of Apple's profits.

The power of this default is so great that in October 2020, the Justice Department, along with eleven states, filed one of the largest antitrust cases in decades. The agreement between Apple and Google was at the heart of the case. *The New York Times* called it "a deal that controls the internet." Google might be a superior search engine, but its market share would be significantly less if another engine, such as Microsoft's Bing, were preinstalled. What might look like a choice actually reflects both your preferences and the choice architecture.

I'm an optimist, so in this book I will usually assume that the designer has the chooser's best interests in mind and is selecting tools in a way that improves the chooser's welfare. But, as mentioned earlier, choice architecture can be used maliciously. If the designer and chooser have different goals, there will always be the temptation to design to promote the designer's interests over the chooser's. This is a serious problem because, as we will see later in the book, choosers are often unaware of the effect of choice architecture. Almost every tool I discuss can be used to benefit or harm the chooser.

Two terms have emerged to describe choice architecture that hurts the chooser. The first is *sludge*, which is easily summarized as using choice architecture that makes it harder for the chooser to do what is in their best interest. If someone wants to opt out of being tracked by advertisers, making it difficult to do that would be sludge.

A different intellectual tradition, user-experience research, gives rise to the term *dark patterns*. Coined by Harry Brignull in 2010, dark patterns are design elements that make people select options that they did not mean to—for instance, signing up for a spam email list or buying something by accident. It is largely focused on the negative effects of design on the web, but dark patterns can often describe cases where a designer makes it easier to do something that is not in a chooser's best interest. If it is easy for you to select a free trial of an online product without realizing that this implies a yearlong commitment, you may have fallen prey to a dark pattern.

They may have different origins, but sludge and dark patterns are closely related. Both involve the outsized impact of perceived effort in selecting how we do a task. One benefit of reading this book, for both designers and choosers, may be to better understand when choice architecture goes bad.

Choice architecture, whether it is good or bad, does the same things: it changes the information we see and changes what we recall from memory. While choice architecture appears to be about things like fonts, colors, and displays, the reason it matters is that it changes what goes on inside our heads. This book examines the different tools that designers have available, how they work, and how they work together. Without understanding the processes underlying choice architecture, we can't be responsible designers. Knowing how choice architecture works will allow us to invent new and more effective tools.

2

Plausible Paths

On the afternoon of January 15, 2009, my wife and I took off from LaGuardia Airport. We walked through the US Airways concourse to board what would be an uneventful flight to Denver. A few gates away, another flight, US 1549, departed for Charlotte, NC, a half hour later. When we landed four hours later and taxied to the gate, there were the usual bleeps and dings of people firing up their smartphones. The beeps were followed by gasps as people read the alerts on their phones. The person next to me exclaimed, "Oh god, there is a US Airways plane down in the Hudson!" Everyone was shaken. We all had the feeling it could have been our plane that went down.

As we wandered, stunned, off the jetway, the usual rush to claim baggage and catch cabs was absent. People stopped to watch the omnipresent overhead screens blaring CNN coverage. Miraculously, the plane had not shattered and sunk. We watched as endless replays showed the mostly un-harmed passengers and crew board fireboats, tugs, and barges. Flight 1549 lasted six and a half minutes and ended with a successful emergency landing in the river. For a New Yorker, this was especially stunning. If I had been home and not on my flight, I could have watched the aircraft descend into the Hudson from my living room window.

Choice architecture is all around us, influencing even the pilots whom we rely on to deliver us safely to our destinations. They are trained to make choices and, as the chair of one flight-training program put it, "We're not building pilots. . . . I like to tell our students we're training them to be decision-makers who happen to know how to fly an airplane."[1] Captain Chesley "Sully" Sullenberger's decision about where to land the plane was made simply and quickly. There were only 208 seconds, just over three minutes, between the time the blades of both engines were stopped by striking a flock of errant Canada geese and the moment the plane touched down. Sully reported that he did not have time to do a careful analysis of his three options: going back to LaGuardia, an airfield whose runways are infamously short, especially for an emergency landing; flying over a densely populated area across the river to the smaller general aviation airfield at Teterboro; or splashing down in the Hudson.

The first thing Sullenberger had to do was make a decision about how he would decide. He did this quickly and automatically, and according to transcripts of the accident report, he was very aware of the decision he made but not as aware of how he chose to make that decision. There simply wasn't time. He was in total control, but his mind was working automatically, as if he was on autopilot.

Earlier, I called this choice of how to decide a *plausible path*, meaning the strategy we use to make a decision. In any situation, there are a number of different ways to make a choice. Early on, we have to decide which options and information to focus on and how to combine the information in front of us. More important, we need to decide what to ignore. We may change our minds, but initially we must make a partial commitment to one strategy for making a choice. Sully had to decide what information to look at, what to ignore, and how to interpret the information he considered. Within moments, he had committed himself to a plausible path for deciding how to land the plane. As we shall see, choice architecture works by influencing the plausible paths used by the chooser. In other words, the choice architecture of the cockpit controls led Sully to a plausible path that resulted in a good outcome.

Sullenberger, in discussing his decision, revealed that he immediately established what was important:

> So I quickly set priorities, I load shed—pared down this problem to its essential elements—did the few things that had to be done, did them very well and I was willing to goal sacrifice. I knew that the highest priority was to save lives, and I was more than willing to give up trying to save the airplane very early on in order to do that. And that was an easy choice for me to make, although as [First Officer]

Jeff Skiles would tell me later, "You put a $62 million airliner in the river and they call you a hero. Is this a great country, or what?"[2]

Sullenberger borrowed the term *load shedding* from electrical utilities: when demand exceeds their capacity, a utility may take parts of its network off-line, shutting down, say, power to a factory, to provide resources to another more crucial location, like a hospital. Pilots use this phrase when they are overwhelmed, and they decide to ignore what they hope are nonessential parts of the problem. Choosing a plausible path is a form of load shedding: it involves making decisions about what is crucial information to consider for meeting goals and what information is nonessential and can be taken off-line.

The way information is displayed to the chooser influences their choice of a plausible path. Lost in the discussion of the bravery of Sullenberger, First Officer Skiles, and the three flight attendants was the role of the cockpit displays. The plane they flew, an Airbus A320, is flown using a single primary electronic display that sits right in front of the pilot. Without that display, Flight 1549 could have had a very different outcome. It played an essential role in the landing (but was not, like the crew of Flight 1549, given the key to New York City by the mayor).

Cockpit instrumentation design has evolved into a precise science, based on an elaborate understanding of human factors and extensive experiments using flight simulators. Designers of airplane displays run many tests to assess their decisions. The goal is to include the most pertinent information in the display while minimizing unnecessary complexity. One major firm suggests asking these questions about any information in the cockpit: "Does it give the pilot what he needs, only what he needs and only when he needs it? And does it give him the information in a way that is intuitive, unambiguous and easy to understand? If not, it's clutter."[3]

Sully did not have much time, but he did establish a simple goal. He wanted to glide the plane, safely and without power, as far as he needed to a safe landing. Keeping the plane in the air expanded his options for landing. Let's look at the key display that faced Sullenberger, the airspeed tape, shown below.

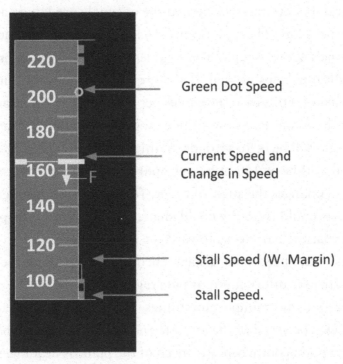

Choice architecture of the airspeed tape[4]

To fly farther, Sullenberger had to track two quantities: the speed of the plane and the flight angle. By keeping the angle of flight and the speed at certain values, he could keep the plane in the air as long as possible, giving him more time to make a decision. While an extremely experienced pilot like Sully could determine these values on his own, the airspeed tape gauge helps him, providing the "green dot speed," or the speed that provides the best lift over drag ratio to get the plane the greatest distance. Sully also needed to make sure the plane did not slow to the stall speed, which would cause the plane to crash immediately.

In the figure, the round dot is at about 200 miles per hour and is green in the actual display. This circle does the math for the pilot: it has calculated the optimal speed to go as far as possible. The pilot simply has to make sure that the plane's speed is equal to the green dot. Another important indicator helps as well: the white bar indicates the current speed—in this case, 160 miles per hour. The arrow attached to the white bar shows the change in speed and what the speed will be in 10 seconds. In this case, the plane is slowing and will be at 150 miles per hour in 10 seconds, unless the pilot changes the angle of flight. To increase the distance the plane could fly, Sully could change the descent of the plane so that the bar moves toward the green dot.[5]

The airspeed tape display encourages a pilot to look at particular information. It puts together, on the same gauge, the two most important things that Sullenberger had to track: the speed of the aircraft and the flight angle. The arrow points out where the speed of the plane is heading, relative to the dot, showing the pilot what he needs to change to get back to the dot. Together, they relieve the pilot of much of the burden of information processing, allowing him to load-shed. Sully could have calculated all of this himself, but the display made it easier, freeing him to consider more important things, like where to land.

Contrast this with other potential and less useful designs for displaying the information. The designer might provide two displays, one each for the current speed and the best air speed. In addition, two more displays could also be added, one for the current flight angle and one for the best flight angle. We might reason that both sets of information are really important and deserve their own meters so they can be easily seen. In addition, because Sullenberger was such an expert, having had about five thousand hours at the controls of the Airbus A320, you might believe that he could easily surmise the dot speed and intuitively know how quickly the plane was accelerating or decelerating. But, by doing the calculations for him, the airspeed tape gave Sullenberger valuable extra time to think about other factors.

Sullenberger knew the A320's airspeed tape intimately and reported that he used it frequently during the landing.[6] He knew this gauge was important. The A320 is a "glass cockpit" aircraft: unlike the mechanical meters in older planes, the electronic displays like the one on page 25 depend upon having power that is normally supplied by the plane's engines. Two seconds after the geese struck Flight 1549's engines, Sullenberger reached up and turned on the auxiliary power units, keeping the vital indicators functional. This is remarkable: he did it on his own with no prompting, breaking protocol. First Officer Skiles was going down a checklist of procedures for dual engine failure, but the three-page list assumed that such a failure would occur above 20,000 feet, providing plenty of time to get through all the items, instructing pilots to turn on the auxiliary power. Skiles didn't even have time to complete page 1 before landing.

What did the gauge enable Sullenberger to think about, and what did it enable him to ignore? How did it help him load-shed? He says that in the midst of everything, he considered the location for a water landing. The Hudson is cold in mid-January. The water temperature was 41 degrees Fahrenheit, and the air a chilly 19 degrees. Hypothermia was a real risk. Even if they successfully landed, the plane might float for only a short time. Sullenberger knew that there were many boats along Manhattan's west side, and a ferry terminal nearby. Because he was able to load-shed, he considered not only where he could safely land the plane but rescue possibilities as well, thinking about what would happen next. The gauge allowed him to pick a location that would maximize the chance of a quick and successful evacuation and rescue.

Cockpit controls are the result of careful design and experimentation, intended to help pilots perform as well as they can. This is not true for all of our decisions. Our choices are often made in environments that are not purposefully designed. The information that we see in everyday life is not the result of extensive testing in the experimental equivalents of flight simulators. A friend suggesting restaurants for lunch is probably simply giving you whatever is at the top of their mind, including foods that you hate. A doctor suggesting alternative treatments might name surgeries that are not appropriate for you but ones they often perform, and they might go into too much detail or use esoteric (to you) terms. You visit an insurance site provided by your employer and see lots of options, including plans for kids (you might not have any) and lots of information about coverage for pregnancy (you are a single man).

Often the choice architectures we encounter lack any serious consideration of how to display information. Instead, the display is haphazard, based on approximate intuitions of what looks good. It is, in general, designed without the realization that choice architecture can influence how and what we choose. But a good choice architecture, like a well-designed cockpit, allows the decision-maker to quickly observe what is important, ignore what is not, and combine the relevant information.

Compare the Airbus A320 cockpit to the typical webpage you might see when buying something on the internet, even from a large, well-regarded retailer like Amazon. If I search for laundry detergent, I am given twenty pages of results, each page containing fifteen options. Each page also has twelve ads (including one for a men's deodorant and another for garbage bags!). Ask yourself if this page follows the advice that the cockpit designer just gave us: Does the page contain only the information I need, presented in an easy-to-understand, intuitive, and unambiguous way, or is it clutter? Of course, Amazon and many other choice architects have motives other than making sure that consumers make the best possible choices for themselves. Nevertheless, the contrast is very informative. It also suggests how subtle things, like how many alternatives the website might show, may change customer choices.

Plausible Paths

The term *plausible path* is inspired by the kinds of initial decisions we make while walking in the real world. Imagine we are friends talking in a park, and we decide to cross the park for an ice cream.[7] There are many ways we can get there: we could go out to the street and take the long way around, we could cut through the carousel ride, maybe even taking a shortcut by climbing on it. But if we are walking in a park and there is a nice gravel path, we take it; we do not climb over the one-foot-tall hedges even if that route would be faster. These decisions are snap judgments. We make them quickly and without a lot of reasoning as we set out, but they end up shaping the rest of our journey. In fact, if someone asks why you took the path, you might have a hard time explaining the choice. Like Sully, you chose your plausible path on autopilot.

When walking, we also do not continually reassess our choice of path. We do other things, like talk with a friend or think about a meeting that just happened. This means our initial choice of a plausible path is "sticky": we might change paths, but our first choice has inertia. Think about getting directions from your smartphone's mapping app. You pick a route at the beginning of the drive. You might change, but you are often (I hope) too busy paying attention to driving to reconsider and choose another route.

If you ever find yourself traveling through Copenhagen Airport, you'll be faced with a similar choice. Once you collect your bags from luggage claim, you can go left to exit via the customs office, which you should visit if you need to pay a tariff, or you can go to the right and exit directly (as shown in the "before" portion of the figure below). The paths taken by people as they move through the airport can save time or cause congestion. Almost 90 percent of travelers would go through the right door, because they had nothing to declare and wanted to avoid the office for declaring goods on the left. That early choice of a plausible path became a problem. People who had gone to the right to avoid customs stayed on the right side of the hallway, resulting in a queue to exit and delays for everyone. The left door was available to all, but people seldom chose the left-side path, and instead stood, frustrated, in the queue for the right door.

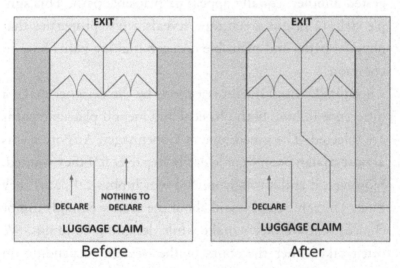

Exiting customs at Copenhagen airport, before (left) and after (right) an intervention[8]

So how do you get people to consider a different plausible path? A consulting firm specializing in behavioral science generated a solution, shown in the "after" portion of the figure. They used dull green lane markers and added signs asking travelers to use both the right and left lanes. Traffic to the left door increased by 54 percent. When they changed the color of the markers and signs to a bright neon green, traffic through the left door grew even more, increasing 128 percent relative to the original setup in the "before" portion.[9]

This large change wasn't driven by costs or information. If people had been sufficiently worried about the cost of the extra time they spent waiting in the queue to exit, the intervention would be unnecessary. Most people were making their decision about which door to choose without much thought, but after the intervention, the bright neon tape suggested another, equally appealing plausible path. This simple strip of bright green tape reveals a few properties that physical paths and plausible decision-making paths have in common.

Seemingly insignificant selections by the designer make a difference in how both physical and mental plausible paths are selected. The green tape at Copenhagen Airport seems almost trivial; people could easily step over it if they wanted. However, it still strongly guided which physical paths they took. The same can be said about the most seemingly minor choices that architects make while designing buildings. We often take either the stairs or the elevator, depending on which is closest—locations selected years ago by the architect planning the building. Similarly, the list of selections made by the choice architect is huge, and while many of those selections seem unimportant, they do influence choices.

These physical and mental influences are front-loaded: they will have more impact the earlier they occur in the user's decision process. Choosing a plausible path resembles a set-and-forget choice, one that, once made, is not revisited (unless major difficulties crop up). Plausible paths, once selected, tend to stay selected. I don't mean to imply that once set, a plausible path cannot be changed. There are certainly monitoring processes that can attempt to correct early errors. But early influences, like the order of options, the fonts used, and everything that determines an initial sense of ease, will be overweighted.

Many of these influences will occur without awareness. Most choice architecture works without the knowledge of the decision-maker. This has obvious implications for the ethics of choice architecture, as I'll discuss in the last chapter of this book.

Because many things that determine plausible paths occur without awareness, many of the common techniques for evaluating forms and other choice interfaces are less helpful when you're designing plausible paths. Asking people how they like a website or giving them a set of options in a focus group will get people to talk, but their answers may have little to do with what is actually influencing their choices.

Paths to Patience

When we choose a plausible path, the choice architect has already influenced our actions. They have influenced what information we will consider and what we will ignore, and that will influence our choice.

When confronted with a choice, we automatically face a series of decisions about how to choose. Instantly, our brain starts evaluating the problem on many dimensions, all at once. The chooser encodes a broad-brush view of the choice quickly. If it's a webpage, we automatically notice the color, whether the font is easy or hard to read, and the amount (or lack) of white space. If it is a friend listing possible places we could meet for dinner, we hear not only the content of the options but the subtleties inherent in how they're talking: Are they hesitant while describing that new sushi place? Are they hinting that they would like to stay nearby? We form an overall impression of the complexity of the choice in front of us: Are there many options? Are there many attributes? Are the labels and units easy to understand? This impression serves to influence our choice of a plausible path.

Let's consider a simple choice between just two options, each with two characteristics. The figure on page 35 presents a choice between two Amazon gift certificates, a smaller one you get sooner or a more valuable one you get four weeks later. In studying decision-making, these two options are called the *smaller-sooner outcome* and *larger-later outcome*.

Smaller-sooner is tempting, and most people—over 60 percent—choose this option. Researchers use choices like this in many studies of self-control. To make sure people take the decision seriously, some participants are emailed the actual gift certificate at the time indicated.

Although this is a simple setup, there are multiple plausible paths. You still have to make decisions about how you will look at and combine information. Even in this simple

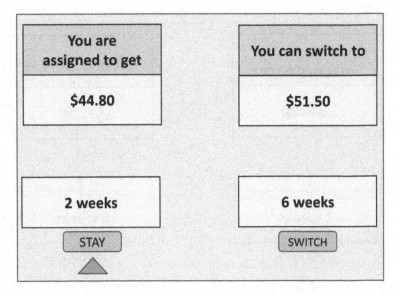

A simple choice between two gift certificates available at different times

problem, different plausible paths will make a difference in what you choose.

You could, for example, look at each amount and try and adjust its value given how long you would have to wait, asking yourself what it would feel like to get the $44.80 in two weeks. We call this path *integrating*. Another path, taken by roughly half of the people in our studies, is to figure out the difference in the amounts—$6.70 in this example—and see whether it's worth waiting an extra four weeks to get the larger-later option. We call this path *comparing*.

Along with Crystal Reeck, now a professor at Temple University, and Dan Wall, a graduate student at Carnegie Mellon, I studied these plausible paths. We did this by tracking the order that people look at information when they make this choice. We use *eye tracking*. Tracking eye movements is

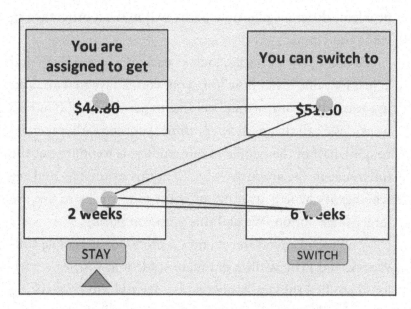

Eye tracks representing two plausible paths for making this choice, integrating (above) and comparing (below)

easier than it sounds. People sit in front of a computer screen and on top of that screen is what looks like a webcam, just like someone might use for video conferencing. The camera focuses on just the pupil and iris of each eye and uses infrared light to unobtrusively track the person's eye movements. The previous figures show typical tracks for integrating (top) and comparing (bottom).

By tracking where the eye stops, a researcher can get a very good idea of what you are looking at. Surprisingly, we don't see anything when the eyes are moving, only when they are still. Essentially, the eye is taking a series of snapshots that our brains stitch together. Eye tracking lets us know what you looked at, and we can see whether you looked first at the smaller-sooner amount or at the time it would take to get the larger-later certificate. While we cannot tell if you are struggling to resist temptation, we can see if you compare or integrate the options. We identify the plausible path you use because we see the snapshots that your eye is presenting to your brain.

Different paths produce different choices. We have given these options to hundreds of people and watched how they made choices. Study participants who compare outcomes, looking back and forth, are more patient. They choose the larger-later outcome almost half the time. The people who integrate the outcomes, looking within the options, up and down, chose the more patient option less than 30 percent of the time. This is because they seem drawn to the immediate pleasure of getting the smaller gift certificate sooner. Comparing, in contrast, points out that you will give up $6.70 if you don't wait.

People seem to persist in one path or the other, across decisions. (Some of the MBAs I teach treat this as a math problem, calculating the annual interest rate implied by the larger-later option. Whipping out your calculator or opening up Excel is certainly a plausible path here, but most people don't take it. If you did, you would find that you are earning 110 percent interest by waiting.)[10]

This kind of decision, known as an *intertemporal choice problem*, has attracted enormous attention in the last fifty years. It involves the fundamental challenge facing most decision-makers when they are making choices involving time. Each option has two attributes: the first, an amount of money, and the second, the date the money will be delivered. To make this choice, people have to trade off between time and money: Sooner is better, but so is more money. In these choices, you have to give up one to get the other.

One of the reasons these choices have attracted so much interest is that intertemporal choices surround us. For some choices, the mapping between these experimental questions and real-life decisions seems obvious. We can decide to spend money today or use the money to save for retirement. But there are other important real-world intertemporal choice problems. Deciding to smoke cigarettes today brings pleasure but has delayed long-term health consequences. As I remind my students, they can decide to go out and party tonight, or stay in and study. By studying, I hope, they get a delayed reward: better grades leading, potentially, to better jobs and higher salaries.

Studying intertemporal problems has shown that costs and benefits that are available immediately have an outsized impact upon decisions. If the smaller-sooner option is available now, it will be much more attractive. Psychologists call such overweighting of immediate consequences *present bias*. Present bias explains why people might like teaser rates, those offers that give you a great deal upfront but then have higher costs down the road. You need only look at most offerings from telephone and cable companies to see examples. Recently, for instance, my cable TV company offered me faster internet service at $49 for an introductory six months. It was almost impossible to find how much it would cost after that.

The act of making any decision might suffer from present bias. With every decision, we must invest effort now for later rewards delivered by choosing better options. We might choose a bad credit card because we like its teaser rate, but I'm talking about another reason we may make a bad choice: we may simply decide that the effort required to evaluate the alternatives is not worth the savings.

This is not to say that we never invest too much effort in a decision. We might get obsessed over picking the best new car or invest enormous effort into buying a new jacket or backpack. But that usually happens because we enjoy thinking about the product. It is inherently something we like. In most cases, the decision itself is not fun, and we try to avoid the immediate costs.

The gift certificate decision illustrates why plausible paths are important. If we can change the path used by people to make a decision, we might help them choose better options. Can changing paths actually change choice, without changing the amount of money or time involved in the choice?

It turns out that influencing plausible paths is very easy. We redid the study, but we made it slightly harder for the respondents, chosen randomly, to integrate or compare. We did this by briefly delaying when each item of information appeared. For half the people, we delayed the information if they tried to compare; for the others, the delay happened when they tried to integrate. This short delay was enough to change the plausible paths that people used. And this small change made people more or less patient.[11]

This is just one example of how a plausible path can be influenced; we have not even begun to exhaust the kinds of selections that a choice architect might make to solve even this very simple intertemporal problem.

Most of the time, we face choice problems that are much more complex than two options with two attributes. Think about picking a restaurant on OpenTable or Yelp: there are many more restaurants and much more information—the star rating, the average price of entrees, the menu, the distance to get to the restaurant, the reviews and listings of the best dishes. If plausible paths can affect choices in a simple decision, just imagine how they might influence the kinds of complex decisions we make using Yelp. And the world we live in is often that complicated: our cereal aisles have hundreds of options, our dating sites have thousands of potential matches, our universities have hundreds if not thousands of courses. Here, choosing what information to look at and how to simplify the decision becomes even more important and has even greater influence on what is chosen. This makes choice architecture even more essential. We will look at the many selections that a choice architect must make in complicated choices soon, but first, it's important to understand how choosers select plausible paths.

Finding Fluency

Ideally, we might think that choosers carefully consider how much effort is required during the entire decision-making process when selecting a plausible path. But that is not realistic. It turns out that people are present-biased when it comes to expending effort, even more so than they are for money. This means that their perceptions of effort at the beginning of making a decision are particularly important.[12]

This helps explain how we could change people's choice of gift certificates. By making some information slightly harder to access, we changed their plausible paths. It made one path slightly easier than the other, and this choice of path happened in the first few moments of the decision.

But there are many ways of making a path seem easier. I will borrow a term from psychologists who call this *fluency*. Fluency is the initial and subjective feeling we have about the ease of taking a particular plausible path.[13] It's similar to the experience of being fluent in a language. Nothing gets in the way of the task at hand: we understand the meaning of what is being said and are not distracted by trying to figure out what a particular verb in a new language means, or how it is conjugated.

Subjective is the key word here. No one is standing with a stopwatch trying to measure how long it actually takes; it is about how hard the path feels. When we understand speech fluently, it's very easy for us to listen to the radio or a conversation. However, objectively, it is very hard for other, nonhuman intelligences. In the early days of artificial intelligence (AI), I sat in a windowless room with one hundred other people watching a demonstration of Hearsay, one of the first speech recognition systems. The crowd was amazed when the system understood, after several minutes, the words "Rook to King's Knight 4," a phrase from chess notation, the very limited domain that the system recognized. The Department of Defense's Defense Advanced Research Projects Agency (DARPA) had given millions of dollars in contracts to Carnegie Mellon to get this to happen. For us, understanding speech is fluent, but for machines, it's very difficult. Similarly, multiplying two ten-digit numbers is fluent for even the least powerful CPU, but not for most people, who find such arithmetic onerous. Fluency is not some objective measure of how hard it is to make a decision, but rather a subjective measure of how it feels.

The feeling of fluency can come from many aspects of how choices are presented, and it is easily manipulated. Think of the bright green line in Copenhagen Airport changing people's selections of physical paths, and how delaying the display of information can change people's level of patience. Another particularly good example is the font used in a book. Hopefully, you are reading this in a font that seems fluent, so that you can concentrate on the meaning of the words and not the process of reading. But not all fonts are fluent. I could write a sentence in one of two fonts: **Helvetica** is a commonly used font that has been shown to be easy to read, and **Haettenschweiler** is a rarely used font that has been shown to be hard to read (and perhaps to pronounce).

Displaying the choice options in Helvetica versus **Haettenschweiler** does not change the information presented to the chooser; it simply changes how hard it is to read. Altering the fluency of the options potentially changes the plausible path used to make the choice. You could also swap in other hard-to-read fonts, like **Impact** and Bradley Hand.

Psychologists Adam Alter and Danny Oppenheimer have given us a nice list of what changes fluency. For example, changing the contrast of a font, making it more similar to the white background, makes it harder to read and less fluent. Converting numerals to words makes the numbers less fluent. Most people have a much easier time reading *12%* than *twelve percent*. Some names are easier to pronounce: studies that compare *Barnings* as a product name to *Yoalumnix* show that English speakers prefer the former, easier-to-pronounce name.

Fluency can also fool us, making us think something is easier when it really is not. A set of studies in psychology asks people to remember words that are presented in a smaller font size, like this, or a much larger font, like this.

The researchers then ask people how well they think they can recall the list before actually asking them to recall it. Participants believe they are more likely to recall the words printed in a big font. As it turns out, however, while the big fonts feel easier to read, any advantage is very small.[14]

When we must choose a plausible path, our perception of initial effort plays an outsized role. Fluency may not be perfect at selecting paths, but it is important. If the designer has made the right plausible paths easy, like in the Airbus A320 cockpit, then we can, to use Captain Sullenberger's term, load-shed. But things do not always turn out that well. Sometimes designers are naive about what plausible paths *should* be used. Sometimes designers want us to use plausible paths that are not in our own best interests. And sometimes, as we will see, adding technology to one of the oldest human activities can produce worse plausible paths, and bad dates.

Dates That Don't Measure Up

My spouse, Elke Weber, is a well-known mathematical psychologist, and we met the old-fashioned way: not online, but in person, at a conference. Her research and writing efforts are directed at understanding another kind of decision, involving the incredibly important topic of climate change. As you might imagine, we have lots of serious conversations, but she has a more frivolous tradition: reading the "Vows" section in the Sunday *New York Times* every week. I have started sharing this small addiction. It is fascinating to find out how very different people have met, dated, and married. And of course, in "Vows," every dating story has a happy ending.

One Sunday, I was captured by one particular couple: She was a stunning African American woman, Erika Woods, from a professional family in Birmingham, Alabama. She worked in the fashion industry, was five foot five, and loved four-inch heels. Her new husband, Assaf Kedem, was an attractive but slight five-foot-two-inch Israeli, ten years older, and the author of *The Investment Writing Handbook*. How did such a dissimilar couple, who characterized themselves as "worlds apart," find each other?

The answer lies, in part, in plausible paths and how they are influenced by the choice architecture of dating sites— and in particular the decisions made by the designers of one dating site, Coffee Meets Bagel.

Looking online for love is a huge industry. Forty million people, almost one third of the single people in the United States, use online dating sites. The industry produces $2.5 billion in annual revenue, and Match Group, the owners of Tinder, Match.com, OkCupid, and others, is valued at $21.8 billion. Online dating is now the most common way that long-term heterosexual couples report meeting, with 39 percent meeting online, as opposed to 20 percent through friends, and 27 percent in a bar or restaurant.[15]

While there may be a handful of major dating sites in the United States, there are more than five thousand worldwide, many made for very specific audiences. For example, there are sites for fans of Disney (Mouse Mingle), clowns (Clown Dating), farmers (Farmers Only), and hip-hop fans (Bound 2). During the 2016 election there was even a dating site dedicated to followers of Bernie Sanders.[16] BernieSingles had about 13,500 members and claimed to "help connect progressives beyond social media to inspire chemistry among folks who share similar visions of the future." Further, they claimed, ironically perhaps in retrospect, that "the 1% are not the only ones getting screwed this election season."

But most people do not have such selective goals for finding a partner, and the role of most sites is to help the chooser decide whom to date. The designers of dating sites are choice architects. They make many selections that influence who messages whom, who dates whom, and, eventually, who become partners. Even something as small as the number of potential dates presented by the site can change an online dater's life.

OkCupid shows twelve potential dates on a screen, but lets you search many screens. More starkly, Tinder lets you see an inexhaustible set of potential dates, as many as you can swipe. This can be exhausting. The Urban Dictionary even has a definition for *Tinder Thumb*: "Localized pain resulting from overuse of the iPhone dating app Tinder, which has users swipe left or right to 'like' or 'nope' other users based on their images and short (often useless) bios. What begins as a fun, game-like experience often results in extreme hand cramps and acceptance that we all die alone."

Erika and Assaf, our unlikely couple, were both users of the then relatively new dating website Coffee Meets Bagel. It was founded by three sisters who were determined to redesign the online dating scene. Early on, they, as designers, made an important selection. According to Arum Kang, one of the founders, "We don't inundate our members with low-quality matches. We do the work for them and keep the work on their part to a minute per day."[17] Part of the reason the founders started the site was they believed that women wanted a different way to consider dates. Men typically spend twice as much time on these sites as women, and they are much more likely to send messages (and less likely to get replies). The goal of Coffee Meets Bagel was to overcome this mass-mailing mind-set by having users contemplate each option more seriously. Arum Kang and her sisters accomplished this by selecting an important feature for the site's choice architecture: you saw only one potential match a day.

Coffee Meets Bagel successfully created a more female-friendly dating site. By changing the choice architecture, Coffee Meets Bagel almost reversed the usual gender ratio of 65 percent men to 35 percent women.

Imagine Erika or Assaf (or yourself, if you would like) using Tinder. They are faced with hundreds of options. How would they look at them? Would they consider each one carefully, reading the details of every profile, or might they instead make a snap judgment based on one or two features, like the picture, age, or (reported) height? On Tinder it seems likely that potential dates are quickly dismissed in a torrent of swipes, each decision based on one or two salient things about the person. Instead, Erika and Assaf were forced by the design of Coffee Meets Bagel to take a closer look. They were intrigued, examined the one profile presented that day more closely, and discovered unexpected things that they had in common. It turns out that Assaf, like Erika, loved R&B and Motown and had a huge collection of recordings.

The quick evaluation encouraged by having many options is called *screening*. Because it seems so fluent, it is a very common plausible path for dealing with large assortments of alternatives. It is easy to take a quick look at a picture, and a lot harder to read text about what someone likes and wants. But that ease doesn't necessarily lead to users selecting the best option.

Imagine, for example, a five-foot-seven-inch woman who skips any potential match who is fewer than five inches taller than she is. George Clooney is using the same dating site, but because he's only five foot eleven, he never makes it past this woman's initial filtering process and they never connect. Imagine, instead, that this woman encountered George as her profile of the day on Coffee Meets Bagel. She might decide his interesting background and charm outweigh her screening criteria, telling herself that his winning smile is worth it, and that she might wear shorter heels.

In this scenario, the choice architecture of a given dating site—not the desires of the user—is determining George's chances. George would be considered and messaged on Coffee Meets Bagel, but not on OkCupid. Similarly, Erika or Assaf might quickly move on to other, more similar potential partners, not taking the time to look more closely at each other's profile.

Screening is even explicitly built into some sites, like Tinder. There, a user specifies an age range and a distance they are willing to travel to meet up. Automating that screening can make the problem worse, eliminating any chance that the chooser will notice something else about the profile. If you were manually screening, you might notice George's winning smile, but automated screening would not even show him to you if he were standing only ten feet beyond the maximum distance that you specified.

There are few choices in life more important than the choice of a romantic partner, so it seems strange that the person we choose to be with should be influenced in part by the number of options presented to us. That is the power of choice architecture: small tweaks, by influencing our plausible paths, can change significant choices.

We can understand a lot about the process of using a dating site because the sites collect information about each visit. This clickstream of data lets us observe what people are looking for in dates without ever needing to ask users what they are looking for or why. It may not feel this way but using a dating site is quite like surfing the web with a small video camera strapped to your forehead. Researchers interested in how people choose dates can see how people search and whom they message. They can see which profiles users are considering, even when they don't choose to look further. In a supermarket, shoppers might look, for example, at the pistachio ice cream but not put it in their shopping carts. Similarly, apps can see when they browse a potential date but don't send a message. This says that there was something attractive about the ice cream or date, since it attracted the person's attention, but there was also something that was not right, since they did not choose it. If they eliminated potential dates based on the presence of an undesirable characteristic, we might call it a *deal-breaker*; if they insist on a desirable characteristic, that's a *deal-maker*.

By watching someone shop, whether it's for ice cream or

love, we learn how they are thinking. Looking at this data reveals the plausible paths that searchers are using when choosing (and rejecting) dates, allowing us to understand how searching works and how it responds to a change in the number of options.

What do we see when we watch people looking for love? At the University of Michigan, Elizabeth E. Bruch, a sociologist, and Fred Feinberg and Kee Yeun Lee, statistical and marketing experts, analyzed 1.1 million choices, looking to see what determined whether members of a well-known dating site decided to look closely at someone's profile or to send a message. What they learned was that screening was common.[18]

As a user of this site, you would confront a page containing at least twelve potential dates (you could ask for more), almost all with a picture (90 percent) and a few facts such as height, age, and weight. Bruch and her team captured that page and documented the characteristics of each of the twelve potential dates that a user saw. They then examined what determined which potential dates were perused more carefully. Clicking through to look at more information is called *browsing*, and if you like what you see, you can message the person. By looking at the profiles that were or were not browsed and messaged, Bruch and company could model what drives the decision to go further. Quite literally, they could watch what the average user was looking for in a partner.

What are the deal-breakers and deal-makers on this dating site? No doubt people differ in their tastes, so the Michigan team looked at different market segments, dividing all daters into groups of men or women who had similar tastes. One large segment of men showed a clear pattern. Their average age was thirty-nine, but they rarely wrote to women of that age. Instead, they were much more likely to write to women ten years younger. The chance of their writing someone four years older than themselves was almost zero. These men used the plausible path of screening by age.

Likewise, there was a substantial group of women who screened for height. Almost all these women preferred to message taller men, and there was a sharp increase as the difference grew from two to six inches. These women were eight times more likely to message men who were six inches taller than they were, and the chances of their messaging someone their height or shorter was practically zero. Bruch and colleagues suggest that this is a *heels effect*: women want to date men who are taller than themselves even when the women are wearing heels. Being the same height as one of these women is a deal-breaker.

Screening makes decision-making more fluid, since you need to look at only a single characteristic of the potential date, like their picture, height, or age, to decide whom to pursue. But this plausible path has flaws, flaws that become quite apparent in dating.

Imagine, if you possibly can, that some men lie about their height. In contrast to these dishonest men, honest men report their height accurately. There is now a relationship between claimed height and dishonesty. The taller the claimed height, the more likely the man is to be dishonest. Screening on height has an awful consequence, leading to more dates with liars. This creates more awkward first dates where the guy does not quite measure up to what he reported!

Screening is a big problem whenever two important attributes have a negative relationship. This happens all the time: cheap insurance premiums mean higher deductibles, high-return investments are riskier, and cheap products are often, well, cheap. Screening might well eliminate options that are good balances between two important but negatively related attributes. Thus, more options can lead to screening, which can lead to dating dishonest men, buying high-deductible insurance, and choosing risky investments.

This is the disturbing thing about choice architecture. Its effects can be huge, potentially even determining your romantic partners, but these effects are often not understood, either by web designers or choosers. Fluency can be a false friend, leading us to plausible paths that overvalue certain options and overlook other, potentially perfect options. Screening potential dates by height or age is easy and makes decision-making simpler, but it simultaneously prevents us from considering options we might well like.

Seeing Clearly

Understanding plausible paths is important—they determine what information we look at and what is ignored. When plausible paths focus our attention on the right information and free us to think about important considerations, we can make better decisions. We make our choice of plausible paths toward the beginning of a decision, by what feels easy, and those initial judgments seem to have too much impact.

Most of the time, people don't think about the plausible paths they use. Unlike researchers, they lack eye tracking or records of mouse clicks. But plausible paths have consequences. Going grocery shopping literally involves choosing a plausible path. If you don't go down the detergent aisle, you won't be seeing, and therefore will not be buying, laundry soap. Indeed, companies now put tracking devices on grocery carts to understand shoppers' paths. But what happens when you see a brand name? You often don't stop to read the package; you remember what you know about and think about the brand. It is acquiring information, not from the outside world, but from memory. What we remember is influenced by choice architecture as well, and to understand that, we turn to the world of memory.

3

Assembled Preferences

Derren Brown, a charismatic British entertainer, has been spectacularly successful. Through his long-running one-man shows and highly rated TV specials, he has single-handedly revived the occupation of the "mentalist"—the supposed mind reader.[1] Brown, however, is different from other psychics or telepaths. He doesn't claim to have any psychic powers. Yet he appears capable of recording, before the fact and with uncanny accuracy, what someone will later think and do.

In one demonstration, Brown has two advertising executives, Tony and Martin, take a cab to meet him at an ordinary-looking office. After initial pleasantries, he asks them to develop a print ad for an unusual new business, a chain of animal taxidermy shops. The ad must contain a logo, a name, and a slogan for the business. They have a half hour. Brown explains he has been fascinated with taxidermy since he was a boy and shows Tony and Martin a few "stuffed animals" as examples. Just before leaving the room, he points out that he has put some of his own ideas for an animal taxidermy shop ad into a sealed envelope. Theatrically, he places the envelope under a stuffed cat seated on the table, so no one can touch it, and walks out.

A half hour later, he returns. Tony and Martin share the results of their work. Their ad has a logo of a large bear, sitting on a cloud in front of an iron gate, playing a harp. They have named the business "Animal Heaven" and adopted the slogan "The Best Place for Dead Animals."

Brown asks Martin to retrieve the envelope from underneath the taxidermy cat, open the seal, and unfold the sketch. It's remarkably similar to the one Tony and Martin just produced. Brown's company's name was "Creature Heaven," the logo was almost identical to the executives', and the slogan differed by only two words.

Both the participants and incredulous viewers wonder how Brown pulled off this little feat of magic. Sleight of hand seems impossible: there was no communication between Brown and the execs during the half hour, and he never touched the envelope after putting it under the stuffed cat. How could he have influenced Tony and Martin's creative process? Unlike other mentalists who leave their audience mystified, one of Brown's trademarks is exposing (or maybe claiming to expose) his secrets, revealing how a trick was performed.

In this case, he showed how his crew exposed Tony and Martin to many of the design elements that would later appear in their ad. The cab that had brought them to meet Brown drove by the London Zoo's imposing cast iron gates, where the car stopped to let a school group cross the street in front of them. On each student's sky-blue T-shirt was an image of the zoo's gates. As they drove on, they passed several signs pasted on a pub, each reading WHERE THE BEST DEAD ANIMALS GO. They later slowly cruised by a coffee shop featuring a blackboard with angel's wings drawn on it, along with the words *Creature Heaven*. And one of the "stuffed animals" Brown shared with them when they arrived to meet him had been a taxidermy bear. The ride subtly planted each concept in the two executives' minds, making it highly likely that they would later recall them. The elements that emerged in their design were so easy to remember that they were nearly irresistible.

When Brown described how the trick worked, it became clear he hadn't predicted the future; he had controlled it. Derren Brown is less a mind reader and more a mind *writer*. He increases the probability that certain already known concepts will come to a person's mind. Psychologists call the ease with which things come to mind *accessibility*. In Brown's demonstration, he increased the accessibility of iron gates, angels, clouds, and happy dead animals.

Sometimes, when we are asked a question, we immediately know the answer. There are foods we know we don't like—ask me if I like liver, and the response will be a very fast no. But if you ask me about sushi, my answer might depend on what comes to mind. If I think of a well-crafted, fresh piece of salmon, I might say yes. If I instead picture an old piece of *uni*, sea urchin roe, my answer will be the same as it would be for liver and just as quick.

What we say we prefer depends upon what we recall. Sometimes we think we know what we want, but often we are faced with a situation that is not exactly like anything we have dealt with before. In these cases, we consult our memory to see how we might feel about the options based on our most relevant experiences. I call these memories, and the feelings they conjure up, *assembled preferences.* You might think that choice is about knowing what is desirable and then locating it. In fact, the hard part is often deciding *what* we want. To do that, we review our experiences to retrieve relevant memories.

This means our preferences are not always stable and fixed, but rather improvised, constructed haphazardly from a large set of relevant memories. While sometimes our preferences are constant, like my lifelong distaste for liver, other times they reflect what just happens to come to mind, which can change depending on the situation and the accessibility of different memories. In the absence of outside influences, our choices don't vary much. Like Derren Brown, choice architects are mind writers—they make design decisions that change the accessibility of different concepts, and in turn change what we, as the audience or consumers, choose.

To better understand this capability, let's visit a team of researchers in Iowa City, Iowa, who changed the accessibility of the familiar American hamburger.

Remembering What We Want

If you walked into the psychology labs at the University of Iowa in the late 1980s, you might have noticed that they smelled more like a diner or drive-in than a center for research and education. The aroma of ground beef on an open grill often filled the halls. The smell itself wasn't the focus of the study in progress but rather a by-product of researching the effects that labels have on people's perceptions of the quality and taste of meat. The meaty aroma was so strong that Irwin Levin, the professor conducting the research, worried his colleagues might think he was running a McDonald's in the building's basement.

Levin's experiments were simple enough. In the first, he asked two groups of undergraduates to rate how they felt about a sample of raw ground beef. For one group, he presented meat labeled "25 percent fat," and for the other, "75 percent lean." Levin found that the second group had a more positive perception of the meat they were shown. They judged it as higher quality, less greasy, and better tasting than the other group saw its sample, which, of course, was the same beef: the proportions of fat and lean meat must add up to 100. However, simply using the words *fat* and *lean* have an effect on what the groups thought about the burgers.

Next, Levin tested how labels could change the actual experience of eating the meat. Levin and his team donned aprons and cooked the meat in front of the individuals involved in the study. Half the "customers" were told that the beef in their burger was 75 percent lean, the others,

25 percent fat. Those participants who were told the meat contained 25 percent fat before eating it found their hamburgers greasier, lower quality, and fattier. Even those who were shown the labels *after* tasting the beef exhibited similar, though smaller, shifts in perception.

Levin, who came up with the idea for the study while having lunch with a marketing colleague, told me that the labels made different aspects of the students' knowledge about hamburgers more or less accessible, changing how they assembled their preferences. Labeling the meat as 75 percent lean might cause the students to think about how delicious the moist, well-seasoned hamburger would taste. A vivid picture of a burger with fresh green lettuce and a red tomato, perhaps next to a salad, might come to mind. Maybe they remember that nice, juicy, high-quality, grass-fed organic burger they had last month.

With the 25 percent fat label, they're more likely to think about the word *fat* and all its negative connotations—the grease, perhaps the rancid smell, the calories in the cheese, heaping loads of limp French fries sitting under a heat lamp, and a factory-farmed cow in a pen, ready for slaughter. In short, the two groups end up thinking about different hamburgers, and different aspects of those hamburgers, simply depending on the label they're shown.[2]

People's associations with hamburgers are rich and complex, containing memories and images both good and bad. Just check out the Small World of Words definitions (the site has collected almost 90,000 responses about the first three words that come to mind when people read another specific word). For *hamburger*, people have responded with positive

The Elements of Choice

words including *tasty, juicy, yum,* and *delicious,* as well as more negative associations like *greasy, fat, yuck,* and *gross.*[3]

These word associations can change depending on the choice architecture. We don't consider everything we know all at once; we recall only part of what we know and use that subset of the information to inform our decisions. Our assembled preferences reflect the choices we make given current inputs, even if those inputs are as simple as the label on a package of ground beef.

Like Brown's taxidermy bears, angel wings, and zoo gates, labels make some memories more accessible, and different labels create different associations. Levin and his researchers in Iowa may not have realized it, but by exposing the students to different labels, they were designing, or writing, the students' responses in the moment. When we make a choice, we don't always report a strongly held opinion; we partially invent that opinion at that time. Just as Captain Sullenberger faced too much information and needed to load-shed—to concentrate on specific parts of the problem—the respondents in the hamburger experiments had many aspects to consider, so they needed to concentrate on whatever they could retrieve from memory then and there, focusing on some memories and not others.

When I described how people choose plausible paths, I talked a lot about fluency, how easy decisions seem initially. People typically choose a path that they expect won't be a hassle. But memory is different. Most of the time, we don't feel like we are in control of what comes to mind. The process is more automatic. If you see the "25 percent fat" label attached to a burger, its negative associated attributes just seem to appear—it's hard not to think of them. Your associations, at any particular moment, are determined by a number of factors—how hungry you are, any scents in the air, how greasy the hamburger's packaging appears, and so on.

The appeal of hamburger meat in Iowa seems totally incompatible with the standard economic model, in which people know what they want and simply need to explore the external environment to find it. In fact, standard economics posits that we have a so-called reservation price for that hamburger. When we look at the menu, we check to see whether the listed price is less than the most we would be willing to pay. If it is lower, we buy the burger. In the standard view in economics, people might have difficulty locating what they desire, but they know what they want. In contrast, psychologists think people can often find many options, but have more trouble figuring out what they actually want.

Assembled preferences may be one of the reasons that choice architecture is difficult to explain in terms of standard economics. In psychology, the crux of making many decisions is identifying what a good choice is. Psychology tends to think about choices as predictions about what we will enjoy, and making these predictions requires that we use our memory.

When our preferences are fixed, accessibility plays little to no role. When I see *liver*, I immediately recall that I hate the taste of liver. When our preferences are assembled at the time of making a decision, however, accessibility is important because our choices can be influenced by all sorts of factors, like packaging labels. There are lots of memories we could retrieve in making a choice based on the quality and taste of ground beef, both good and bad, which means we can make inconsistent choices determined by what we retrieve at that time. Walt Whitman put it well in his poem "Song of Myself":

> Do I contradict myself?
>
> Very well then I contradict myself,
>
> (I am large, I contain multitudes.)

Accessibility

Almost every time we visit a company's website, we are greeted with a luscious, artistic background photograph somehow—usually tangentially—related to the company's product or service. With the music streaming service Qobuz, for example, some visitors find a bearded, earnest listener wearing expensive headphones, lost in music, or a young, waifish singer holding a vintage wooden guitar, eyes closed in front of a microphone that looks right out of a 1940s radio studio. The images seem more like magazine covers than webpages. Why do companies take the extra time and expense to license or produce such high-quality imagery, even if it doesn't relate directly to the product?

One answer is provided by the Danish company Arono, the developers of a successful weight-loss diet plan and workout app. Arono's customers are usually recruited through the company's newsletter and its fourteen-day free trial offer, after which they can buy a monthly, quarterly, or yearly subscription. Originally, the customer sign-up page featured a seemingly relevant photo of an in-shape, sporty model stretching against a nondescript gray background. Today, however, instead of the model, the photo is of a delicious-looking healthy meal with lots of avocado, lush greens, and a tasty bit of cheese, with some copy asking us if we want to receive a personalized diet plan. Why the change? It turns out the image of the meal was 53 percent more effective in producing sign-ups than that of the model.

Arono conducted an A/B test comparing the two images, randomly showing half the potential customers the model and the other half the food. But why was one picture more effective than the other? One possibility is that each image causes different memories to be more or less accessible, and therefore more or less likely to be retrieved. When we see these images, we assemble our preferences for weight-loss plans and the experiences we've had with controlling our weight. The two pictures make different aspects accessible: the model as the potential long-term benefit and the meal as a delicious reward now. As discussed, we are more likely to retrieve the memory that is most accessible at the time—here, we feel like the meal is within reach, whereas the glamorized image most likely is not. If we've never been that trim before—most of us aren't models—we aren't able to access such memories, as they simply aren't there. But most all of us *have* eaten a delicious salad, and we can easily conjure up the crunch of the lettuce, the sweetness of the avocado, and the sharpness of the cheese—accessible memories that say, "Yes, I want *that*!" Next thing we know, we have another app on our phone.[4] By changing the accessibility of different memories, a website's background can affect our decisions.

In the early 2000s, the internet had just become a commercial medium, with stores starting to sell all sorts of products through websites that did not look particularly good. A graduate student at the time, Naomi Mandel, now a professor at Arizona State University, came to me with an idea that I admit seemed unlikely to me back then. Naomi's crazy idea: she could change people's choices by changing the wallpaper on a website, affecting the memories that would be accessible to the viewer. Certain wallpapers could be associated with different aspects of the products, so making those features more accessible made them more likely to come to mind, emphasizing their importance.

For example, for a furniture website, Naomi believed that people who saw a background full of fluffy clouds were more likely to think comfort was an important feature of the couches being sold. Naomi's speculation was that changing the wallpaper could change the sofas that customers would choose to buy. Like the creative and energetic PhD student she was, Naomi set out to disprove my skepticism.

She constructed multiple versions of the same website with different backgrounds: one with a background of fluffy clouds, one with a background of dollar bills, and so on. In a separate study, she showed that clouds made comfort more accessible, money made costs more accessible, etc.

Then it came time to let respondents go shopping. On a website, she asked participants to select between two sofas, one expensive and luxurious, one cheaper and less comfortable. In other words, it was an A/B test. For those who saw the clouds, if comfort became more accessible, would participants spend more time thinking about how nice it feels to sit on a really comfortable couch? Would they then be willing to pay more for that comfort?[5]

Naomi's hunch proved correct. People who saw the clouds chose the more expensive, more comfortable couches 61 percent of the time. When they saw the dollar bills, in contrast, this declined to 52 percent, a remarkable change in customer behavior for a minor adjustment to the site that carried no information about the product or its appearance.

We asked participants in the study who purchased the more expensive, more comfortable couches if the background influenced their choices. While we knew it had, they told us it did not. Like many decisions made because of choice architecture, the website backgrounds changed people's behavior, but they were unaware of the effect. They would never know they had been influenced. Changing accessibility changed how they assembled preferences, leading to different choices.

Of course, since Naomi's insight, A/B testing has become central to how companies design their websites. But it doesn't end online. Things we take for granted every day can affect our accessibility. Take the weather—not only can it change our accessibility, but it can do so even for closely held beliefs, like climate change. On February 5 and 6, 2010, a blizzard moved up the East Coast of North America, dropping 20 to 35 inches of snow on Virginia, Maryland, and

Washington, D.C. The media called this storm "Snow-pocalypse," followed four days later by another snowstorm, dubbed "Snoverkill."

Together, Snowpocalypse and Snoverkill closed businesses and local and state governments for days. People were forced to stay home and deal with the usual inconveniences of heavy snowfall. Some media outlets suggested that global warming was over, or that this one-two snow-mageddon punch was proof that climate change was a fraud. Senator James Inhofe, a noted climate-change skeptic, built an igloo in front of the U.S. Capitol complete with a hand-lettered sign reading AL GORE'S NEW HOME. Climate-change deniers crowed about a conference on the climate crisis that was postponed by the storm.[6]

Despite the total lack of scientific evidence, something seemed understandable about Inhofe's claim. Looking out my window at 40 inches of snow, I could see how global warming was, perhaps, a little harder to believe for some people. I did a quick online survey with Ye Li, now at University of California-Riverside, and Lisa Zaval of Columbia that asked two questions: "How much do you believe in global warming?" and "Is today's temperature above or below normal?" We used the respondents' zip codes to look up the actual temperature of their location when they answered.

We found a significant correlation between the relative temperature (how much warmer and colder that day was compared to average) and concerns about climate change. We called this *local warming*, in contrast to global warming, since the correlation showed that the temperature at that particular place and time behaved as if it was an important factor in deciding whether or not to believe in climate change. Since today's weather is easily seen and accessible in our memory, it receives too much weight, even though in the grand scheme any individual day's weather plays very little role in the overall climate crisis we face.

This finding has been replicated by many others, including in lab studies where researchers surreptitiously changed the temperature in the room to be hotter or colder than normal while asking participants for their opinions about climate change.[7] Raising the thermostat increased belief in climate change, lowering the thermostat decreased it. This ambient temperature even affected participants' actions. At the end of a similar study, we asked those involved if they wanted to donate some of the money they had earned by participating in the study to fighting man-made climate change. When they experienced much colder than usual temperatures in the room, they donated only about $0.75, but when it was much warmer than normal, they donated about three times as much, $2.25.

The weather also changes all sorts of consumer behavior in ways that seem consistent with accessibility. Choice architects may not be able to change the weather, but they can certainly change accessibility. Using a database of over 40 million car sales in the United States, a group of economists and marketing scholars including Meghan Busse, Devin Pope, Jaren Pope, and Jorge Silva-Risso compared sales on sunny and cloudy days for convertibles and four-wheel-drive cars. Just like local warming, the particular day's weather held influence: there was a 12.6 percent increase in the probability of buying a convertible on a clear day. Busse and company found the opposite effect for four-wheel-drive vehicles: they were more likely to be sold when the weather was bad. In fact, a 10-inch snowfall stimulated sales of four-wheelers by about 6 percent for the following two to three weeks.[8]

Similar results have been found with other kinds of purchases. Economists Michael Conlin, Ted O'Donoghue, and Timothy Vogelsang found that cold-weather items, such as heavy jackets, were more likely to be purchased on particularly cold days. However, unlike cars, we can easily recover from this mistake—just return the package. Not surprisingly, they found a significant increase in returns in the days that followed. On average, there was a 4 percent increase in returns when the temperature on the day of the order was 30 degrees lower.[9]

Inhibition

There is one more wrinkle in understanding the relationship between memory and assembling preferences. When we recall a memory because it's accessible, something surprising happens: other related memories become harder to recall, even if they would be useful. Psychologists call this blocking *inhibition*; accessibility makes some memories easier to remember, but the very process of recalling these thoughts or experiences blocks or reduces our ability to remember other related ones.

Inhibition happens all the time. Say you walk into your dry cleaner the day after you get a new phone number. The dry cleaner asks for the new number and you strain to picture it in your mind. Just as you feel it on the tip of your tongue, the dry cleaner, trying to be helpful, looks at your last order and says, "Is it 212-. . . ." And as soon as he states the last digit, the new number vanishes entirely and you can't picture any phone number aside from that old one. Hearing the old number seems to wipe out any hope of retrieving the new one—the increased accessibility of your old digits has inhibited the accessibility of the new ones. You surrender and sheepishly pull out the piece of paper where you've written the new number down. This type of experience takes place in particular when the two kinds of information under consideration are similar. The new phone number does not inhibit unrelated memories. If the dry cleaner asked for the date of your wedding anniversary, for example, you'd probably have no problem reciting it right away.

The iconic game show *Jeopardy!* provides further insight into inhibition. The most climactic part of the show is Final Jeopardy, where the contestants must write down the answer to the same, often difficult, question. In 2020, *Jeopardy!* held a tournament of tournaments, "*Jeopardy!*: The Greatest of All Time," where three all-time champions faced off to prove who was the best of the best. This contest took place shortly after Christmas and New Year's, was well covered by the media, and had huge ratings, with millions of viewers tuning in for the dramatic moments that *Jeopardy!* is known for. The winner was Ken Jennings, who had won over $4.5 million throughout his appearances on the show and famously held the record for most wins, with seventy-four victories in a row in 2004. But I'm interested in what happened on the seventy-fifth appearance, when he lost on what seemed to be a simple question.

In Final Jeopardy, the contestants were given this clue: "Most of this firm's 70,000 seasonal white-collar employees work only four months a year." When posed with this clue, many people would naturally think about obvious seasonal work times, like the winter holidays or summer vacation when students often take temporary jobs. That's what first came to Jennings's mind as well: "I assumed the answer would have something to do with summer or the holiday season." Our minds, like his, try to think of companies that must hire to meet this seasonal crunch. Maybe a department store? Amazon? The Post Office? We could quickly count those out, as most of the positions those companies are hiring to fill would not be white-collar jobs. What about other similar employers? Jennings came up with "What is FedEx?"

When he revealed the answer, there was an audible gasp from the audience. Many knew he was wrong, and that after seventy-four matches, he was about to be defeated. You might think the correct answer, H&R Block, would be easy. But Jennings claims that he never even considered tax season, and although he knew the company, H&R Block never entered his mind. How did he make this mistake?

Thinking about the holiday season made holiday employers more accessible: Amazon, brick-and-mortar retailers, and the Salvation Army probably all came to his mind, as they likely would to ours. But at the same time, inhibition makes it harder to think about tax season, census taking, and other kinds of temporary employment. We unknowingly suppress some memory to focus on the task at hand. For Jennings, holidays acted as an inhibitor, making tax season disappear from his mind.

Choice architects, knowingly or not, often direct attention, and in turn memory, in one direction at the cost of another. In writing this section of the book, I tried to lead you astray by telling you that the tournament was held right after Christmas and New Year's. This comment made the holidays more accessible, and presumably, led you to inhibit tax season, just like what had happened with Jennings. If instead, I had told you that Jennings's loss had occurred on April 15, Tax Day, you might have focused on tax season and inhibited the holidays. So here we see how the environment can affect not only what comes to our minds but also what does not.

If I asked you to write down the names of all fifty of the United States, how do you think you would you do? Would you be better than Emory undergraduates, who, on average, could list only forty? Some, like the state you live in, would be very accessible. Now imagine I offer you a little help by giving you a list of twenty-five states you can study for five minutes before the test. Would you use the list? Surely you would do better than having not reviewed the list; after all, you would have been given half the answers, so you're halfway home.

But my help is actually no help at all. While you will remember more of the listed states, you will remember fewer states overall. Reviewing the twenty-five states you were given made them more accessible, but it also made the states not on the list harder to recall. Typically, when people are given the list, they "lose" three to five states, recalling about thirty-six, instead of forty. Inhibition lowers the ability to recall states not included on the list,[10] even when those on the list are easier to remember.

Whenever we have issues remembering something, we are tempted to write it down. That process can help. Benjamin Franklin—publisher, inventor, essayist, and diplomat—was famous for suggesting a system for decision-making involving paper and (quill) pen. It turns out he was an early choice architect and anticipated the role inhibition has in assembling preferences.

Joseph Priestley, the English chemist who identified oxygen and invented soda water, asked for Franklin's advice about an important choice he faced: Should he take a job as a tutor and assistant to a rich gentleman? The position would provide a steady income, something Priestley desperately wanted, but might take time away from his research. Franklin famously told Priestley to write down a list of pros and cons. What is often left out of the story is something crucial to this discussion: Franklin worried Priestley's pros might inhibit his cons, and vice versa:

> When those difficult Cases occur, they are difficult chiefly because while we have them under Consideration, all the Reasons pro and con are not present to the Mind at the same time; but sometimes one Set present themselves, and at other times another,

the first being out of Sight. Hence the various Pur-
poses or Inclinations that alternatively prevail, and
the Uncertainty that perplexes us.[11]

Franklin had a solution to address this problem:

[During] three or four Days Consideration I put
down under the different Heads short Hints of the
different Motives that at different Times occur to
me for or against the Measure.

Franklin called this decision-making process his "moral
algebra," in part because he added up the pros and cons,
weighting them by importance to make a decision.

Why write things down over three or four days instead of
making the list while the pros and cons are fresh in our
minds? It seems that Franklin was worried about inhibition.
He actually considered remembering the hardest part of
making difficult decisions. The piece of paper was important because, unlike human memory, it overcame the effects
of accessibility and inhibition. Human memory exhibits an
ebb and flow, with some things coming to mind and then
disappearing, quickly replaced by others. When certain memories become accessible, they inhibit others. So, if we always
make our decisions on first blush, without the list as guidance, the first considerations that come to mind will domi-
nate.

Franklin's list of pros and cons minimized this concern.
He realized not only that preferences are assembled, but
that retrieving memories is tricky. When most people talk

about Franklin's advice, they neglect the role of memory, often omitting it, and concentrate on his adding up the pros and cons. When that happens, we lose sight of the piece of paper for what it really is: a choice architecture for improving decisions by removing the foibles of memory from our assembled preferences. Over time, accessibility fades, leaving other reasons, initially inhibited, to come to mind.

Inhibition is not permanent. Eventually, you would walk out of the dry cleaner and remember your new phone number. As Franklin suggested, over the course of a few days, considerations that were "first being out of Sight" will reappear. In our example of recalling the fifty states, North Dakota does not take a permanent departure from our mental map—after some time, the midwestern state will return, snugly surrounded by Minnesota, South Dakota, Montana, and our friends to the north, Canada. If Ken Jennings had more time to consider his Final Jeopardy answer, at some point he would have went "Duh," and said, "Of course, H&R Block." If you are a crossword puzzler, you have probably experienced that same feeling. You can't find what seems to be a good answer to a clue and keep coming up with answers that don't fit the given number of spaces. But if you come back to the clue a half hour later, suddenly the answer seems obvious.

The temporary nature of inhibition suggests that people might change their minds depending on what memory or attribute they think of first: Think first of the fat in a hamburger, and you will believe it is less healthy. Think about the lean meat, and you will feel better about the same burger in the bun. Elke Weber and I, along with a varying set of excellent co-authors, have tried to put this idea into a model of how preferences are assembled, something we call *query theory*.[12]

The basic idea of query theory is that when we make a choice, we assemble our preferences by thinking about the different aspects of the potential options. We first consider one set of aspects, then the other, what Weber and I see as queries to memory, thus the name. Because of accessibility, the first query will produce a richer set of reasons than the second. By directing our attention toward one query, we change how our preferences are assembled, which affects our ultimate choice. In our burger example, the percent fat label makes the unhealthy aspects more accessible, and inhibition makes the healthier aspects less accessible. The percent lean label does just the opposite. In this simple case, we consider both options, but the label given to the attribute changes the order of the queries, and that change in order can affect our decision. Query theory is a specific way of applying accessibility and inhibition in choice architecture.

Not to overstate its power, but query theory can add years to your life . . . or at least make you *think* you will live longer. One's impending worldly end is not necessarily a pleasant topic, so people don't consider it often, particularly when they are young. But "How long will I live?" is a good example of a question where we recall a set of facts to come up with an assembled answer.

Life span is one of the most important factors to consider when making long-term financial decisions. Estimating how long you will live will help you choose a mortgage rate, decide when to retire, and determine how to invest, withdraw, and spend your retirement savings. If someone expects a long life, they may plan to save more during their working years. But because we assemble answers spontaneously, even when it comes to our longevity, those answers will be influenced by how a question is posed. Unknowingly, these assembled preferences might have an outsized influence on your financial choices.

There are two different ways to think about longevity. Let's say you wanted to know whether you will still be kicking around at age eighty-five. You could ask:

What is the probability I will live to eighty-five?

or

What is the probability that I will die by eighty-five?

Obviously, the answers are related. Either you are alive at eighty-five or you are dead at eighty-five. If you think there is a 70 percent chance you will be alive at eighty-five, there is a 30 percent chance you will be dead at eighty-five.

But you might think of different memories, attributes, or events when asked about your life span in different ways. Imagine I asked you the probability of your living to eighty-five. You may well first think about why you might make it. For example, you might recall any relatives that made it to a ripe old age, say an Aunt Betsy who lived to 103. Maybe you think about how you work out occasionally, or how you quit smoking years ago. Maybe the lightning speed of twenty-first-century medical and scientific advances enters your mind. These ideas have become accessible, while their counterparts, answering why you might not live that long, have been inhibited.

Now imagine that I then asked you the probability of your dying by eighty-five. Would the same thoughts come to mind? Probably not. Instead, the reasons you might not make it to eighty-five become the first queries you consider. You forget all about dear old Aunt Betsy, and home in on your Uncle Mort, who had a massive heart attack at fifty-three. Your occasional workout routine and pride in quitting smoking is replaced with the fact that you are twenty pounds overweight and your cholesterol levels have been climbing in recent years. You're more likely to remember an article you read about growing resistance to antibiotics, or perhaps the perception that the world is becoming increasingly violent. All your optimistic thoughts when asked the "live to eighty-five" question may be hard to recall—they have been inhibited.

The question's wording alters the order in which you consider why you might live to eighty-five versus why you might die before then. The "live to" phrasing encourages accessibility to positive reasons, because those are what you will think of first, and it inhibits negative reasons. The opposite might be true when you are asked the "die by" question, with the negative thoughts prevailing.

Along with a group of researchers, I have asked thousands of Americans over the age of forty-five about their life expectancy. To keep things simple, I convert their answers to the same scale and look at how respondents replied to ques-

The Elements of Choice

tions about a 50 percent chance of living to a certain age. When we asked what age they would *live to*, respondents believed there was a 50 percent chance they would be alive at eighty-five. When they were asked when they would *die by*, they reported a 50 percent chance that they would be alive at seventy-five. The same question with slightly different phrasing resulted in a ten-year gap.[13]

To make sure this result was due to differences in what they recalled in response to the different queries, we also asked what they'd thought about as they made their estimate. In the "live to" question, people thought more about parents, aunts, and uncles who lived a long time; how good their health was; and breakthroughs made by modern medicine. In the "die by" question, the accessible memories were much different: they recalled early deaths and other misfortunes in their families, along with random dangers, like terrorism, that could result in the deaths of younger people. Everyone typed these thoughts one per line, hitting return after they thought they had finished a thought, so we could count what they were thinking. Every additional thought recalled about living longer increased their perceived estimated life expectancy by 4.6 years.

These findings raise another important point about choice architecture, one that we must all be careful to remember. Not every designer has our best interests in mind. Knowing how respondents reply to the "live to" versus "die by" questions means people peddling products or services dependent on longevity can use the same accessibility and inhibition to market and sell their wares. Consider an annuity. It really should be called longevity insurance: annuities are insurance plans that provide guaranteed income no matter how long you will live. They protect you from living longer than your money. The basic idea is that you give the insurance firm an amount of money now, and they will give you monthly payments back as long as you are alive.

If you think you are going to have a long, healthy life, clearly this deal is a good one for you. Annuities, however, are hard to sell, as many potential customers are skeptical of the model. Some clever salespeople seem to think ideas like query theory might be able to assist them in changing this opinion. A website for financial services salespeople suggests this advice:

> How often do you search for a way to get the conversation with a prospect rolling on the right track, particularly taking the discussion into retirement planning territory? You can use the phrases below . . . to help shape a thought-provoking conversation and encourage your clients to spend a few minutes "predicting" how long they might live and what a potentially long life could mean. . . . [W]hy not arm yourself with some thought-provoking statements you can use while looking your prospect in the eye across that proverbial kitchen table? Statements like:
>
> "Let me ask you this. Do you come from a family that has a history of living into their eighties or nineties, or beyond?"

> "Has anyone in your family ever lived to age 100 or more?"
>
> "Do you have expectations of being the oldest living member in your family?"
>
> "If I asked you how many years you think you will live in retirement, what would you say?"[14]

These are not queries in theory, these are queries *in practice*. This post advises sales representatives to replace any natural order that potential clients might use to answer these questions with the one the salespeople want them to use. Manipulating retrieval like this not only makes it easier to think about living a long time but inhibits our ability to think about why we might not live that long. If used to sell annuities to the wrong customer, this is the salesperson's equivalent of a dark pattern.

While query theory looks at how we convince ourselves, this insurance sales advice suggests that salespeople can use the same theory to persuade others—including asking a set of questions that assemble memories and beliefs to indicate you will live a long time—and, no doubt, to sell you an annuity.

Preferences as Memories

Not all of our preferences are constructed. No choice architect in the world will ever make me enjoy eating liver. But we are busy, and many situations in which we face a decision are unique. Either the details differ (like facing menu choices in an unfamiliar restaurant) or the situation is one that we don't think about often (like longevity or changing jobs). Drawing our attention to one aspect of our memory or another can influence our choices. This intended direction would be fine, except we don't always know when we are being influenced. Decision-makers almost always deny that the weather, the way a question is framed, or a subtle webpage background can affect their choices. This belief is because, in part, we have a terribly naive understanding of how memory works and how it influences the decision-making process. Perhaps the best contribution this book can make is to lift the curtain, at least a little bit, on how designers and choice architects manipulate memory to their benefit. If we understand mind writing, we may be a step ahead.

4

Goals of Choice Architecture

I n the early spring of 2020, everyone wanted to talk to their doctor. COVID-19 changed many things, but right then, many people—too many people—had a single question: "I think I have symptoms of the coronavirus. What should I do?" Implicit in the question was a choice among several options: doing nothing, self-isolating (including from family), trying to get a test, or going to the emergency room.

There was a no shortage of information. Indeed, there was a tsunami of stories, theories, information, facts, and fantasy. At the beginning of the COVID-19 crisis it was all a blur, and making decisions was not at all fluent. Figuring out what information to look at was discouraging. At the same time, picking the right course of action—what we will call an *accurate option*—seemed essential. We all felt we needed a helpful conversation.

All choice architecture is a conversation between the designer and the chooser. Sometimes, like when you're talking to a car salesperson, it's a real-life, face-to-face conversation. Other times, like when you are using a website, the conversation is virtual. The people on the other side of the conversation are far away, perhaps no longer even working on the project. Websites are conversing with hundreds, thousands, or even millions of choosers, while the car salesperson is talking to just one. But the car salesperson and the website both have something in common: they need to know about you to provide you with information and options.

Conversations often involve exchanging knowledge between the participants, and in a good conversation, you can learn from each other. We all know the characteristics of good and bad conversationalists. If your partner is a good conversationalist, they might tell you something like "The local grocery is changing its hours and has special times for older people," and you may tell them in return a trick you learned for getting groceries via Amazon. A bad conversationalist, however, does not seem to understand you and provides tons of boring and irrelevant information that seems off topic. A bad conversationalist tells you at length about how the virus ruined their vacation trip to someplace you couldn't care less about. COVID-19 conversations—and conversations in general—share two important goals that are also central to choice architecture:

- **Fluency:** A good conversation is fluid, and we can concentrate on the substance of what is being said. In fact, we often say that a conversation *flows* when it is good. Ultimately, the feeling of fluency helps determine whether we will engage in a conversation at all, as well as for how long. If the doctor is hard to understand, using a vocabulary that you do not comprehend, it is unpleasant. By now, you may see the analogy between a good conversation and choice architecture. For both conversations and decisions, we may disengage and avoid situations that lack fluency. More important, fluency might be used to guide us to the right plausible path, one that could lead to a better decision. But what exactly does a good decision mean?

- **Accuracy:** A good conversation helps us select options that are best for us and most accurate for the situation at hand. The COVID-19 conversation with our doctor helps us figure out if our symptoms suggest a course of action. Our doctor should help us find the options that make us feel the best, both in the present and in the future. An unneeded trip to the emergency room could expose us to infection and consume resources that could be used for people who are really sick. This would not be an ideal, or "accurate," outcome. We will see that accuracy is not always easy to define, but it is essential to understanding whether a choice architecture is performing well.

Sometimes there is tension between these two goals: a very thorough discussion might be less fluid, but it also might lead to a more accurate choice. We will discuss this tension throughout this book, but first we must better understand fluency and accuracy.

To understand both goals, we might think about what a good conversation with a doctor would be like. To do this, we might want to know what both the patient-chooser and the doctor-designer know. The chooser could report any symptoms, such as whether they have a fever or a cough. They could also tell the doctor about their personal demographics, recent travel, and close contacts. The doctor knows what types of people are at risk, which symptoms suggest further testing, and what experts think are the best decisions to make in each situation. In addition, a good doctor might also make us feel a bit better emotionally.

Due to the pandemic, there are too many patients and too few doctors, so such a conversation between doctor and patient might happen via an app. On March 27, 2020, Apple released such an app, Apple COVID-19, designed to facilitate precisely this conversation. It asks the user a set of questions and provides a course of action. Living in New York during this time of high stress, I naturally wanted to have a "chat" with this app. It's a portrait of fluency: only relevant text appears on each page. I compared it to a website run by the State of New York that performs a similar function. In addition to asking me questions about my symptoms, the state page gave me a lot of unnecessary information. With every question the website presented—indeed, on every *page* of the site—the names of the governor and the state health commissioner, as well as a list of file formats used on the website. Granted, this is not a time for website niceties, but having to actively ignore this information did not make the site more fluent. If the Apple app is like a doctor who listens attentively to you and gives you only relevant information, the New York State site is more like the person who drones on about irrelevant trivia.

The Apple app doesn't tell you the name of the Apple president. It gets right down to business, first identifying the symptoms that warrant an immediate trip to the emergency room. Then comes the real interview. It starts by asking your age, but the way it does so is informative. You can imagine one of those terrible pulldown boxes appearing, listing every year from 2020 back through sometime early in the last century. These require you to scroll through dozens of options to locate your birth year. Not very fluent. Instead, the Apple app presents you with three categories: "under 18," "between 18 and 64," and "65 and older," as that is all the information it needs. The subsequent tile then lists seven simple questions, each of which has a simple yes or no answer. It then asks three more questions and suggests which choices you should make. The app was quite successful; when released, it was the number-one app in the health and fitness category for a week and number four overall.[1] A similar app, COVID Symptom Tracker, developed by King's College London, Guy's and St. Thomas' Hospitals, and ZOE Global Limited, was the number-one medical app in the United Kingdom and was used by more than 2.6 million participants in the United Kingdom and the United States. That app asked you to report your symptoms daily and was used to improve our understanding of what symptoms were helpful in diagnosing the disease.[2]

Both these apps provided good conversations. I was asked a simple series of easy-to-answer questions, which made them fluid, and received information that was useful and—according to the Centers for Disease Control and Prevention—accurate.

My Two Uncles

There is another decision that is nowhere near as fluid as it ought to be, and it is faced by almost all Americans of a certain age: when to start claiming Social Security benefits. It might seem mundane, but it turns out to be one of the most important questions about finances Americans face as they grow older. To help explain why it's such a challenge, I like to compare two of my favorite uncles.

Here I'll call them Uncle Don and Uncle John. Neither was a proverbial "rich uncle." Uncle Don was from my mother's side of the family. He was gregarious, single, and from a large family. Uncle Don's parents didn't live long—neither made it past their midseventies. Uncle John was on my father's side. He was a bit quieter, even taciturn, and also single. That side of the family is much smaller but tends toward longevity. Both of John's parents (my grandparents) lived into their nineties, remaining sharp and mobile all the while. While I hope I have inherited genes from Uncle John's family, I often had a better time hanging out with Uncle Don. He had better parties!

My uncles, along with everyone else about to claim Social Security retirement benefits, faced a choice. Don and John could start claiming as early as their sixty-second birthdays and get about $1,334 a month. They could also wait as their benefits increased, by about 8 percent a year, until they reached $2,347 a month at age seventy. For a question so important to their future and retirement, many Americans make this decision astonishingly badly.

Let's assume that, like the median American family, neither of my uncles had a large 401(k) or other retirement account stashed away for retirement. The median family has about $76,000 in their retirement accounts, and that $76,000 has to pay for eighteen years of retirement. That works out to $350 a month—not a princely sum wherever you live. This means that for both my uncles, and for the median American family, their Social Security checks would be important. For the majority of Americans, the bulk of their postretirement income will be their Social Security benefits. Their retirement savings are only a supplement.

This choice has serious economic consequences. If Don and John claimed early, their annual benefits would be lower—if they claimed at sixty-two, they might get about $16,000 a year. If they waited to start collecting at seventy, they would collect more, about $28,000. So, should they wait? This is a surprisingly complex question, one that has produced many pages of academic writing.

In deciding whether to claim early or late, Uncle Don and

Uncle John may have visited the Social Security website, which would not be much help. There they'd be confronted with strange and unfamiliar terms (like *excess earnings* and *delayed retirement credits*), as well as information that does not apply to them. One of the stranger terms is *full retirement age*, which describes a particular age that the government has given that label, based on history, but that age is nothing special. Your benefits will grow at 8 percent on either side of that age, and the age depends upon your year of birth. It is an arbitrary term.

There is one factor is obviously important: How long are you going to live? The longer you live, the better it is to wait. If you knew you were to live to only seventy-five, claiming at sixty-two is a good idea: you would collect a total of $208,000. This is almost a 50 percent increase from the $140,000 you would collect if you started at seventy. Waiting means that the benefits are larger, but you collect for a shorter length of time, only five years in this case.

Most people in the United States live longer. If you were to live until eighty-five, a reasonable expectation, you would collect about $368,000 if you started collecting early at sixty-two. But if you waited to claim at seventy, you would collect $420,000 total. Remember that Uncle Don and Uncle John, based on their parents' longevity and their own health, knew something about their respective prospects of long life. As a result, my uncles might have needed to make very different decisions.

The 31 million Americans projected to retire in the next decade face a similar decision.[3] This decision is more important than ever for two reasons. The company pension, known technically as the *defined benefits plan*, is decreasing in importance as fewer and fewer companies provide such programs. And Americans are living longer. The average American now spends about nineteen years in retirement, about 60 percent longer than they did in the 1950s.[4] It may cost some of them money, but many Americans claim benefits early. Roughly half claim benefits by sixty-four.

Are they making a mistake? Are their choices accurate—and by *accuracy*, we mean "Does the chooser pick the option that is best for them?" Defining "best for them" is not simple, given that different people may want or need different things. You might be tempted to suggest that all people wait to collect Social Security, because they get bigger payments. But that may not be a good idea.

For Uncle Don, who was likely not going to live as long as Uncle John, claiming early would probably *not* be a mistake. Had he consulted longevity calculators (online programs that ask questions to determine life expectancy), he might have found out that he was expected to live to seventy-five. He would collect, over his expected lifetime, about $68,000 more by claiming at sixty-two than if he had waited until seventy.

But longevity wasn't his only consideration. Since he was not married, he did not have to worry about benefits for his partner. He didn't love his job and dreamed of quitting. Because of these factors, claiming early might make even more sense. After taking everything into consideration, Don might wisely conclude that delaying was not in his best interest.

Uncle John, on the other hand, would probably benefit from delaying. He might have used his retirement savings to supplement any salary he was making and waited as long as he could. It would be as if he had a very low-risk investment with an 8 percent return.

The example of my two uncles illustrates that the conversation about when to start claiming Social Security must be customized to the individual making the decision. To identify an accurate decision, the answer will depend upon factors, such as longevity, that will differ across people. For some people, like my Uncle John, claiming benefits at sixty-two would be a mistake. Without knowing more about the people claiming benefits, we can't know who is making mistakes and who is not. When I first learned about how many people claimed Social Security early, I thought I knew how to fix it: default everyone into claiming later—for example, at seventy. But the lesson I learned from my uncles is simple. Moving everyone to later claiming may help some people, but it would certainly hurt others. This is just one demonstration of why choice architecture must reflect differences in circumstances.

Finding the Right Box

The story of Uncle Don and Uncle John reflects a major theme of this book. The goal of choice architecture is not to get people to choose one particular outcome, like claiming Social Security at seventy across the board. Instead, it is to encourage people to pick the right option for them. We can draw a simple table illustrating this. On the top are two options, claiming Social Security at sixty-two or claiming at seventy, and in the rows below are my two uncles. The goal of choice architecture is to get each uncle to make the decision that is right for him—to get him into the right box.

Good and Bad Decision Outcomes
for Claiming Social Security

	Claim Early (Sixty-Two)	Claim Late (Seventy)
Short life expectancy (Uncle Don)	Good decision	Mistake
Long life expectancy (Uncle John)	Mistake	Good decision

We could construct a similar table for most choices. It might have more options, like the different options presented by the COVID-19 app we talked about earlier (self-isolating, seeking treatment, and so on). For each person, there will be one better outcome, and the job of the app is, again, to get that person in the right box.

Sometimes it is easy to know which box is best. When it comes to saving for retirement, we could imagine that most Americans must make a choice between saving more and saving less. Remember that the median American has only about $76,000 in retirement savings at sixty-five. For most people this is not enough—64 percent of workers say they are behind schedule in saving for retirement. So, for most people, the right box is saving more. Many of the early successes of choice architecture have come in cases where most people make the same error in the same direction, putting many people into the same (wrong) box. Increasing retirement saving across the board would help the majority of people, though we might be making a small mistake for some. While increasing the savings for those who have saved enough is not ideal, it is probably not that harmful. There is an implicit cost-benefit analysis in the decision to nudge everyone in one direction: the benefits of moving most people into one box (making them more likely to save, for example) increases the welfare of many people. Making a few people save a little too much is a small price to pay.[5]

In other situations, one-size-fits-all interventions may do more harm than good. *Heterogeneity*, a term used by behavioral scientists, reflects the fact that different people have different needs. To improve decisions around claiming Social Security, we could have tried to increase everyone's claiming age, but that would create another problem. Such a nudge might help Uncle John, who would be able to collect more money, but it might move Uncle Don from the correct box (claiming early) to the wrong one (claiming late). That would be a mistake that would cost him $50,000 if he lived to seventy-five. To put that in context, remember he has only saved about $76,000 for his retirement, and that would be eight years (from age sixty-two to seventy) without any Social Security.[6] If he didn't continue to work in retirement, he would have less than $800 a month to live on if he tried to wait until seventy to claim.

This need for customized help runs counter to the way most people use the term *nudging*, as a synonym for choice architecture. Too often, nudges are interpreted to mean changing everyone's behavior in a single direction. But we can customize choice architecture. Richard Thaler and Cass Sunstein call this *customized nudging*—that is, applying different architecture to different people, so that each person is encouraged to make the right choice. There are cases, like in the example of my two uncles and their Social Security options, where people differ more dramatically in their preferences and needs, and one-size-fits-all choice architecture will be harmful for some of them. If we can, we should use a more customized approach that gets everyone into the right box.

The Reality: An Important Decision Gone Bad

Let's return to what my uncles would have seen if they went to the Social Security website for help:

Who Can Use the Retirement Estimator?

You can use the Retirement Estimator if:

- You have enough Social Security credits at this time to qualify for benefits **and** you are **not**:

    - Currently receiving benefits on your own Social Security record;

- Waiting for a decision about your application for benefits or Medicare;
- Age sixty-two or older and receiving benefits on another Social Security record; **or**
- Eligible for a pension based on work not covered by Social Security.

Then you would see the following under "How to Move Around in This Application":

The "Next" and "Previous" buttons are at the top and bottom of each page to move forward and backward page by page. Using the "Next" button takes you to every page where you may need to enter information.

You also may use the tabs at the top of the page to move between sections.

Important:

Do *not* use the "Enter" key on your keyboard to move around the application or make a selection from the drop-down lists.

Do *not* use your browser's "Back" button to move around the application.

Do *not* close your browser or use the "X" button to leave your application.

Not exactly fluid, is it? Instead of concentrating on the decision at hand, I need to understand terms like *Social Security record* and *Social Security credits* (and I need to click through to another page to figure that out!). I also have to remember not to use my browser's Back button or the Enter key, things I normally do on other websites. Clearly, the Social Security website is making me think about lots of things other than what is important for my decision-making process.[7]

Fluency determines plausible paths, but we have not talked about one particular plausible path: avoiding the decision entirely. An absence of fluency can increase the tendency to avoid or delay a choice.[8] In other words, making a decision difficult can cause that decision to *not* be made. Making decisions more fluid can help people actually make that decision in the first place.

Decisions surrounding retirement are delayed (if not avoided entirely) because they are unnecessarily unpleasant. People know that retirement exists but don't want to face retirement planning. Surveys often ask people who have recently retired when they first started thinking about actually retiring. About 22 percent of people first start thinking about the decision one year before they retire, while another 22 percent first think about it only six months before they retire.[9] Obviously some decisions, like the amount you will save toward retirement, should be made much earlier, and saving is most effective (thanks to the magic of compound interest) when we are far from retirement.

Thinking about retirement is difficult. It feels like it is in the distant future, and people do not like thinking about their older selves. But the tendency to avoid thinking about retirement is encouraged when the very tools one must use to make these decisions are, in fact, awful to use. Given how important retirement decisions are, this is a problem worth solving.

What Is Accuracy?

Uncle John's and Uncle Don's decisions had a pretty clear definition of *accuracy*: they wanted to be comfortable in their retirement. But it's not always so easy. If we assume that more money collected over the course of a lifetime is better, then we can easily identify mistakes in the claiming age a person selects. But Social Security has another benefit. It pays you as long as you live, so it is a form of insurance. If you live longer than you expect, you are covered.[10]

How can a choice architect identify when people make an error? How can we say that one choice architecture provides more accurate choices than another? Researchers tend to use three different approaches: *dominance*, *consistency*, and what I will call the *decision simulator technique*.

Dominance simply says that one option is better than (or at least tied with) another in every way. This is the easiest way of identifying errors. Imagine you visit a travel website to shop for flights. You have two flights to choose from: the first flight is direct and not very crowded. It has spacious seats and costs $450. Another flight takes more time because it makes stops in the middle of nowhere. It is also more expensive, has

The Elements of Choice

seats with less leg room, and is very crowded. Choosing the first flight is the right thing to do because it is better in every way. Choosing the second is a mistake because it is worse in every way. We say the first flight is a *dominating* option and the second flight is a *dominated* option.

If we were testing a choice architecture for this decision, how would we know it is doing its job to help people pick the best flights? Imagine that the website presented ten flights. We would want to make sure choosers pick the dominating options and avoid the flights that are dominated. If there was one option that was better than all the others, then not picking the superior option would be a clear error, and we could pretty confidently conclude that the user who did not pick it made a mistake. Choosing dominating options and avoiding dominated ones is a clear way to judge the accuracy of a choice. This is a great criterion for accuracy, but as you will see in later chapters, missing the best dominating option and choosing the worst dominated options happens in the real world. Furthermore, not all choice sets have dominating and dominant options. For those cases, we need other ways of judging accuracy.

A second way of identifying errors is consistency. If we change the choice architecture, does that change your choice? If so, at least one of those choices is a mistake. In fact, that is one way we know that choice architecture matters: give people exactly the same information, change the way it is presented, and if they choose different things, the choice architecture is driving the choice. The problem with looking at consistency is that we don't know which choice is wrong.

Let's go back to our flight example. Imagine you go to a

well-known website like Expedia and pick a flight from American Airlines. But imagine a parallel universe where you had gone to another site, say Google Flights, and picked a United flight. Let's assume that those flights are both available somewhere on each site. They are different. One costs more or has a shorter flight time or better seats. Since they are different, they cannot both be your best option. Ideally, you would be consistent and pick the same flight on the two sites, but you did not. Why? It has to be because the sites used different choice architectures. We cannot say which flight is a mistake, but we can say that a mistake *is* being made, even if we do not know what it is. Clearly something about the choice architecture of one of the sites led you astray.

Demonstrating inconsistency has been at the heart of decision research for the last forty years and has been a major driving force in behavioral economics.

One of the first and most influential demonstrations that people have inconsistent preferences involves evaluating gambles. Imagine you were given the choice between playing one of these two gambles:

- Gamble A: A 75 percent chance of winning $14

- Gamble B: A 25 percent chance of winning $41

Which did you select? If you're like most people, you probably picked the first bet, Gamble A. After all, it's a good chance at getting some money.

Now imagine you walk down the street and visit Paul's

Gambling Place, where they sell gambles. In real life this is called a casino, where you might put different amounts of money down at a roulette wheel, for example. Now, in this hypothetical scenario, Paul sells only Gamble B, and he asks you how much you will pay to play it. You look at it, and you assemble your preference: $41 is a nice amount of money to win and you don't think much about the 75 percent chance of getting the outcome of zero, so you say $11. You continue your stroll and walk into Sarah's House of Gambles, which sells only Gamble A. You take a look and Sarah asks you how much you would pay to play Gamble A. It pays out only $14 but the odds are good, so you say $9.

Do you see the inconsistency? You initially chose A over B. When you went into Paul's, you said you would pay $11 for Gamble B. And then at Sarah's you said you would pay less, $9, for A. This means you prefer Paul's Gamble B to Sarah's Gamble A. But when you chose between them, you said you would prefer A! There can only be one better gamble, but it looks like you don't know which one it is.

The choice architecture here is in how I, Paul, and Sarah asked you to express that preference. In one case I asked you to choose, and in another case Paul and Sarah asked you to price the gambles. Your favorite *should* be the same, but for most people it is not.[11]

This research was done by Sarah Lichtenstein and Paul Slovic. It has been done many times and is so reliable that I use it in classes, confident that it always works. Lichtenstein and Slovic even replicated their experiments on the floor of the Four Queens, a casino in Reno. It drove economists absolutely batty, because after all, preferences should be consistent, whether you are choosing or pricing. Of course, choice architecture itself is pretty irritating to economists for exactly this reason: many things that should not matter end up changing choices. These inconsistencies are important in testing theories, but they are less so in improving people's choices. Why? Because they tell us that something is wrong but can't tell us what the right option might be. It is hard to fix a choice architecture when we don't know which option is right. Choice architecture might benefit if it moves beyond inconsistency, identifying which option is better than another.

There is a third way; by use of an analogy to flight simulators, I will call this a decision simulator. A flight simulator is used in cockpit design. The cockpits we talked about in chapter 2 are very much the products of hundreds of hours of simulation, used to identify good placement and design for controls and displays. Professional pilots, like our friend Captain Sullenberger, can spend hours flying a simulator of the Airbus A320 before qualifying to fly the real thing. A simulator models how the aircraft responds to the pilot's decisions. Most often, pilots are given a specific task to practice, like simulating a takeoff of an A320 from Heathrow Runway 09R or landing a Cessna Citation CJ4 at Teterboro Runway 19. Bad decisions result in bad outcomes, like a crash, but because it is a simulator, they do so without the cost.

Just as a flight simulator might test your ability to fly from Newark Liberty Airport to Des Moines International, decision simulators test your ability to accomplish a certain decision goal: buy the cheapest option, try to get the best balance between price and quality, or, more generally, find the most fitting option. This is like buying presents for a friend: you are not shopping for yourself but rather trying to pick the option that would please your friend the most.

Let's try using a decision simulator to evaluate a dating site. Imagine you are a customer of a dating site, and that designers are trying to see how the site is doing. They might tell you to imagine your ideal "type" of date and ask you to find the person who is the closest match. For example, you might be looking for a partner of a certain height, looks, and personality. Maybe it's tall blond men who are interested in extreme sports, yoga, and opera. The goal is to see how close you come to finding this "ideal" match. The closer the match, the better the choice architecture. The hope is that the choice architecture has enabled you to find someone as close as possible to this ideal.

Giving people a goal might seem unrealistic, but it allows us to see whether the choice architecture helps you find the right option. If a flight simulator shows that one cockpit design enables the pilot to make a smooth landing and another cockpit design is confusing and almost produces a crash, then we are comfortable saying that the first design is better. Similarly, if one choice architecture produces better choices than another, then we think it is a better design. Choice simulators are particularly useful in showing that one choice architecture is better than another, because we can see if people find what they are looking for. To use our dating example from chapter 2, we would want to make sure that it allows Erika to find Assaf and vice versa. Of course, before we conclude that any particular choice architecture is best, we would want to see that it serves a broad set of goals. Just as we would like a flight simulator to show us a particular cockpit design is better for short and long flights, we would want our dating simulator to find the best match across daters with different goals.[12]

A great example of the decision simulator technique is work by the economists Sendhil Mullainathan, Markus Noeth, and Antoinette Schoar. Financial advisers, people who suggest investments, are living and breathing choice architecture. These researchers wanted to see how well financial advisers performed for customers. To do this, they hired actors as "mystery shoppers" to visit the advisers. Think of the financial advisers like you would a website. They should, in theory, have conversations to discern your needs and help you pick the right investment options. But do advisers help investors?[13]

The economists wanted to make sure that their assessment of advisers was not due to one particular type of customer. They had actors play different kinds of customers. For example, one customer made a classic mistake: he kept investing in last year's hot stocks. The problem is that while these stocks did well and got positive press the previous year, they tended to do worse than average the next year. There is even a name for this—*chasing returns*—and a good adviser should tell a client to stop doing that. The second investor type was actually doing the right thing, according to expert advice: holding a broad set of stocks in low-cost mutual funds. Here the adviser might have made minor adjustments, but they should have said the client was on the right track. It helps that contemporary financial theory has a fairly clear idea of what most people should be doing, depending upon their circumstances.

Each actor paid visits to different banks, retail investment firms, or independent advisers, all serving the lower end of the wealth spectrum. On each visit they stuck to a detailed script, playing their role.

How did the conversations go? Well, if the visit had been a flight simulator, most of the planes would have crashed. Our "good" investor was told she was doing badly; only 2.4 percent of the financial advisers supported her strategy. In contrast, the investor who was making the mistake of chasing returns was told he was doing well about 20 percent of the time.

From the point of view of the investor, the conversations did not result in accurate recommendations. The advisers suggested options that were objectively more expensive: they had higher fees paid to the firm and the adviser. For example, the actor who had done the right thing was told to sell all her low-cost index funds and invest over 60 percent of her money into more expensive actively managed funds. The economists think these are costly mistakes because these fees would increase the amount the investor paid to the company by $500 to $1,000 a year.

This calculation illustrates a real advantage of the decision simulators: since you know what should have been chosen, you can identify how big of a mistake was made. In the case of these advisers, they turn out to be costly conversations.

Talking about Decisions

If a conversation is difficult, we tend to avoid it. Just because we are having a conversation that flows, however, does not mean we are receiving useful information. Similarly, choice architecture is not just about fluent choices. We could make Uncle Don's choice fluent, showing him a screen with a Social Security claim of seventy already checked. This could lead him to make an inaccurate choice.

Again, the analogy from Churchill's observations about the House of Commons to choice architecture is apt: someone who designs buildings struggles with the two goals of making a building both attractive and functional. A choice architect must struggle with the two goals of making their product both fluent and accurate. In the best buildings, these goals complement each other: an attractive building invites use, welcoming the visitor, and a functional building makes it easy for the visitor to accomplish their purpose once there. The best choice architectures will be inviting to the decision-maker but still produce decisions that are in their best interests.

5

Decisions by Default

W hy aren't more people organ donors? I became interested in this question twenty years ago during a subway ride far below the streets of Manhattan. I was on my way uptown to New York–Presbyterian Hospital. I had been diagnosed with advanced stage IV Hodgkin's disease, a cancer of the lymph system. Now, thanks to two stem cell transplants, I have recovered.

Fortunately, I could be my own stem cell donor. Stem cells mature into the cells that make up your blood and immune system. Having these cells is important during treatment for Hodgkin's. When the procedure starts, powerful chemotherapy agents are dripped into your system. These drugs, with luck, kill the cancer cells. But, as collateral damage, they destroy your own bone marrow and immune system. So, doctors harvest stem cells from Hodgkin's patients before chemotherapy. After the chemotherapy has done its work, these stem cells are transfused into your arm to create a new immune system. The cells circulate for a few days, then, like a flock of migrating birds, they find their way home to your empty bone hollows and reproduce your bone marrow.

I was on my way for an initial doctor's appointment for my stem cell collection when I did something I never do: I talked to a stranger on the subway. A young woman broke the silence and asked me a question (she obviously didn't live by my rule): "Is 168th Street the stop for New York–Presbyterian Hospital?" I said yes, and since I was getting off there, I offered to point her in the right direction.

When we emerged aboveground, I asked her where she was going in the enormous medical complex. She mentioned a floor and building that I knew was used for organ transplants. As we chatted, she explained that she was being evaluated as a kidney donor for her sister.

Later, during my stem cell collection, I had lots of time to think. The process is long: you sit for hours after a port the size of your fist has been sewn into a large vein in your neck. Your blood is circulated through a large machine that separates the stem cells from the rest of your blood. You lie covered with a blanket as your blood circulates out of your body and returns. There is not much you can do, and I was too nervous to nap. My mind wandered to the decision that woman made to donate a kidney to her sister. This generous act would save her sister from long and frequent dialysis sessions, likely extending her sister's life. I thought this must be one of the hardest decisions one could make. There is a reason we are born with two kidneys. Giving one up, even for a loved one, is a risk and takes courage. You are making a difficult trade-off: you are profoundly helping someone but subjecting yourself to the anxiety and discomfort of major surgery, rendering yourself a little less robust with potential long-term consequences. How do people make this decision? What influences them?

This reminded me of a conversation I had with some academic friends a few months earlier. From this discussion, I learned three stark facts about organ donation. First, about 20 Americans die daily because they cannot be matched with a donor; 107,000 people are on the waiting list. Second, most people (surveys say 85 percent) agree that donation is a good thing, and that people should donate organs. But there is a massive disconnect between approving of the idea in a survey and taking lifesaving action. At the time, fewer than 28 percent declared their intention to be a donor. This is surprising because it is easy. In most states, you simply have to check a box when you renew your driver's license.[1]

The third thing I learned was that the rates to agreeing to be a donor differ across countries. The graph on the next page tells the story visually.

Some people, like the Danes, appear to be very squeamish: only about 4 percent agree to be donors when they die. Compare them to the seemingly generous Swedes—almost 86 percent of them agree to be donors. The Germans agree to be donors only 12 percent of the time, but the nearby Austrians almost universally agree to be donors.

Later, as I was recovering from the stem cell transplant, I wondered what kept more Americans from being donors

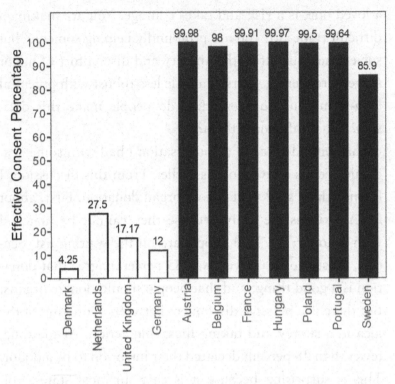

Observed willingness to be a donor: rates for low-enrollment
countries (white bars) vs. high-enrollment countries
(black bars) from Johnson and Goldstein (2003)

and why seemingly similar people, like the Danes and Swedes
or the Germans and Austrians, were making such different
decisions. Being a living donor, like my subway friend, was
quite dramatic, but agreeing to be a donor at death seemed
to be very beneficial to other people and not nearly as difficult.

Saving Lives One Click at a Time?

In the months that followed I had a lot of time to think. Posttransplant, you spend weeks in a sterile hospital room. The room has negative pressure—it is carefully ventilated so that the air only flows out, in order to prevent infection. With all this extra time, my obsession turned into a research project. During that time, I started to outline a series of studies that would explain the differences in the graph and maybe help increase organ donation.

Soon afterward, Dan Goldstein, who had recently become a postdoc at Columbia, and I started to ask people to write down what they were thinking about while deciding whether they would be a donor. While being a living donor is dramatic, we concentrated on a decision that applies to many more people: becoming an organ donor when you die. The things they said were interesting and contradictory: "How will this help the life of the recipient?" "Is this okay with my religious beliefs?" People were also disturbed by the image of what happens when organs are transplanted. It seemed that, by asking, we were making people assemble their preferences, and that for most people this was very unpleasant. It requires them to think about their own demise, an image and decision they would rather avoid.

This might explain why people avoid the decision but it can't explain the differences in donation rates by country. What could be causing them? Do people in different countries think differently about donation? Why?

I've often talked about this research and shown that graph. It has taken on a life of its own and has been called one of the most famous graphs in the social sciences.[2] When I show it to people, I ask them to explain the differences. Most people have guesses. They talk about differences in religions across countries: Austria is more Catholic than Germany. They speculate that attitudes toward medicine and science differ, or that some countries have a stronger sense of community.

In fact, the truth is surprisingly simple: much depends merely on what happens if people *don't* make a decision, something called a *no-action default*, or simply a *default*. The countries on the left of the graph ask you to choose *to be* an organ donor, and those on the right ask you to choose *not to be* a donor. If you do not make an active choice, you are, by default, a nondonor in Germany and a donor in Austria.

Dan and I wanted to understand this. We started by asking a sample of Americans whether they would be donors or not by presenting them with a choice on a webpage. One group, the opt-in condition, was told that they had just moved to a new state where the default was not to be an organ donor, and they were given a chance to change that status with a simple click of a mouse. A second group, the opt-out condition, saw an identical scenario, except the default was to be a donor. They could indicate that they did not want to be a donor with a mouse click. The third group was simply required to choose; they needed to check one box or the other to go on to the next page. This neutral question, with nothing prechecked, is a *mandated-choice condition*; it's important, because it shows what people do when they are forced to choose.

The effect of the default was remarkably strong: when

they had to opt in, only 42 percent agreed to donate, but when they had to opt out, 82 percent agreed to donate. The most interesting result was from those forced to make a choice: 79 percent said they would be a donor, almost the same percentage of donors as in the opt-out condition. The only difference between the group that was asked to opt out and those who were forced to make a choice was that we forced the respondents in the mandated-choice condition to pick either box before they could go forward. It shows that if forced to make a choice, most participants would become donors. Otherwise, if they were given a default, most simply took it, whatever it was.

This looks impressive, but what happens in real life? We looked at ten years of donations across many (mostly European) countries. Using statistical techniques, we were able to control for differences between countries, such as the quality of the transplant infrastructure, education levels, and religion. Not all relationships were obvious. For example, Roman Catholics are more likely to donate, who knew? However, the bottom line is that changing the default—what happens if you don't make a choice—appeared to increase the number of donors. Each donor can provide multiple life-saving organs—a heart, kidneys, and corneas, for example—so each donor can help many people.

If donations can save and improve lives, it is not surprising that countries spend lots of money and effort trying to encourage them. In 1998, the Netherlands sent 12 million letters, one to every household, encouraging individuals to become donors. This was accompanied by a massive educational campaign on television, radio, and in print. If you look at the Netherlands in the graph, it looks like all these efforts helped, but only a little. It has the highest agreement rate of the opt-in countries, but the effect was small compared to the effect of the default. For example, in neighboring Belgium, which is an opt-out country, 98 percent of the population are potential donors, compared to the Netherlands' 28 percent.

Since then, several different researchers have compared opt-in and opt-out countries using different data and models. According to some economists,[3] this simple change could "considerably alleviate" the shortage of organs in general and eliminate entirely the shortage of important organs, like hearts. Others estimate that opt-out countries have a 25 percent to 30 percent increase in the number of actual donors and have shown an overall increase in kidney and liver transplants, even when accounting for donations from living donors.[4] A recent review of the role of defaults in donation decisions summarizes data from many subsequent studies. It concludes that the rates of consent, donation, and transplantation are higher under "presumed consent" (opt-out) policies than under so-called explicit consent policies. But that review suggests that there are other important factors involved the organ donation decision, and both Dan Goldstein and I agree.[5]

Donation policies have changed in several countries in the two decades since my subway ride. Singapore in 2004 changed its law to opt out for most citizens, and in 2009 it extended the policy to cover all citizens and permanent residents. Argentina changed to an opt-out law in 2005, Chile in 2010, and Wales in 2015. Finally, the beginning of 2017 saw the

French change to an opt-out regime. England, the Netherlands, and Nova Scotia changed the default starting in 2020, joined by Scotland in 2021.[6] Significant efforts toward opt-out regimes are under way in Ireland and elsewhere.

Still, it would not be right to advocate simply changing the default and stop at that. First, it is difficult to say that the switch of default causes the changes in donation rates. We titled our paper "Do Defaults Save Lives?" as a question, and we think there are several reasons it is not entirely settled. When a country adopts a new policy, the change gets a lot of press coverage. It also often does additional advertising. No one has, understandably, been able to do an experiment where people are randomly assigned to either opt-in or opt-out, and observed what happens to donation rates.

Second, the process of becoming an organ donor has many steps, and there are many things that could be done to improve the situation beyond just automatically checking a different box. That does increase the number of people classified as donors, but it does not guarantee that person becomes a donor. When a potential donor dies, their next of kin is often asked for permission before any organ transplants take place. This, of course, is another place where choice architecture can have an influence.[7] Spain has been particularly successful in encouraging donation, increasing donation from 14 donors per million in 1989 to 34 per million in 2014—an increase of 143 percent. Although Spain is often considered an opt-out country, that is not the view of all of those responsible for running the program. They argue that its success lies in a focus on making sure that families are comfortable agreeing to donations and that potential donors are identified. Spain is quite successful; only 16 percent of families do not give consent. There are transplant coordinators, typically doctors, specially trained in making the request. Many hospitals have special rooms dedicated to the kind of difficult conversation that occurs between the family and the coordinator. This "Spanish model" has been adopted elsewhere, first in several Latin American countries and later in Australia and Italy.[8]

The way the choice is posed to families is its own choice architecture. The question to the family can be framed as either explicit or presumed consent. One example is a "presumptive approach" designed to increase agreement. It focuses on the benefits of donation to the recipient and the opportunity to save lives, and uses the assumption that families have little knowledge of donation. Writing in the journal *Critical Care Nurse,* Sheldon Zink and Stacey Wertlieb argue that "[b]y focusing on the benefits of donation, the requestor shifts the tone of the conversation from discomfort and doubt to compassion and possibility. . . . Enabl[ing] the family to understand donation as an incredible opportunity."[9] This strikes me as an excellent way of helping people assemble their preferences at a difficult time, even if it is a bit directive.

I am often asked why the United States has not seriously considered a change from its current opt-in policy. First, for an opt-in country, the United States already has a high rate of donation, and it has been increasing.[10] Part of that success may be due to improved requesting, using the techniques like presumptive consent. A second reason is the American belief in personal choice.

Not only do 90 percent of people approve of donation in general but also 55 percent specifically support an opt-out regime. In addition, a recent simulation analysis suggests that changing U.S. policy could extend many lives, if not entirely meet the need for donations.[11] Flipping defaults, alone, is not the sole solution, but it could be part of how we deal with death by denied donations. It is quite possible that the choice architecture of asking the family is even more important.

Alternatives

There are many diagnoses for the problem of insufficient organ donation. Some observers, like Gary Becker and Richard Posner at the University of Chicago, think that the failure to donate is caused by a lack of incentives. Their logic is that organs have a value to the potential donor. This is easiest to see for a living donor—for instance, in the case of kidney donation. Donors think they should be compensated for undergoing surgery, the short-term risk of surgical complications, and the longer-term risks of not having a second kidney. This suggests, to advocates of this position, that there should be a legal market for organs. Without compensation, there will be a lack of willing donors, and there will not be as many transplants. One consequence of banning organ sales is a black market: many kidneys are illegally sold by living donors, usually from the poorest countries. Only Iran allows a legal market for organ sales. Trafficking in organs is a billion-dollar industry, with the going price for a kidney approaching $62,000.[12]

The pro-incentives view is based on the belief that people know the value of their organs. While some people do donate because they are altruistic, more would donate if compensated. Even for donations that occur when someone dies, advocates argue that donations will increase because people would want to leave money to their family and will not donate unless their heirs are compensated. If there was a sufficient incentive, they would participate in a transaction.[13]

But what if economists are wrong and we don't know the value of a heart, kidney, or lung? Many people have not thought proactively about organ donation and must assemble their preferences when faced with the decision. They haven't, for example, estimated what one of their kidneys is worth. If I do not want to think about donation, I might just take the default. Or, if I were forced to—say, by being confronted with a question on my driver's license application—I have to decide, on the spot, what a reasonable answer might be. Assembling this response can be affected by how the question is posed. Perhaps the path to better outcomes lies not in giving people money for their organs but in helping them think about the problem.

Richard Thaler and Cass Sunstein suggest something they call *prompted choice*: asking in a nonthreatening environment, where potential donors can consider the options more carefully, like during their annual physical. It is reasonable that this might be better than the current practice: people are often deciding whether to be an organ donor in the Department of Motor Vehicles while renewing their driver's license.[14]

Israel takes a different approach that appeals to people's sense of fairness. It asks: why should people who are unwilling to be donors themselves be allowed to be recipients of donations? Under this system, priority in assigning donated organs to recipients is given to people who are willing to be donors themselves.

While these alternatives are important, they are either much more expensive or require more effort than changing defaults. Having trained people in hospitals to help facilitate requests requires funding. Asking your doctor to have a meaningful conversation with you about donation takes time away from other important conversations they could have with you and with other patients. Legal organ markets require payments and infrastructure for matching buyers and sellers.

The goal of well-designed choice architecture for organ donation is not to maximize organ donation, but rather, as we discussed in chapter 4, to get people into the right box. If opt-out policies do that, it is wonderful, but only if choosers end up being classified correctly. Currently, many people are in the wrong box: they would like to be donors, but they have not become one.

One recent survey, conducted by the U.S. Department of Health and Human Services, reported that 70 percent of people are willing to be donors, but only 50 percent have signed up. This means that the way we ask for these choices misclassifies 20 percent of people. Other questions in the survey confirm this; when asked, half of those who were not signed up said they wanted to be donors. This means the current choice architecture has a cost: many willing donors are not considered donors. They are in the wrong box. A more accurate choice architecture would save lives. The next table illustrates something else as well: it would be possible but very unlikely in an opt-in scheme to make the other mistake, classifying someone as a donor who would not want to be one. People who say they want to be a donor, but in reality do not, should be very rare.

Misclassification by Default:
Lives Lost by Using the Wrong Default

Intent (when asked in surveys)	Actual Status (as treated by the transplant system)	
	Signed up as a donor	Not signed up as a donor
I want to be a donor (70%)	Correct classification (50%)	Mistake (20%) (lost lives, wishes not met)
I do not want to be a donor (30%)	Mistake (near 0%?) (wishes not met and anguish to family)	Correct classification (30%)

Each of these mistakes has a cost. If I want to be a donor, and am not classified as one at my death, there is the cost that my wishes are not fulfilled, and lives are lost or lived with diminished quality. However, in an opt-out system, we may see an increase in the other mistake: I may be classified as a donor and I don't want to be. Here my wishes are not fulfilled, and my family may face significant anguish. Different defaults make certain costs more or less likely, and the right default depends upon the costs of the mistakes and how frequently they are made.

Ultimately, the question of what the right default is depends upon how you weight the costs and benefits of each outcome in the table, as well as the cost of making the decision. After all, choosing a default saves you from contemplating what happens to your body after you die.

As a kind of transplant survivor myself, I put a lot of value on preventing the deaths of the 108,000 people on the waiting list for organs. I acknowledge that others may place a lot more value on family anguish and autonomy than I do, but it seems to me that if we make it clear that people are able to opt out, and if we make it an easy process that is respected, we could potentially save lives. Doing this would impose the effort of registration on those who are certain that they do not want to be donors.

Others, including my friends Thaler and Sunstein, disagree. They believe an opt-out system is likely to decrease people's willingness to be a donor. One reason is that many countries do not have an easy way of tracking those who decline. But no matter what you think about this important issue, I hope this suggests a framework to think about the defaults. The argument about what is the right default is not a matter of one's being right and the other wrong, but rather what trade-off you make between these different kinds of costs and benefits. One thing we should all be able to agree on is that any choice architecture that gets potential donors in the right box, while respecting the feelings of families, would be a good thing.

If we are going to produce more accurate outcomes—and it really is a matter of life and death—it would seem important to dig deeper into how a designer's selection of defaults changes the decision-maker's choices.

How Defaults Work

Studies show that walking is surprisingly good for you: it leads to longer life and increased cognitive function. But how does walking produce these benefits? There is no one simple answer, but rather multiple ways this happens. Walking increases health because it has different effects on your body. It works, in the language of a social scientist, through three different channels. First, it strengthens your leg muscles through use. Second, like any exercise, it burns calories, reducing weight. Finally, the exercise stresses your cardiovascular system, improving heart function. Walking works so well because it does all three things at once. In principle, you could separate these three channels. For example, reduce the amount you eat, and you will change the number of calories you retain, but you won't have the cardiovascular and muscular benefits. The power of walking comes from these multiple channels working together.

Defaults are similar; they work not just in one way but via three channels, each of which helps to change choices. Like walking, the effects are strongest when all three channels kick in.

One channel is apparent to anyone: defaults make choices

seem easier. Just as you feel a brisk walk increasing your heart rate, your feel that a default makes your choice easier because you choose more quickly.

But that is not all that defaults do. Understanding defaults requires us to understand two other channels as well: endorsement and endowment.

These channels use the principle we have talked about in chapters 2 and 3. Changing the ease of making a decision alters a chooser's plausible paths. A default can cause someone to not engage in a decision; they simply choose the default, the easiest plausible path of all. Endorsement and endowment change how preferences are assembled. Knowing that a default has been chosen—or endorsed—by a trusted source may make you think about different things than if the default was set by someone you don't trust. Your preferences may also be assembled differently if you think as if you already own the default—that it's already been endowed to you. To make them easier to remember, you can think of these effects—ease, endorsement, and endowment—as the three Es. Let's start with ease and look at how defaults used during the rise of the original iPhone helped launch an internet superstar.

Ease

Justine Ezarik grew up in Scenery Hill, a hardscrabble township forty miles south of Pittsburgh. Her mother was a home-health aide, and her father was a coal miner. Growing up, Justine was fascinated by computers and technology. She moved to Pittsburgh as a young adult, where she worked as a sketch comic and graphic designer.

On Saturday, August 11, 2007, a default catapulted her to internet stardom. That week she received her first bill for the newly launched iPhone from AT&T. But there was something very unusual about the bill, and she decided to post a video of it online.

The bill was three hundred double-sided pages and delivered in a box requiring $7.10 in postage. What important details did such a massive bill report? Justine was a heavy texter, and most of the pages consisted of a list of every text, web search, and phone call that she had made. Since she had an unlimited plan, every line ended with the cost for that transaction, $0.00. Justine thought it was hilarious that AT&T and Apple went to so much effort to document so much nothing. She shot a video in her local coffee shop featuring her flipping through all three hundred pages of the bill in fast motion, accompanied by the snappy, happy sounds of the first iPhone jingle. A YouTube star was born. Justine became iJustine, and, within a couple of weeks, the video had been viewed more than 3 million times. iJustine went on to be one of the most popular internet "life-casters," with 6.8 million subscribers on various YouTube channels, almost half a billion views of her videos, guest appearances on *Law & Order: Special Victims Unit*, *Criminal Minds*, and *The Vampire Diaries*, and a memoir that became a *New York Times* bestseller. Little did she know that her career was launched by a terrible selection of choice architecture by some unknown manager or programmer at AT&T.

The bill was impressive and excessive, but it was not a random accident. Justine could have chosen *not* to receive the enormous bill, so in a sense, she chose to get it. But the reality, I suspect, was that she had no idea that she'd made a choice in the first place. When she activated her new phone online, the webpage presented Justine with three billing options: The first option, to get a detailed paper bill, was the default. The second option was a summary bill detailing just her bottom-line total due. The third option was an electronic bill. In her excitement to use the new phone, Justine (and as far as I can tell, almost everyone else) did not read or consider the other two options. She just accepted the default. Most new iPhone users "chose" to receive these complete (and completely uninformative) paper bills. They may not have all been three hundred pages long, but most of the 145,000 iPhones activated the first weekend were purchased by people "choosing" a long, itemized bill.[15] The voluminous printouts made *Computerworld*'s list of "Technology's 10 Most Mortifying Moments" and attracted nationwide media coverage.[16]

Someone at AT&T was a poor designer. They had selected the wrong default. This selection was bad for the customer, who did not want rafts of uninformative pages; bad for the environment, since trees died unneeded deaths; and very bad for AT&T. It was an expensive mistake that made them look very foolish. The major new product launch was central to the rebranding of AT&T. They had worked hard to be the exclusive provider for the iPhone to highlight themselves as a technology leader, and instead they produced rafts of useless paper bills making them look like anything but.

The Wednesday after the bill arrived, Justine and everyone else who had chosen the default received a text message from AT&T:

> We are simplifying your paper bill, removing
> itemized detail. To view all detail, go to att.com/
> mywireless. Still need a full paper bill? Call 611.

AT&T then started charging $1.99 for detailed bills like the one sent to Justine for free by default.

One of the ways that defaults work is by presenting an easier plausible path, in this case both in how it feels and how long it took. Just like iJustine, I bought an iPhone that same weekend and took a plausible path, the one that required almost no effort. We both clicked a web button that said "accept and continue" and decided not to read the long, detailed disclosure of the firm's billing policy. Little did we realize that we were agreeing to receive a boxful of bill that month. The choice of this path was driven by an initial judgment of *fluency:* a subjective judgment of how easy the decision felt.

Fluent plausible paths are sometimes reasonable when the stakes are low, but an easy decision may not be an accurate decision. Just because a choice is fluent does not mean it necessarily leads to an outcome you want, particularly if a designer may have bad intentions.

In 2015, DirectTV was charged by the Federal Trade Commission with abusing a default. If you signed up for DirectTV's services, you were given three months of free access to premium channels like HBO and Showtime. But there was a default that the FTC claimed was hidden from buyers: if you did not actively cancel your subscription after the three months, you started paying for these channels. This is what we called presumed consent when we talked about organ donation. Lawyers have another name: they call opting out a *negative option*. By accepting the promotion at the initial decision, buyers were accepting a default, one that could be costly to them three months later. While the suit was part of a complex litigation that the FTC eventually dropped, the FTC now has a Negative Option Rule to address similar problems.

An even clearer example of a badly intentioned choice architect using dark patterns to exploit ease are the websites run by a certain company that provided payday loans. After providing all the information needed to apply to the loan, consumers were taken to a page with special offers (see page 128). A quick look leads you to the obvious next button: "Finish matching me with a payday loan provider!" There are four special offers above that. If you look at the first box, you note that "No" is preselected, but that is hard to see because the dots are so small. Almost no one realized that by clicking the obvious button at the bottom of the screen, the fluent path for finishing the deal, they were agreeing to the offer in the upper right-hand column, which was also hard to read, but had "Yes" prechecked. Despite the title, "Get a $2,500 Visa Card," you were agreeing to getting a prepaid debit card, with no initial value, that cost the consumer $59.95. (The $2,500 value was the maximum the consumer could transfer onto the card!) The image is from a court filing by the FTC. The commission finally won a judgment against the firm and returned $1.9 million to consumers who had taken the easy path. Unfortunately, that is not as happy an end as it may seem: when divided over the 110,000 consumers, each received less than $15 back.

Before you get your loan, check out the limited time offers below!

Improve Your Credit Score

○ Yes ◉ No

I want C Credit to repair my credit report.

By accepting this offer I authorize Academy Credit to use the same information that I provided earlier. I hereby authorize Academy to debit my bank account for a one time credit report and setup fee of $97.00. Academy Credit will continue working on my case of a monthly fee of $49.95 until cancellation. I agree that as soon as my initial fee is withdrawn Academy Credit will pull my credit report and begin disputing the inaccurate, erroneous, untimely and unverifiable items therein. I also acknowledge that I have read the Disclosure Statement and Cancellation Notice and give my Digital Signature and Limited Power of Attorney. For C Credit to complete the credit Report Audit and Verification Service.

Get a $2,500 Visa Card

◉ Yes ○ No

Everyone Qualified for a $2,500 VisaA® Prepaid Card – NO CREDIT CHECK.

A VisaA® Prepaid Card with EverPrivate is the only way to shop online without anyone else knowing. Just load the card with cash and make purchases anonymously. NO credit check, NO link to personal credit information, NO bill mailed. INSTANT APPROVAL! It's perfect solution if you want to protect your privacy. Check "Yes" and you will receive your VisaA Prepaid Card including lifetime free access to EverPrivate Card privacy tools to protect your identity. YOU HEREBY AUTHORIZE EVERPRIVATE CARD to debit your bank account for the one time enrollment fee of $54.95. See Terms and Privacy information.

Get a FREE Color Printer

○ Yes ◉ No

Would you like a NEW Computer with a FREE wireless keyboard and mouse or a brand NEW iPod?

MyComputerClub allows members to purchase quality computers while also rebuilding their credit. Receive your Free 21-day trial today. If you decide to keep your membership, an annual membership fee of $89.00 will be automatically charged to your account of record as 2 monthly payments of $44.50 after your Free trial. Click Here for Terms and Conditions.

Get CASH for a New Car

○ Yes ◉ No

I want a FREE Auto Loan Quote.

Get a fast, FREE, no obligation quote for an auto loan whether you need a used car or a new car. All credit welcome. By clicking the button below, you agree to the CarsBlvd privacy policy and terms and conditions. You also authorize a credit check to be performed by our lending partners in order to evaluate the financing options that can be provided to you.

Finish matching me with a payday loan provider!

Deceptive defaults. Notice that only the upper-right-hand choice is checked "Yes."

Ease can make a path work like a default even when nothing is prechecked. We saw that in chapter 1, with cabs presenting suggested tip amounts. But these suggestions can also be dark patterns, when a designer with malicious intent makes one option much easier to find.

You see "almost defaults" all over the internet. Most times when I try to unsubscribe from a junk email list, I'm taken to a page where the button for unsubscribing seemed smaller and inconspicuous. A large button asks me if I want fewer emails instead. My recent favorite had the unsubscribe link— it is required by law, after all—but in a dark gray font on a black background. The federal law that requires commercial email to provide an opt-out option, the CAN-Spam Act, states that "creative use of type size, color, and location can improve clarity." Unfortunately, that creativity has gone in the wrong direction this time.

These are not defaults. The designer is not preselecting an option for the chooser. The malevolent designer works by exploiting ease. Color and size make it easier to press one button or hard to see the unsubscribe link. These are dark patterns using ease to purposefully lead you astray.

The consequences of taking these defaults vary in importance. But even when the stakes are very high, changing the default can make a surprisingly large difference, particularly when the effort required to change the default is small. One of the most important financial choices that people make is the amount to save for retirement. In 2006, Congress passed a law that allowed employers to change the default for retirement savings. Traditionally, employees had to opt in to save. By default, they saved nothing from their wages.

Many people do not save, despite the large economic consequences. After Congress passed this law, many employers changed the default option on their employees' retirement plans from the traditional zero to a default savings rate of 3 percent. In addition, many employers also defaulted employees into increasing their savings rate at the end of each year. This radically changed people's behavior. In 2011, it was estimated that this change in default was worth over $7 billion in increased savings.[17] A small change in the default meant a big increase in savings. Why? Again, thinking about your retirement savings is no fun and far from fluent for most of us. The result is avoiding an hour or so of hard and unpleasant work that has long-term consequences that are worth tens of thousands of dollars.

Defaults derive some of their power from the large role that ease can play in making a decision. Sometimes, like when we are deciding whether or not to be an organ donor, the decision feels very painful. Who wants to think about what happens to their organs when they die? When choosing between thinking about your own demise or skipping the decision altogether, you might choose the plausible path of not making the choice. It feels as if the effort to think about which box to click is insurmountable.

But ease is not the only ways defaults work. To understand this better, we need to talk about another of the world's all-time favorite topics: auto insurance.

Endorsement

If choice architecture is like a conversation, then we might want to think about the intent of the designer, particularly when they suggest a default. It might be that the designer sets as a default the choice that they think is best for most people. Less scrupulous designers could set the default to the option in their best interest, like in the DirectTV example.

In 1993, as mentioned earlier, the states of Pennsylvania and New Jersey allowed companies to sell two different varieties of auto insurance coverage. In both states, buyers could now choose between a more expensive policy that would pay them for pain and suffering resulting from an accident in addition to their medical expenses and a less expensive policy that would cover only medical bills. The difference in insurance premiums was not small. I lived in Pennsylvania at the time, and the cost for full coverage was about $300 more a year than for the limited coverage.[18]

I was part of a team, along with Jacqueline Meszaros, Howard Kunreuther, and Jack Hershey, that conducted one of the first studies of defaults.[19] We asked people to pick between two policies, simply changing which policy was the default across conditions. We wanted to study people who had actually bought car insurance, so we stopped people in a hospital cafeteria rather than asking students at the University of Pennsylvania. Half randomly were given full coverage as a default and could change to the less expensive, more limited coverage, and the others were given the other default. The defaults caused a large difference in policy choice. When the full coverage was the default, it was chosen 53 percent of the time, even though it was more expensive. But when the other policy was the default, full coverage was chosen only 23 percent of the time.

We were interested in whether defaults would have this

effect in the real world. We were lucky; the two states allowed companies to offer the two policies at the same time, but with one important difference: the default. In Pennsylvania the expensive policy was the default; in New Jersey it was the cheaper policy. This was just like our experiment but this time with real decisions costing people real dollars. The effect was even larger. Only 20 percent of the folks in New Jersey picked the full coverage policy, but 75 percent of Pennsylvanians did. Ten years later, my colleague Dan Goldstein and I estimated that more than $2 billion in additional insurance coverage was sold in Pennsylvania because the more expensive plan was the default. Clearly ease played a role here. To change your choice from the default, you would have to read and mail in a form that was written in the usual insurance talk (which is not easy to understand). But talking to participants in our experiment suggested another possible reason people chose the default: people thought that the state had chosen the best option as the default for them. In other words, they thought the state insurance authorities *endorsed* that option.

Defaults can change choices when people believe that the designer, either implicitly or explicitly, endorsed the default option. They use the endorsement implied by the default to make their decision rather than thinking independently about what is right for them.[20] People consider the default a suggestion, something that the choice architect thinks they should choose. The plausible path here is to accept the suggestion—when the chooser sees the default, they may conclude that the designer is preselecting the option that they think is best. This would be true even if the choice was presented in a way that was fluent.

Similar thoughts might have been in the minds of customers when Deutsche Bahn, the German national railroad, changed the default for whether or not riders reserved seats. When you buy a ticket on a Deutsche Bahn train, like on most railroads, you can get on the train, but you are not guaranteed a particular seat. You can also buy a seat reservation separately from the ticket for about €2. Deutsche Bahn simply changed its website to make the purchase of seat reservations the default, unless customers unchecked a box. Before the change, 9 percent of ticket purchases included reservations. Afterward, 47 percent of ticket purchases included reservations, increasing the railroad's annual revenue by an estimated €40 million. The railroad told us that their customer surveys indicated that customers were happier with the new default, and many customers thought that the railroad had made the change to make sure customers were more comfortable.

A final example: Remember that most firms set the default for retirement savings at 3 percent. Many people believe this is what the firm thinks is right, but the reality is that for most people, it is too little. This is an endorsement gone bad.

The effect of endorsement implied by default is not the same as the effect of ease. Whether people believe an option is being endorsed depends on who sets the default. Reactions to the insurance default might have been different if the default was set by the insurance company. People suspicious of their insurance company's motives might well have looked more closely. People trusted the German national railroad; the same thing might not work for airlines if people trust them less. If a default is set by someone trusted, endorsement might well persuade the chooser not to look further. And those who are suspicious of the designer might think about their choice more carefully.

Endowment

Electricity generation is the second largest source of greenhouse gases in the United States. It accounts for more than a quarter of all carbon dioxide emissions. These emissions could be reduced through the use of renewable sources of electricity and through adopting products that are more energy efficient. People often say that they want to reduce their energy use, but they don't take steps to do so. In Great Britain, for example, only 3 percent of consumers get their electricity from renewable sources. Yet a majority of people in most countries say they would buy renewable energy, even at a small premium. There is a big gap between willingness to adopt green energy and behavior. If you change the default to renewable energy, however, it turns out they will select, and keep using, green energy.[21]

One nice example of this is a field study conducted on German electricity buyers by Ebeling and Lotz. Researchers directed over 41,000 utility customers to one of two websites, identical except that one had a default for a more expensive green electricity supplier that provided 100 percent sustainable electricity. The other site had a default for the less expensive nonsustainable supplier, called "gray electricity" in the industry. People were making real decisions with real costs, and the effect was large. For those who bought electricity, 69.1 percent chose green electricity when it was the default, but only 7.2 percent chose it when gray electricity was the default. Ebeling and Lotz wanted to make sure that people were not just picking the prechecked option by mistake, so they also showed that most people, more than 85 percent, understood which kind of energy they chose. It doesn't seem that they were "tricked" into picking the default.[22]

These decisions about what kind of electricity to buy are lasting. Almost everyone keeps the option that they choose, even if it was heavily influenced by the default. In addition, they seem content with their choice.

Is this acceptable? Lucia Reisch and Cass Sunstein conducted a worldwide survey to see if people endorsed setting green energy as the default. They found that across countries, a majority are in favor of making green energy the default, with support varying between 50 percent and 75 percent. In the United States, even the majority of people who identify as Republicans support green energy defaults.

How do defaults work in this case? Ease plays a limited role, since you merely need to click a button on a website to change your option, and the rates are presented clearly. Endorsement might contribute to the effect, but does everyone trust their electricity supplier? This is an example of the third way defaults work, and it involves how choosers assemble their preferences for power suppliers.

Think back to when we talked about assembled preferences, inhibition, and query theory. We showed that asking people how long they would live caused them to name different ages than when we asked them when they would die. They did that because they thought about different things in each frame. When asked how long they would live, they first thought about why they might live long and then, later, about why they might not. Because recalling reasons they might live longer inhibits recall of reasons they might not, people asked how long they would live gave longer estimates than those asked when they would die.

Defaults work similarly. We think about the default option first, which inhibits the second option. When we default people into the green, sustainable option, they think about why they might choose that option first, inhibiting reasons they might choose the gray option. Electricity from wind turbines and solar cells comes to mind, along with teenage climate activists and the future of their kids and grandkids, suppressing the recall of any cost advantages. They might also think of the disadvantages of nuclear and coal power. When it comes time to think about why I might want the gray power, I might not even recall its big advantage—its lower cost. If gray energy is the default, then I might think first about the added expense, my tight budget, and what else I could spend the money on first. Later, it would be hard to think of the advantages of green energy, and windmills may not come to mind at all.

Isaac Dinner, Dan Goldstein, Kaiya Lui, and I showed this in a study where we asked people to choose between two different kinds of light bulbs: the ordinary, incandescent bulb and the more energy-efficient compact florescent light (CFL). Each has its advantages and disadvantages: incandescent bulbs are cheaper to buy but more expensive to use. Because they are less efficient at converting electricity to light, they are more expensive to operate, and you will need a new one more quickly, since they die in much less time. On the other hand, while CFLs are less expensive in the long run, the early bulbs looked funny and often had an unusual cold light, among other disadvantages. We invented a situation where ease and endorsement would have little effect, and we asked if people thought about the two products differently when the default changed.[23] People were told that they had hired a contractor to do a home renovation and their contractor had given them a choice with a default. We made it clear that the contractor didn't care which light bulb you ended up with and was more than happy to switch the bulbs. They saw this instruction:

> Your contractor, whom you trust, has just finished the new addition to your house and had to install some light bulbs. He says that the crew put in six brand-new *CFLs for a cost of $18 but he would be happy, when he stops by tomorrow, to put in incandescent bulbs, which would save you $12.*

Other respondents made the same choice, but we had changed the default:

> Your contractor, whom you trust, has just finished the new addition to your house and had to install

some light bulbs. He says that the crew put in six brand-new *incandescent bulbs for a cost of $6 but he would be happy, when he stops by tomorrow, to put in CFLs, which would cost you another $12.*

In both set of instructions, you have the same set of options, but you need to decide to take an action, described in italics, if you want to change from one kind of bulb to the other. Would you make the same choice in these two frames? When CFLs were the default, they were chosen about twice as often (44 percent) as when they were not (22 percent), despite the fact that the options were identical. All we changed was the default. Since the scenario didn't require any effort on the part of the chooser, and the choice architect had no preference, we were pretty sure that the large effects of default were due to neither ease nor endorsement.

We asked people what they were thinking about when making the choice, and it was different for the two defaults. The results were in line with query theory. When the CFL was the default, people thought more often about how buying CFLs would save them money on electricity and about how CFLs last a lot longer than incandescent light bulbs. If the incandescent was the default, they thought more often of how CFLs are expensive, how they emit cold light, and how they have an unappealing squiggly shape. These differences in what people think about predicts what they choose, explaining, in this study, how defaults change choices.[24]

There are many who argue that defaults are an important part of changing people's environmental behavior.[25] For example, in a study at Rutgers University, researchers changed the default for printing from single-sided to double-sided and reduced the amount of paper used by 44 percent, a total of 55 million sheets of paper a year.[26]

Changing how you assemble preferences also happens in a well-known behavioral economics demonstration called the *endowment effect*. Every semester, I do this demonstration in the first class in behavioral economics. I feel a little like a magician: the trick never fails, and the results always surprise my students.

You walk into a room and randomly give half the people in the room a mug, making it really clear that you are choosing who gets the mug at random. Since you decided who owns the mugs at random, the value of the mug should be the same, on average, for both the people who happened to get a mug and those who didn't.

But then the trick occurs: you ask the people who do not have a mug how much they would pay for one, and you ask those who have a mug how much they would sell it for. Because of random assignment, the average price should be very close.

The reality is different: those who were randomly given a mug actually value it twice as much as those who were not, on average. A $7 mug will be worth $10 to those given it randomly, but $5 to those who did not receive one. This is the endowment effect in action: people who currently possess an object seem to endow it with additional value. This is shown in the work of two Nobel laureates, Daniel Kahneman and Richard Thaler, along with their co-author, Jack Knetsch.

Again, the difference is due to how we assemble our preferences. We don't know, off the top of our heads, exactly how much we think a mug is worth, so we have to estimate or assemble our value. Gerald Häubl, Anat Kienen, and I redid this classic experiment, but this time we asked people to tell us, by typing into a computer, what they were thinking about, reporting the thoughts that occur naturally. Owners first thought about the many wonderful characteristics of the mug, and only later did it occur to them that they might do something with the money they would sell the mug for. The people who did not have the mugs, on the other hand, thought first about what they might do with the money. One mugless individual, who was participating in the study at eleven thirty in the morning, told us quite a bit about the lunch they would buy with the money. Only later did they contemplate the mug, and because of inhibition, they didn't think about the mug for long.

In these studies, Gerald, Anat, and I are confident that this difference in preference construction is causing the difference in the value of the mug. We used the number of participants' typed thoughts, positive or negative, to predict the prices they would pay for the mug. Each positive thought raised the price they would pay by thirty-seven cents. We also made the endowment effect disappear by asking them to consider the opposite of what they normally would. For example, when we asked people who received the mug to list things they would do with the money they would gain from selling the mug *before* asking them to list things they would do with the mug, their value for the mug decreased, erasing the endowment effect.[27]

The Elements of Choice

Do Defaults Always Work?

Defaults seem to be a triple-barreled threat, working because they make choices easy, imply endorsement, and endow the chooser with ownership of the default option. Some of the examples we have seen have had huge effects, increasing the number of people donating organs or using green electricity. This raises an important question: Do defaults always work so well?

There are two reasons to ask. First, getting designers to change defaults is not always easy. More than once upon asking about changing defaults, I've been told, "That is the way we have always done it. Why change?" A designer may have to spend a lot of political capital to get a default change approved, and they want to be sure the money, time, and effort they invest will be worthwhile. Designers need to know how much defaults will change behavior. Will changing the default double the number of people taking that option, or will it increase uptake by a mere 1 or 2 percent?

Second, we talked in chapter 1 about the reproducibility revolution. To see whether an effect is real, we need to look across many studies to see if results replicate. It is natural for people to talk about big successes, but big successes may be flukes.

Fortunately, since we started to study defaults in the 1990s, there have been many studies of defaults and new ways of summarizing them. Jon Jachimowicz, now a faculty member at Harvard; Shannon Duncan, now a graduate student at Wharton; Elke Weber, who teaches at Princeton (and, as you know, is my spouse); and I pulled together every study that has used defaults, both published and unpublished, so we could see how well defaults work in different settings.

We used meta-analysis, a statistical tool that summarizes what we know about a topic. Meta-analysis is often used in medicine to give doctors quick summaries of dozens, sometimes hundreds, of studies. This way they can see how well

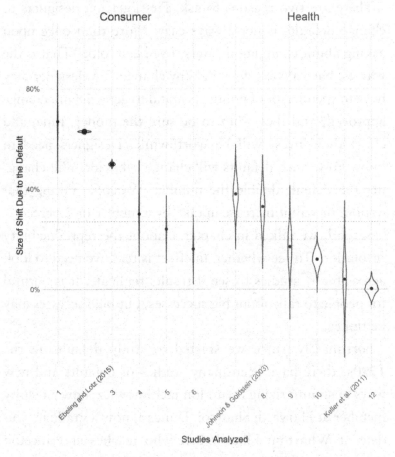

Differences in choices caused by changing the default

an intervention, such as a new drug or a new surgical procedure, works on average. In the last ten years, meta-analysis has become much more important in psychology and policy. Just like in medicine, it helps us understand how well an attempt to change behavior will work.

The figure on page 142 is a forest plot. It's called that because some forms look like trees, but I prefer to think it has that name because it helps you see the forest instead of the trees. I've drawn twelve of the fifty-eight studies from our analysis to keep things simple. The position of the dots show how big the effect of the default was in each study. For example, the Ebeling and Lotz study showed that the default produced a 62 percent increase in the choice of green energy. The size of the dots represents how many people were in the study, and the "blob" represents how much variability we expect in the result. As the sample size gets larger (a bigger dot), the blob gets smaller, so small that it disappears is some studies.[28]

The beauty of this figure is that it gives you a broad overview of many studies involving thousands of respondents. With a forest plot, you can take in dozens of results in a glance. Looking at this figure, you can see several things immediately:

- In the studies that I plotted, the default effect never backfires. Choosers do not appear to reject the default and pick the opposite. You can see this because no experimental results are below the solid horizontal line indicating no preference for the default.

- In most of the experiments, the differences are statistically significant and fairly large, since the dots are far above the solid line. The defaults changed choices.

- We can try to see average effect, weighted by the size of the studies. This is the dashed horizontal line. Defaults seem to be, on average, a strong intervention: these simple changes, like changing one argument in the HTML code presenting a choice, can increase the frequency of choice of an option by 27 percent, even when we include in our weighting studies that showed no effect.[29]

- There are three studies that are not significant. For example, Study 9 was a very small study, and its distribution overlaps with the zero line. We cannot say it is statistically different from zero. In other words, defaults do fail to produce statistically significant change in some cases.

For designers, this is very important. Changing the default produces, on average, a big change in what is chosen, but the effect size varies. In applying choice architecture, it is important that we have realistic expectations for what we can accomplish. Earlier, I talked about the fantastic results with green energy (the second study, the one by Ebeling and

Lotz, in the figure). It's a great study, and very statistically significant, with 41,000 utility customers participating. But its effect is not typical: a 50 percent increase in buying green electricity caused by the default is about twice what we see across studies. We might ask why, in this case, the default was so powerful? Part of the reason is that it is a consumer choice, and made infrequently, and once made it is difficult (i.e., not fluent) to change. Knowing that allows the designer to have a better guess of both what effect they should see and how to increase the strength of the default. If you have read just one study of defaults, you may not be aware of how much the size of the effect varies and may overgeneralize the single result to your situation.

There is one more thing about the figure worth talking about. The six studies on the left are all in situations that involve consumer decisions, and the six studies on the right are health decisions. As you can see, defaults have a larger effect in consumer decisions than in health decisions. This is important. If you are a designer thinking about using defaults, you can expect more of an effect in a consumer application than in a health application. In other words, all other things being equal, we would expect a study like the green energy study to have a larger default effect than a health study like the organ donation paper.[30]

Meta-analysis can help us understand why default effects are stronger in some cases than in others. Our meta-analysis looked to see if each study changed the ease, endorsement, or endowment aspects of the choice. We found that, in general, default effects were strongest when the default changed all three effects and weaker when they changed only one or two.

Picking the Right Default

Let's say you're about to buy a car—a really fabulous car—and are visiting the website of a certain well-known German auto manufacturer. Since a confidentiality agreement prevents me from disclosing the name of the firm, I'll just call it German Large Auto Manufacturer, or GLAM for short.

When you visit the GLAM website, you build your own car using what the auto industry calls a *configurator*. You get to choose all the options for the car: the engine (there are sixteen different types available), body paint, upholstery, gas tank size, and even the type of wood for the gearshift knob (walnut, birch, or maple). You make more than fifty different decisions!

How should GLAM set the defaults on the configurator? Do they matter at all? People at GLAM had heard about our work with organ donation, and they wanted us to see whether it would work for autos. It could be the case that defaults might not play a large role when buying cars; some managers thought defaults would not make a difference. After all, this is an expensive purchase and most German car buyers spend a lot of time thinking about their choices. Besides, buying a car entails not just one choice, but many.

Maybe defaults won't have an effect when a consumer is making over fifty decisions.

They wanted to be convinced that defaults made a difference, and only then would they deal with the problem of what the *right* default was. I was not at the meetings, but I imagined some people on the marketing board, dressed in dark Hugo Boss suits, sharing skeptical glances.

What are the possible default settings GLAM could select? We thought of at least three possibilities:

- The default could always be the least expensive default.

- The default could always be the most profitable default for GLAM: if defaults affect choice, GLAM might substantially increase its profitability simply by changing the underlying HTML code on its website.

- The default could be the option that is the most popular if there was not an explicit default.

You might be tempted to think that GLAM would always pick the most profitable default, but that might not have been in their long-term interest. They wanted customers to be loyal and buy another car, and if the default gave the consumer the wrong option—for instance, engines that were too small or bodies that were too large or the wrong color—GLAM might lose a long-term customer.

Interestingly, GLAM always set the default to the lowest-cost option. It looked like GLAM had thought through this, but that did not appear to be the case. We asked senior managers about the decision to set the cheapest options as the default, and it became clear that no one would admit to having made that selection. There was talk, in fact, that some low-level programmer had selected the lowest price as the default. It is clear that the decision was not made at the high levels of the company. This surprised us; we *thought* defaults would matter, but managers who do not know choice architecture didn't think defaults would have much of an effect. This "default neglect" could be costing the company a lot of money and making consumers worse off, but it gave us a chance to improve profits and customer outcomes.

How would consumers be worse off with a cheaper product? At first glance, defaulting customers to the least expensive option might seem like a good idea, at least from the customers' viewpoint. If defaults influence choice, people will end up with a less expensive car. But not every customer wants the cheapest car. Different people want and need different things. The least expensive engine was the most fuel efficient. If choosers care about gas mileage and carbon emissions, that is a good default. But it hurts those who feel a need for speed provided by a larger engine. They might end up with an underpowered car that would be a safety hazard on the sometimes speed-limitless German Autobahn, where cars drive on some stretches at speeds in excess of 180 kilometers (110 miles) per hour. Larger engines might also be good for someone who tows a camper or boat. Consider other features where the cheapest option might not be the best: low cost meant minimal airbag protection, no child safety restraints, and no first aid kit. The cheap default might reduce the car's safety. If defaults affect choice, setting the cheapest options as the defaults was a problem.

To see whether defaults did make a difference, GLAM invited us to do a set of studies. It was a researcher's dream: an experiment with real customers. For GLAM, getting defaults in the configurator was important, particularly in Germany. Unlike in the United States, most cars sold in Germany are built to order, not bought off the lot. I, along with a team including Andreas Hermann and Mark Heitmann (now professors at the universities of St. Gallen and Hamburg, respectively), constructed clones of GLAM's configurator. We became real designers affecting the choices of real car buyers configuring their autos. A small percentage of GLAM's customers were directed to our clones of its site instead of the official site itself, and we selected different defaults to see if they changed choices.

The effects of the defaults were surprising, even to us. I'll focus on just one of those fifty-plus choices each buyer made: the engine. This is the most important choice for most people, according to market research. It also has significant impact on the car's cost. The most expensive engine cost €18,000 more than the cheapest one. Consumers saw one of three clones of GLAM's current configurator: one where no engine was preselected, one where the benign (most popular) engine was preselected, or one where the cheapest engine was preselected (GLAM's current default). Making the cheapest engine the default made it more popular than when there was no preselected option. This alone lowered the average overall price of the car by €476. In contrast, using the most selected engine as the default made it, and other more expensive engines, more popular, raising the average price of the engine alone by €302. More than half of the consumers made different choices when there was a default. Management was now convinced that defaults mattered, but they faced another question: What is the right default? They were not happy when we explained that they needed to consider the cost and benefit of different defaults, so they asked us whether we could do better.[31]

GLAM wanted its site to be fluent so that customers would be engaged with their choice. It didn't want customers visiting the competition's configurator because GLAM's was cumbersome. GLAM also told us that accuracy was essential: it needed customers to be happy with the car they bought. Customer satisfaction is important in the auto industry. Firms even advertise their satisfaction ratings. If a customer's car is slower or less safe than needed, GLAM has a problem. So GLAM wanted to get each customer into the right box, not just once, but for more than fifty decisions. This is particularly challenging when the "right" box differs across people, as it does with cars. To help overcome these challenges, we need to realize that defaults come in different flavors. There are two basic default types: *mass defaults*, where the same default is presented to everyone, and *personalized defaults*, those that change for each user.

GLAM, like many companies, used a one-size-fits-all mass

default. This is how defaults are normally used—everyone gets the same outcome unless they make an active choice.

How should you set a mass default? One option that we suggested to GLAM was to preselect the options customers chose most often when there was no preselected option. In the case of a car's color we might set the default to the most popular color, since it is best for most customers. If I have reason to believe that most customers will pick a plain steering wheel when there is no preselected option, then defaulting to that option is probably a good idea, particularly when there is little harm if the customer gets a slightly different option than is optimal because of the default (say, a black versus a dark gray steering wheel). You might call these *benign defaults* because the cost of getting people into the wrong box is small, for both the designer and chooser, and because the selection of this default is intentional.

Not all mass defaults are benign. Most people ordering a car may not purchase attachments for a baby seat as an option, but for those choosers that are parents, this could be a costly mistake. For many other goods and services, people sometimes want very different things. Making the hottest sauce the default on the menu of a taco shop might delight some customers, but even if it is the most popular option, some eaters will be upset. Economist and marketers use a technical term, *heterogeneous preferences*, to describe these cases.

This is a challenge of mass defaults. For organ donations, changing the default could mean saving a life through transplantation, but it could also mean causing a family's anguish after a transplant whose donor might not have intended to donate. This is a difficult cost-benefit trade-off. In fact, it seems like the kind of trade-off that makes us wish we had different alternatives.

Fortunately, there are alternatives to mass defaults. When choices are presented online, defaults can be changed based on what we already know about the customer or decision-maker. If we know their past behavior, purchases, or demographics, then we can give them a personalized default. This default is set to be our best guess of the option that the decision-maker would want in the absence of the default.

You can select the default for choosers based on what they have done in the past. These are *persistent defaults*, like when the barista at Starbucks remembers you like almond milk. If an airline remembers my choice of seat and meal from past flights, it can present a persistent default. Websites can learn from my past preferences to produce defaults as well. This can be simple, like when Amazon asks whether I want to keep using my shipping preferences whenever I check out. They can also be more complex. One online food-shopping service offers to put your entire last order into your online cart to start. Persistent defaults are widely used, as they overcome the problem of differing preferences by remembering the data that chooser has already shared. They can please customers. Walking into my favorite breakfast place and having the staff ask, "Do you want the usual?" is a good default.

Persistent defaults are based on what the user chose in the past. They can't be used for important decisions that are unique, like choosing a college or house, where little or no past data about choices has been shared.

Sometimes the designer has significant knowledge about

the chooser and the decisions they face. They might even know more than the chooser does. For example, a chef can construct a menu of things that they think you would like, even if you don't know the dishes. A good personal shopper might suggest things you would not have thought to try on, never mind buy. They use both knowledge about you and about people like you to make suggestions. This is another kind of personalized default, called a *smart default*. These defaults recognize that choosers have different needs and solve the problem of what a good default is by using their knowledge of customers to preselect that option.

Many people hate to think about retirement planning, so it is not surprising that a kind of smart default is part of many retirement savings plans. In many plans, the default is a *target date fund*. These plans use your age and knowledge of financial theory to decide your allocation between stocks and bonds. Assuming I tell the retirement plan provider that I want to retire in my midsixties, the retirement plan then defaults me into a fund that uses a strategy consistent with that goal. The standard advice in finance is that I should shift my investments from riskier securities, like stocks, to less volatile cash assets as I approach retirement. So, for example, if I am forty when I start with my employer in 2015, I might tell the retirement plan provider that I want to retire in my sixties, or twenty-five years from now. It might then default me into a mutual fund called something like "Target2040" that will reallocate some of my funds from stocks to bonds automatically every year as I get closer to retiring in 2040.

Target date funds have been hugely successful in the U.S.

retirement marketplace. Over 71 percent of U.S. 401(k) plans offer these funds, and more than half (52 percent) of all retirement investors hold these funds. Holdings in target date funds are more than $1 trillion. Clearly, smart defaults can be big business.[32]

Both mass and personalized defaults have a place in the designer's toolbox. They fit different situations depending upon what the designer knows about the chooser. If you know nothing, mass defaults are your only option. You still must make a decision about what is the right default.

The advantage of personalized defaults is that they can help minimize the kinds of harm to consumers that a one-size-fits-all mass default can cause. They get more people into the right box, delivering more accurate decisions and providing a fluent plausible path.

Two key takeaways apply to all default selections:

- If you must use a mass default, try to identify the one that maximizes benefits by helping most consumers find the right option for them, while minimizing harm to those who make the wrong choice. Cost-benefit analysis of this kind often involves difficult trade-offs. These hard trade-offs do not go away if you ignore them. Just like defaults themselves, they are always there, even if you don't admit it.

- If you can customize the default based on something that you already know about the customer, you can improve outcomes and get more people to make the choice that is right for them. Persistent defaults, when people have stable preferences, can be based on past behavior. Smart defaults, when we have some idea of what people should or will choose, can improve people's decisions. In both cases, personalized defaults are at least as good as, and usually better than, mass defaults.

Finally, I want to point out that while smart defaults can improve outcomes for both customers and companies, a company might instead choose defaults that simply maximize their own profits or fulfill their own goals.[33] That raises questions of awareness and ethics that we will talk about later, but I suspect that would at best help the firm in the short term. Firms that manage defaults strategically and ethically can expect to be paid back with loyalty and trust.

Getting the default right can be a big boon. In early March 2020, at the dawn of the pandemic in the United States, Zoom went from a fairly obscure video conferencing platform to a lifeline for schools, companies, families, support groups, and even imbibing neighbors. Later that spring, when Zoom first sold its stock to the public, it was the rare successful IPO in a down market, valued at $9 billion. The fascination was so intense that the stock of a similar sounding but much smaller company, Zoom Technologies, with a market capitalization of about $14 million, increased in price by 100 percent. No doubt the increase was aided by the fact that the smaller company had the ticker symbol ZOOM.

Enthusiasm for the larger Zoom quickly waned, however, as users became concerned about security. The most public concern was "Zoom bombing," when an uninvited guest would join a scheduled meeting or class and hijack the feed, broadcasting undesirable content, such as obscenities, threats, racial slurs, and pornography. The FBI's Boston office was concerned, and the New York State attorney general wrote a letter inquiring what the company was doing to prevent this. Zoom, under pressure to improve its security, urged people not to distribute their personal ID and instead use a meeting-specific link with a password. Those suggestions had little effect, but surprisingly, some small changes in defaults did. These involved not new encryption—that came a few weeks later—but instead making the suggested changes to the default. Meeting passwords, the use of randomly generated meeting IDs, and the use of waiting rooms, all features that were available before, became the default. Reports of Zoom bombing were greatly reduced, and very little negative feedback was received about the implementation of these defaults. Google Trends reports that searches for "Zoom bombing" peaked on April 2, just before the defaults were changed, and by April 27 they were down by 95 percent. Apparently, in the new pandemic world, most people were much better served by the new defaults, as was Zoom.[34]

Defaulting to Democracy

A couple of years ago, I was contacted by the Brennan Center for Justice at New York University, an organization that was advocating automatic voter registration. This is a system that automatically registers a citizen to vote unless they affirmatively opt out, whenever they interact with their state government (for instance, when they register their car or get a driver's license). That information is then shared electronically with the election office, and they are registered to vote.

I hope that after reading this chapter, you could predict some of the effects. How would the three channels for default effects—ease, endorsement, and endowment—work here? Because it makes registration easier, and because you are endowed with becoming a registered voter, automatic registration should increase the number of registered voters. For those who trust the government, it is also an endorsement and should boost registration. For those who do not, it might have the opposite effect. But the one lesson you might take away is that we would expect automatic registration to have a large effect. It does. In Oregon, one of the first states to adopt automatic registration, you previously could have registered to vote at the Department of Motor Vehicles, but you had to opt in. In the four years prior to the switch, about 4,000 people a month registered there. After automatic registration went into effect, that number increased almost fourfold, to over 15,000 a month. We don't know whether those people actually ended up voting, or if some of them would have registered in other ways, but the effect seems large.

I also hope this chapter has helped you think about whether automatic voter registration is the right default. If we think about the costs and benefits, like we did in chapter 4 and earlier in this chapter, regarding organ donation, it seems we are dealing with a different picture. Someone who was misclassified as a donor who did not want to be and their family might bear a great cost, and the individual's autonomy is not respected. But in both organ donation and voting registration, there are many people who would like to be donors or voters who don't get around to it. The key difference in voting is that there seems to be very little cost in mistakenly registering someone who does not want to be registered. No one is forced to vote, and you could decline to be registered to vote: the default is very easy to change. In fact, proponents of automatic registration think there are advantages to security. The electronic system keeps records more up-to-date than the old paper-based system and can make detecting duplication and changed addresses more easily.

People can disagree about what is the right default, but as is shown in many cases in this chapter, they should agree that defaults will make a difference. As of December 2020, twenty-one states—including Alaska, West Virginia, and Georgia—have decided that being registered to vote is the right default.[35]

The Elements of Choice

6

How Many Options?

For generations, students applying to college found out whether they got into their favorite school by going to the mailbox. Bad news came in a thin envelope containing a single-page rejection letter: "We were impressed with your application but regret to inform you. . . ." A thick envelope meant acceptance; it contained information on how to pick dorms, how to register, and how to make all the other exciting decisions that came next.

Eighth-grade students in New York City similarly apply to high schools, but for them thick envelopes mean bad news. Their rejection envelope is thick because it contains instructions on how to apply for the leftover spots at other schools in the city.

Radcliffe Saddler, a thirteen-year-old honors student, had a 94 percent grade average and was the valedictorian at his middle school.[1] His parents immigrated to the United States from Kingston, Jamaica, when he was six, in part to provide Radcliffe and his siblings a better and cheaper education. When it is time for high school, the New York City public school system asks students to rank the schools that they would like to attend. Radcliffe applied to nine very good high schools, but like 10 percent of all New York City high school students, he was not accepted by any of the schools he'd selected.

Radcliffe was immensely disappointed. He held his emotions in during the forty-five-minute ride home on two city buses, but when he finally arrived, he went to his room and cried. "I felt like I never worked hard enough," he said a couple of days later. "To see other people get in, I feel like I did something wrong."

Why didn't Radcliffe get into a better school? Perhaps it has to do with how the designers of the system presented his choices.

Having students compete to attend the high school of their choice has become common over the last twenty years. Many cities in the United States, including Denver, Minneapolis, New Orleans, New York, and Tucson, present students and their parents with options—that is, they ask families to choose their preferred schools. Roughly half of the fifty largest districts across the country offer students some degree of choice of high school.

While school choice is controversial, I am not going to talk about the politics of the question. Instead, let's concentrate on another very important aspect: how parents and kids choose schools. Parents know more about their children's skills, preferences, and values than the school system does. They know whether their child likes small classes, enjoys learning languages, wants to be a medical technician, or plans to attend a world-class college. If administrators knew all of this as well, they might be better able to suggest the right school for a child. They don't, and besides, they are quite overwhelmed. The counselor assigned to work on high school applications with Radcliffe oversaw 350 students. Given that families make this choice with their children, can we develop a system that would help them achieve better outcomes? A good outcome would be a school that fits the needs of the student, their interests and abilities, and other preferences. This school will be different for different students because they have divergent interests, say for sports and arts programs, or how they feel about other attributes, like travel time to school, or the student mix.

How can school districts that ask students to apply to high schools design a choice architecture that most effectively presents families with the options available to them? I was involved in a research project to find the ideal way of presenting information about schools to parents and kids, and I quickly became aware that the choice architecture used to present information about schools can determine someone's future. Choices were very much influenced by how information was presented, and that determines quite a bit about your future.

School choice is a topic that highlights one of the most basic questions in designing choices: How many options should we present? Some districts may have just one or two high schools, but in big cities there are dozens, even hundreds, of options. Should we present the entire list, no matter how large? If the designer decides to limit the number of choices, how do they reduce that amount? Any decisions made in the design process will have a substantial effect on the student's selections and, ultimately, the high school they attend. After all, if a school is not listed, it is unlikely to be chosen.

New York City was one of the first localities to use school choice for public schools. In 2003 it reached out to Harvard University economist (and future Nobel laureate) Al Roth. Along with Atila Abdulkadiroğlu and Pathak Parag, he designed a system intended to encourage families and schools to make good choices and to get kids to attend better schools—which would, theoretically, put pressure on poor-performing schools to improve.

Roth is no ivory tower ideologue. In fact, he is a product of the New York public schools himself, the son of two public high school teachers, Ernest and Lillian, who taught typing and shorthand in Queens to working-class women training to become secretaries. Roth attended Martin Van Buren High School but never graduated, skipping his last few courses to go to Columbia University for his undergraduate degree. (Ironically, this would make him one of the students responsible for lowering Van Buren's graduation rate.)

Years later, after getting his doctorate, he became one of the world's leading experts in market design, a phrase that economists use to describe cases where players in a market, like schools and students, must figure out how to get the best possible match.[2] For example, Roth redesigned the nationwide system that is used every year to match more than forty thousand medical students to hospital residencies in almost all specialties, using principles from the economics of market design. When Roth got the phone call asking if he would apply the concepts of a matching market to the New York City high school admissions system, it seemed like a natural fit. Schools wanted the most appropriate students, and parents wanted the best school for their kids.

The theory behind the system is complicated, but the basic idea is that families rank schools by preference while schools rank potential students. An algorithm uses this information to match students and schools, simultaneously giving both the best outcome. The key to the matching system that Roth and his colleagues designed was getting families to express their preferences honestly. The instructions on the forms, asking families to rank up to twelve potential schools, explicitly says: "It is important to list program choices in your true order of preference."

Well, how hard could that be?

First, consider the number of options available. In 2019, New York City had 769 public high school programs housed across 437 buildings. How many of those schools did New York show to every potential high school student? All 769 of them.

How much information did the designers present about each school? Quite a bit. Each school is described by at least seventeen specific attributes in a 628-page book, given to each student in middle school, the *New York High School Directory*. It's aptly named: at 380,000 words in length and weighing about three pounds, it resembles an old-fashioned telephone directory—and it's about as hard to carry. (Reflecting the diversity of the school population, it's also available in ten languages, ranging from French and Spanish to Bengali, Korean, Urdu, and Haitian Creole.) It is easy to imagine that an eighth grader might balk at adding that weight to their backpack, letting it lie, instead, at the bottom of their locker, never finding its way home.

Schools vary a lot in quality, so the stakes are high: in the best schools almost everyone graduates, while in the worst only about 40 percent get a high school degree. This system, as unwieldy as it seems, has produced some improvement. Choice, combined with an aggressive program of closing failing schools, has increased graduation rates and other metrics that measure success in New York City. But that improvement has not been universal. Those kids who are most disadvantaged have shown the least improvement, and there is a remarkable lack of diversity in New York high schools.[3]

To Radcliffe's parents, having so many choices seemed overwhelming. According to his mother, Claudette Saddler, the process was "like a big maze and you are the little creatures just walking around. . . . It's like, 'Somebody please help me.' I thought it would be simpler for the parents."

Why did Radcliffe fail to get into one of his selected schools? We already know that in other areas, more options can lead to inferior decision-making. In chapter 2, we saw how a person overwhelmed by the options on an online dating app might initially screen for attractive photos, reducing the number of possibilities to something more manageable, but often missing their best matches as a result. A similar problem arises when families start picking schools. Some parents reported screening based on graduation rate. The directory listed this information for the first time the year Radcliffe made this decision. At first, this seems sensible: going to a high school with a high graduation rate would increase your chances of getting a diploma. But if lots of people use graduation rates to make a choice, they will all apply to the same handful of schools. The Baruch College Campus High School, which has a 100 percent graduation rate, received 7,606 applications for 120 seats in 2011, giving it an acceptance rate of 1.6 percent. (By comparison, Harvard accepted 6.2 percent of its applicants that year.) The admission chances for anyone but the very, very best students become almost zero, even for a very good student like Radcliffe. In school choice, just like in dating, more options can discourage a deeper understanding of those options.

The system designed by Roth and his colleagues assumes that a chooser can rank schools in terms of overall preference. Accordingly, a chooser should report their "true preferences" for all the schools that they could rank. But in New York that requires that a chooser pick a list of the best 12 schools from the 769 in the book, and then think carefully about the relative merits of all 12 of them. They need to be able to distinguish between, say the tenth-, eleventh-, and twelfth-best schools. Given that 769 options are presented in New York City, this seems unlikely.

Assembled preferences might also be at work: parents may not be able to articulate trade-offs among the seventeen very different attributes, like graduation rates and time spent on the subway commuting. Many families might find it difficult to decide whether their fourteen-year-old daughter should spend twenty more minutes on the subway for a 10 percent better chance of graduating. All in all, the system designed by Roth and his colleagues assumed that families would think much more systematically than they actually do.

If 769 choices are way too many, how can we identify the right number? The current directory leads choosers to select plausible paths that might lead to bad outcomes. But how could we do better? To know that, we need to look at two things that happen when we increase the number of options.

Building Choice Sets

Much has already been written about *choice overload*, or as it's known in some circles, "the tyranny of choice."[4] Too much choice, according to this view, is bad, causing people to feel less confident in their choices and to delay deciding. While the idea is popular, as we will see, the logic of providing the right number of options is more complex, and the data suggests that "less is better" is not always the right answer. For example, Benjamin Scheibehenne, Rainer Greifeneder, and Peter Todd, researchers associated with the Karlsruhe Institute of Technology, the University of Basel, and Indiana University, respectively, conducted studies where they gave Berliners a choice of either five or thirty restaurants. While people found it marginally more difficult to make a choice in the larger choice set, they nonetheless made choices just as often.[5]

This is a clear case where synthesizing the many studies with a meta-analysis would be useful. There have been two major meta-analyses of number-of-option studies and their effects on people's feelings about choice. The first shows that changing the number of options has no effect on how people feel about the choice, and the second shows that the effect of adding options is very complicated.[6] By complicated, we mean that adding options sometimes hurts but can also help. Barry Schwartz, who popularized the phrase "the paradox of choice" in his book of the same name, reflects on this:

> In academic literature, there have been a couple of papers published that question how generalizable the choice problem is. Some studies show the effect . . . some of them show the opposite effect—people like more choice, and they end up doing better and feeling better. If you put all these studies together and look for an average effect, the average effect is no effect. But that's not because these studies have no effect; almost every study has an effect. It's just that sometimes choice is paralyzing, and sometimes it's liberating.[7]

That is intellectually interesting and honest, but makes it difficult for the designer, doesn't it? How do we decide the right number of options? To answer this question, we need to understand that two different things happen when we increase the number of options.

In chapter 4, I discussed fluency and accuracy, the two goals of choice architecture. Adding options affects these two goals in opposing directions. To see this, think about an example where you are the choice architect for a city with fifty high schools. As in New York City, you must design a system for high school applications that will be the same for every kid. Since it must be printed on paper—not every home has internet access—you cannot customize the list for each child. So, how does adding options affect these two goals?

Schools focus on different topics. Some are vocational; others emphasize an area of study like the arts or computers; still others are great at college prep. Schools also differ in quality, and location is important. There are other key attributes: sports programs, the look of the campus, the kinds of Advanced Placement courses available, tutoring options, extracurricular clubs, and many more. The *New York High School Directory*, for example, delineates the percentage of students who "feel safe in the hallways, bathrooms, locker room, and cafeteria" of each school.

Presenting all these factors to create a simpler choice for parents and kids is a daunting design problem, even with fifty schools. To begin, let's put these two conflicting goals in context:

- **Fluency.** We want people to feel comfortable with the information facing them, so that they will actually engage in the decision-making process. They should not feel like Radcliffe's mom did: overwhelmed, wandering "a big maze and you are the little creatures just walking around." Presenting fewer options leads to greater fluency. Presenting more options reduces fluency and leads people to screen out options.

- **Accuracy.** We want a choice most likely to get them the best outcome, given their preferences and abilities. With the right ranking, Radcliffe might have been admitted to a school that better fit his needs. He had selected schools with good college prep programs. His first choice was Millennium High School, where 97 percent of the students go on to college. Adding schools to the list we present to students increases the probability that they will find a good match. But adding options causes them to consider fewer factors. Radcliffe might not have considered his competition in applying to these schools, for example. In his case, this meant that he went into a second round of matching with schools that had leftover spots—not the outcome that he wanted.

To see this in action, let's walk through our example as we increase the number of options. Imagine we presented a single option. We will simplify our view of accuracy a little and look at the probability that we *present* the choosers with the best option.[8] Since we have to present the same list to everyone, we cannot customize the list for each student. Since we don't know anything about the student who will be seeing the option, we can't match the school to the student. We are picking blindly, essentially picking each additional school at random from the fifty. The chance that the school is the best for that particular student is one in fifty. Blindly presenting one school won't be good, since the chances are that this school would not be the best one for any particular child. Kids looking to study languages might get a school heavy on engineering, or someone looking to train in retail might get a school emphasizing marine science. (Besides, the school system needs to balance demand across schools, complicating logistics.)

Presenting two schools gives the family a choice and doubles the probability that the child will find a good match. It is still very unlikely to be the best but the probability that one of the two schools will be the best is one in twenty-five.

As we increase the number of options, from three to four to five, all the way up to displaying all fifty schools, we increase the probability that the best school for that student is presented. Adding more choices increases the probability of presenting parents with a better option until, when we present all fifty, we are certain the best school is somewhere in the list.

But as we have seen, having too many options may cause people to give up on making a choice altogether, or to pick a simplified plausible path. There may be fifty schools presented, but they might only look at a few. There are many sad stories of quick decisions. In one, a kid quickly fills out the form the morning the rankings are due, without their parents knowing. This is like doing your homework on the school bus, and it's not likely to turn out well. Another student, who was a native English speaker, picked a school specializing in English as a second language, ranking it as their first choice because their friends were going there. Many rank only one or two schools—a clear mistake according to Roth—and overwhelmed guidance counselors can only do so much.

Increasing the number of options increases the chance that families will be *presented* with the best school for them, but it does not mean they will *see* it. As the choice becomes more complex, people will look at less information, either by looking at fewer options, or by looking at fewer details about each option. There is a trade-off here, between increasing potential accuracy and decreasing fluency and search.

When we see trade-offs like this, however, there is a point where the increases in accuracy are balanced by the decreases in fluency. This is the best we can do with constraints—the point of equilibrium where the two factors balance out. We might call this the "sweet spot" for presenting the choices, representing the best accuracy we can achieve without overwhelming people with options.

If we want to present the right number of options, we need to pay attention to both the potential accuracy we achieve by adding options and the impact those options have upon fluency. But there is good news for both the designer and for families. Changing fluency can make looking at options easier. Imagine we use a better format, with easier-to-read fonts. This will change the trade-off, making families less likely to stop searching. This does something important: we can add more options to the choice, increasing the probability that we have shown the family the best option, since they won't stop their search quite as quickly.

Another way to make decisions more accurate is to increase the quality of the set that we present. If we can remove any terrible schools from the set, choosers, even if they were picking randomly, would on average get better outcomes. Remember that we talked about dominated options, those that were truly bad, in chapter 4. These are alternatives that are worse in every way. Imagine that there was a school that was unsafe, had very poor graduation rates, and had no redeeming programs in any field. Even if no family would actively pick the school, they would still have to go through the work of weeding it out. And if they weren't paying attention, they might actually choose it. Why should we include that school in the set of choices? An obvious way of improving the choice set is to eliminate that option. This means that the probability of seeing the best school increases, since families don't have to waste time viewing such losers.

This teaches us an important lesson: the designer has enormous control over the impact of adding options. There is no simple rule for providing the right number of options, but a good designer can help by making choices more fluent, presenting the right set of options, and paying close attention to that sweet spot between an accurate set of options and an overwhelming one.

How to Present More Choice

On October 1, 2013, many middle-class and poorer Americans woke up to a new world: they could now buy health insurance, some of it heavily subsidized, through a set of exchanges. The Patient Protection and Affordable Care Act (otherwise known as Obamacare) was, in the overheard words of then vice president Joe Biden, "a big f—ing deal." But the optimism of the opening days was quashed by a series of very visible missteps. Many of the exchanges suffered information technology meltdowns, with people facing long waits to access websites made unresponsive by excessive demand.

That was bad, but there was a bigger, though almost invisible, problem. Even if they could log on, people still might not choose the right insurance for them. That could be a serious issue: the very people that Obamacare was meant to help, people living near the poverty line, could wind up with the wrong insurance, possibly wasting money that could be used for groceries and schools on an inappropriate policy that did not meet their needs. Since the policies were subsidized, taxpayer dollars would be wasted as well.

Researchers have been studying the general question of how well employees do when they select among the health insurance plans offered by their firms as part of their benefits. Most firms try to offer a good set of options to their employees. After all, by encouraging employees to buy good health insurance, they will most likely enable those employees to stay healthier—and more productive—in the long run.

On the whole, however, people choose health insurance badly. One study by behavioral economists Saurabh Bhargava,

George Loewenstein, and Justin Sydnor looked at an actual company that believed in offering lots of options.[9] There were forty-eight policies that provided users access to the same networks of doctors, hospitals, and other providers. The difference was how the costs of the plan were managed. Some provided lower out-of-pocket costs, which was great, but those policies had more expensive premiums. For some policies, once you added up the higher premiums, it turned out that you would have ended up paying more than you would have saved with the plan that offered lower out-of-pocket costs. No matter how much health care you used, you would pay more for these plans. These low out-of-pocket policies are the essence of dominated options. If you pick one, you end up paying more for the same coverage. Choosing one of those plans would be like seeing two identical packages of soap on the store shelf and buying the one that is more expensive.

One fact that has long been known in the insurance industry is that people really hate paying out-of-pocket fees for medical care. After all, you've paid all this money in monthly premiums, and now you have to pull out your wallet again to actually receive the service. People seem to be willing to pay higher premiums just so they can pay less at the doctor's office, even if it costs more overall.

Of the forty-eight plans at the company that the three economists examined, thirty-five were simply bad deals all around. Yet over half the people who worked for the company chose one of these more expensive plans, costing them an average of about $370 a year more for the same health insurance. To make matters worse, these mistakes were more common among those workers who could least afford to make them—the ones earning less than $40,000 a year, along with women, older employees, and those with chronic health conditions.

Could people make similar mistakes on the new exchanges? Depending upon where they lived, consumers saw very different sets of options. Some states presented a small range of options, while others, like Utah, offered more than one hundred. Could that have been too many? Did it change how people felt about making a choice (the fluency of the choice)? Could it affect whether or not they picked the right policy (whether they made accurate choices)? Health insurance choices have many facets, but let's see if you can pick the most cost-effective option. Take a look at the eight options in the following table.

Eight Health Insurance Options Presented to Choosers

Health Plan	Monthly Premium	Doctor Visit Copay	Annual Deductible
A	$435	$10	$200
B	$376	$28	$735
C	$425	$18	$380
D	$545	$15	$150
E	$600	$5	$100
F	$369	$40	$850
G	$417	$10	$550
H	$392	$20	$680

If I told you to find the cheapest policy, ignoring factors like the quality of the plan for now, you might find it difficult. Even if I tell you how often you will visit the doctor and how much you will pay in out-of-pocket expenses, the choice is very daunting. I've presented this decision to groups of intelligent economists and psychologists, including Mac-Arthur Fellows. They all find this decision painful, and after a few minutes, most plead with me to tell them the right answer. Yet this is a simple version of the very choice people buying health insurance face.

I was worried about whether choice would work on the exchanges. If competition was to succeed, people had to make good choices. Along with a group of co-authors,[10] I looked at decisions like this before the exchanges were launched. Would people find choosing policies fluent? How accurate would they be? To look at what Obamacare might bring, we used a decision simulator, as described in chapter 4.

We showed hundreds of potential customers, online participants who could have been in the market for insurance on the exchanges, realistic policies. This was on our own simplified exchange, which looked like the table above, and asked them to pick the most cost-effective option. We told them they would make five doctor's visits, with $200 in out-of-pocket expenses. In the real world, they would have to estimate how much care they would use, but knowing how much they would use for the sake of the experiment should have made the choice easier. To make sure that they would really think it through, we offered more money if they were able to select the most affordable policy from the available options. If they picked the most cost-effective option, they would earn $10. If they picked the worst, they would get the minimum payment, $2.[11] Paying them did make them work harder. It took them about 30 percent longer to make a choice.

One set of participants chose from among four options and the other chose from eight. We asked them afterward how confident they had felt about making a choice. Even though it sounds a lot like accuracy, this is a measure of how people feel about the choice and not about if they really picked the right option. The result was unequivocal: they were less confident about choosing with more options. And while subjective feelings of confidence and making the right choice are surprisingly unrelated, their choices were worse when they saw eight policies.

This suggests that our website should be limited to only four policies, but that isn't practical. Insurance policies and insurance buyers differ in important ways, just like schools. Some have great mental health coverage, while others offer good coverage for kids. The exchanges need to offer enough options to handle all these differences. But as we have seen, more options can also lead people to disengage from the choice, not look at all the options, or adopt a plausible path, like screening, that can lead to bad choices.

It's a tough challenge for the designer. Health insurance resists fluency. For one thing, it's simply unpleasant to contemplate you or your loved ones getting sick. For another, there are many unfamiliar and difficult terms and concepts. Take *deductible*: that's the amount you must pay out of your own pocket before insurance coverage kicks in, although you'd never know it from the name. Some people misunderstand what a deductible is, thinking that it's the amount you save because of insurance. Or *copay*: this is the amount you pay for treatment out-of-pocket. Again, not necessarily an intuitive label.

It seems like the designers of health exchanges are stuck. They need to present more options, but if they do, people will mentally check out of the process and make worse choices. How could you make these choices more fluent? If we could do that, we might be able to offer more options without people tuning out.

Choosing the most cost-efficient policy is difficult because there is not a single price tag. There are monthly premiums, but also deductibles, copays, and other things, like in-network and out-of-network costs. Even if you know how much care you are going to use and you understand the terms, it is a lot of work to figure out what a policy would cost, and the work increases as you add more options.

To figure out the cost in the example in the table, a chooser would have to:

1. Multiply the monthly premium by 12;

2. Multiply the copay by the number of times they expect they would have to go to the doctor;

3. Figure out whether their out-of-pocket costs or the annual deductible is smaller; and

4. Add the three sums from steps 1–3 to arrive at the total.

That is a lot of work, and they would have to do it eight times, once per policy. It feels like filling out a tax form, doesn't it?

Our solution for fluency? We simply did the math for them. The table below and the task are the same as the one above, but we added a fifth column that displays the cost. When we made this simple change, people found this complex choice more fluent, and the differences between presenting four or eight options disappeared. People were just as confident and accurate even though we doubled the number of options.

The Same Choice, with Calculator

Health Plan	Monthly Premium	Doctor Visit Copay	Annual Deductible	Total Annual Cost
A	$435	$10	$200	$5,470
B	$376	$28	$735	$4,852
C	$425	$18	$380	$5,390
D	$545	$15	$150	$6,765
E	$600	$5	$100	$7,325
F	$369	$40	$850	$4,828
G	$417	$10	$550	$5,254
H	$392	$20	$680	$5,004

This is not an isolated example. While the meta-analyses of the many studies of the effects of increasing the number of options on fluency show there is a small choice-overload effect, with more options leading to less fluent choices, the effect is relatively small (negligible, in fact, in one of the meta-analyses), and it turns out it is easy to make disappear. The meta-analysis conducted by Alex Chernev, Ulf Böckenholt, and Joseph Goodman shows that choice architecture, like the calculator in our example, has much more impact than increasing the number of options. Chernev and his colleagues looked at studies that changed both the choice architecture and the number of options. The bottom line is that the effect of good versus bad choice architecture is over three times as large as the effect of increasing the number of options. This is excellent news for the designer. You *can* make people feel good about having more options.

Here is an example from school choice. In some cities, the lists are organized alphabetically, like a telephone book. While this might be useful if you were looking for a school that you had heard of, it is doubtful that anyone wants to choose a school that starts with a given letter of the alphabet. We might do better by organizing schools by something more relevant, like type—college prep in one section, vocational in another—or location.

Going back to health insurance, more options not only made people feel worse about their choice (what people usually mean by choice overload), but they made objectively worse choices as well. In our first study, for example, the choosers got the right option 42 percent of the time with four options, but with eight, they got the right policy only 20 percent of the time, data that suggests that they might as well have been guessing.

Because we are using a choice simulation, we know what the best option would be for a family and can estimate how much missing choice architecture costs. For example, looking at the table on page 179, the cheapest option is F. Imagine that a shopper didn't want to do the multiplication of premiums and decided instead just to look at the cheapest copay and deductible, Option E. That plausible path might seem sensible, but it is really expensive. The difference between the cost of E and F is almost $2,500! We can also see how well insurance buyers in our study do with and without choice architecture. Without choice architecture, people do badly, overpaying by an average of $533 per family.

We tried many things, including giving them annual cost totals like those in the table on page 179. This not only made them feel better about their choice, but it also made their decisions more accurate, cutting their errors in half. Since we knew the right answer, we could set those as defaults. When we combined calculators with defaults, choosers did really well, and their mistakes only cost them $72. Most important, with choice architecture, there was no significant difference in choice quality whether they chose among four or eight options. Choice architecture overcame choice overload.

You might think this is a special situation, since we told people what their usage would be, but other researchers have shown that providing estimates of the cost of policies, even when people don't know their usage, can improve choice.[12]

Our studies suggest that better choice architecture would have saved health insurance buyers over $450, half a week's salary for the average buyer on the Obamacare market. The potential savings of providing effective choice architecture for health care plan selection is, in total, more than $9 billion.

Inspired by this, we decided to do our own meta-analysis. This differed from the prior two analyses because it asked a different question: not how people feel about their choices, but whether increasing the number of options affects accuracy. We concentrated on studies that used a decision simulator, studies where the researchers knew the right answer. This work with Shannon Duncan, now a graduate student at the Wharton School, and Ulf Böckenholt, an expert at meta-analysis at the Kellogg School, looked at how accuracy changed as more options were added. While we found that more options could hurt accuracy, that was only when decisions were made without choice architecture. With choice architecture, there was no adverse effect.

The intelligent use of choice architecture lets us add options without reducing fluency, therefore getting closer to the best choice for each person. As such, "How many options?" is the wrong question. The right questions for choice architects to ask are:

1. How can we present the options more fluently?

2. Which are the options most likely to produce an accurate choice?

Going Back to School

Let's close by revisiting Radcliffe Saddler, whose story ultimately has a happy ending. Usually, the schools available in the second round are low-performing ones that have low graduation rates, often large neighborhood schools or schools that have been put on warning that they may be shut down. Fortunately, Radcliffe applied and was admitted to a new program that was just starting and had openings. It was not the kind of college prep school that he wanted, but it was an innovative school focusing on information technology jobs. The Pathways to Technology School, a program cosponsored by IBM, includes two years of college leading to an associate degree following the traditional four years of high school for students who perform well. Radcliffe was an exceptional student there: two years after he started the program, he had twenty-one college credits and passed all five of the New York State Regents exams. That year, there was a school-wide contest to pick a student to introduce a special speaker at the school, President Barack Obama. The winner was Radcliffe. His two-minute introduction went well. According to Radcliffe, "It was really cool. I expected him to shake my hand, but I wasn't really expecting the hug."[13]

Radcliffe, now twenty-four, works for IBM as an associate designer. This is a happier ending than we might expect. But remember his original goal: going to a school to prepare him for a four-year college degree. One wonders what would have happened if the designers of the New York City school match program had helped him make a better choice in the first round.

7

Putting Things in Order

I n late 2000, the nation anxiously followed a news story
that involved choice architecture, even before the term
was coined. The vote count in Florida was incredibly close, with 537 votes out of 5.8 million cast separating
the two candidates. The result would determine who won
the Electoral College: George W. Bush or Al Gore.

The choice architecture issue was fundamental: Did the
votes as recorded reflect the true preferences of the voters?
There was significant doubt. Perhaps people didn't understand the strange "butterfly ballots," where the response
box and the candidate's name were not aligned. Even if they
did, there were questions about what constituted a vote:
people watched daily broadcasts of recounts where inspec-
tors argued over whether or not a ballot was clearly punched
through—creating a "hanging chad," in the vernacular of

the time. There was another effect in play, though, and it's one that still influences election choices today.

In Florida, George W. Bush's name was listed first on every ballot. Why? Some assumed the ordering happened because Governor Jeb Bush was George's brother, but the real reason was less nefarious. As it turns out, it was required by state law. In 1951, the Democrats who controlled Florida's state government passed a law requiring that the candidate of the party of the sitting governor be listed first in every race. Since Jeb Bush was a Republican, his party was listed first across the ballot. Given the slim margin, could this subtle selection of choice architecture have helped decide who would be president?

Woodrow Wilson earned his PhD in political science from Johns Hopkins University before becoming the twenty-eighth president of the United States. He believed that order mattered. In an essay called "Hide-and-Seek Politics," he wrote:

> I have seen a ballot which contained several hundred names. It was bigger than a page of newspaper and was printed in close columns as a newspaper would be. Of course, no voter . . . can vote a ticket like that with intelligence. In nine out of ten cases, he will simply mark the first name under each office, and the candidates whose names come highest in the order will be elected. There are cases on record where shrewd seekers of office have had their names changed to names beginning with some letter at the head of the alphabet preparatory to can-

The Elements of Choice

didacy on such a ballot, knowing that they had no chance of election otherwise.

Changing your name so you are first on the ballot shouldn't qualify you for office. Appearing first, either because of electoral law or a random choice, shouldn't determine the outcome of an election. Was Wilson onto something?

Some states randomize the order of candidates on ballots, usually by county,[1] and this allows us to see whether order matters. We can take the percentage of the votes that a candidate gets when they are first and compare that to when they are, say, last. Researchers like Jon Krosnick, a political psychologist at Stanford University, have studied these so-called ballot order effects for years. In the 2000 presidential election, Krosnick and his colleagues examined how order affected voting in three states—California, North Dakota, and Ohio—that randomized order. In all three states, Bush received a larger share of the votes when his name was first than when it was last. The difference was 9.45 percent in California, 1.65 percent in North Dakota, and 0.76 percent in Ohio.

Across all two-candidate races, the average advantage of being first turns out to be between 1 and 2 percent. The effects are larger for nonpartisan and primary elections. Why? Nonpartisan and primary elections remove an easily plausible path that people might otherwise use to make a decision: voting by party. A study of voting for lesser-known primaries in Texas, where ballot order is randomized, showed that the first-listed candidate enjoyed a 10 percent increase in votes. The conclusion is that order effects are larger when the candidates are less well-known or, in the language of political science, when the electorate consists of "low-information" voters. A paper by Darren Grant, an economist at Sam Houston University, describes a "perfect storm" of ballot order effects. Two little-known candidates had the same last name, Green, and common first names, Paul and Rick. They were running for the state's Republican Supreme Court nomination, so party was not a cue. The study found that whichever Green was listed first on that county's ballot received a 20 percent advantage.[2]

To put the size of these effects in perspective, campaigns spend millions of dollars on get-out-the-vote efforts and consider a 2 percent increase in turnout a big win. Even modest ballot order effects get them the same bounce for free.[3]

Of course, the 2000 Florida ballot involved well-known candidates. But with Bush and Gore separated by just 537 votes, only a handful of voters needed to mark the first name they saw in order to win Bush the election. If a handful of voters—about 1 in every 25,000 voters, or 0.0045 percent—checked the name because it was first in the list, order alone would have determined the next president of the United States. Had the order been different, putting Gore first or varying randomly from county to county, history could have been different. Order might have been a factor in Florida. Order effects overwhelm this difference in total votes and the influence of the much publicized hanging chads or butterfly ballots.

We will never know for certain if the outcome in Florida depended upon whose name was first. But it seems obvious that we should randomize order on all electoral ballots. No one would propose choosing presidents, senators, mayors, or city council members based on a coin flip instead of by holding an election. But think about it: if we use a coin flip to determine ballot order, that is exactly what we are doing in close races. If the order effect is larger than the difference between the candidates, the outcome of one coin flip could determine who is elected. Only about twelve states change name order fully in some or all of their elections. The best scheme might be like that used in Ohio. They start with an alphabetical order and rotate that order across precincts. Other states do it, but only for some elections. For example, Texas changes order only in primaries, perhaps because order effects might be larger there, given that people can't vote by party.

The other thirty-eight states that do not control for order might adopt methods that minimize its influence. It certainly is not a good idea to do what Delaware does, requiring by law that Democrats are always listed first. Having the incumbent listed first, as is done in Massachusetts, increases the advantage of being the incumbent. In theory, it might be best to change the order so that everyone sees a different arrangement, but that seems unwieldy, particularly with paper ballots. A good approximation would be to change the order across voting precincts, election districts, or counties. It is important to realize that systematically changing the order does not make the effect of ballot order disappear. Instead, it balances out its effect. Contrast that with the alternative, practiced by about seven states, where an official controls the ballot order, giving them the power to influence elections.

Has anything changed since 2000? Krosnick, the political psychologist most associated with order effects, is convinced that order made a difference in 2016. Donald Trump's name was first in critical states, like Wisconsin, Michigan, and Florida, and he won by small margins in those places. Of course, Hillary Clinton was listed first in some close states as well. In 2019, the Democrats sued in a number of states, including Florida, to randomize order. In Florida they won an initial ruling, since overturned, and the Republican candidate was listed first, again, in 2020.[4]

How Order Matters

You might recoil at the idea that something outside of our control, like the order of options on a list, can influence our decisions. Or you might think order could affect our unimportant decisions, like what ice cream to buy. But would order matter for important choices, like where to go to school, or what mutual fund to purchase?

The reality is that these effects can be large, but the explanation is complicated at first glance. After reading about voting, you might think being first is always best, but there are times when being last is best.

These results seem so complicated that a designer might want to simply throw up their hands and give up. In fact, I struggled when writing this chapter because of the difficulty of explaining order's effects clearly. But then I realized two things. First, the effect of ordering can be very large, often as large as the effect of defaults. Remember that changing defaults can increase the choice of a candidate by more than 20 percent. And, as with defaults, it is easy for the designer to change the order of options. Online, you can sort a table differently with a simple change in code or a mouse click. Second, while the results might seem complex, the drivers of order effects are pretty simple and fairly easy to explain. By understanding the drivers, we can understand the effects.

The first driver is a set of factors that make the initial item in an ordered list more likely to be chosen than if it were later in the list. When being early in the list helps, we call this *primacy*. Imagine you were given a list of ice-cream flavors, and let's say there are fifty-seven options. If being first on the list makes it more likely that you will pick that flavor, we are seeing primacy. We will delve deeper into this shortly, but the drivers of primacy are close cousins of factors we have already discussed. People do not always search enough, and different orders change the ways we consult memory to assemble our preferences. You might start reading the list at the top, and stop before you reach the bottom.

The second driver is a set of factors that favor being last in the list, something we will call *recency*. Recency means that things later in the list get an advantage. If I recited the list of ice-cream flavors and you consistently chose the last, you would be exhibiting recency. Recency again depends upon memory, but in a very different way. As we proceed through a long set of options, we may forget some things about the prior options.

This will often be the case when we don't control the flow of information. When we look at a ballot, we can decide what to look at and when. The same is true of a written menu. But contrast seeing the fifty-seven flavors of ice cream in a list to hearing someone recite them one by one. In this case, they and not you control what information is presented. You need to remember whatever they say to have a chance at choice. If you forget it, it is not going to be selected. The same is true for judges of figure skating. The performers present sequentially, so to compare one skater's performance with another's, a judge must rely on their memories. As each subsequent figure skater performs, the judges' memories of the previous performers inevitably fade. By the time the last skater appears, memories of the first will have degraded substantially. The comparison is now anything but fair.

Primacy and recency will each be important in different situations. For example, primacy might happen when we are using a website, but recency might happen if discussing our options with a colleague. To understand this, we need to understand what causes primacy and recency.

When Being First Is Being Best

The long, written menu of ice creams, listed from top to bottom on the wall, is a good illustration of primacy. Imagine it is just twelve artisanal flavors and each item has an extensive description, almost an essay, including ingredients. The first is called fruit parfait. The essay describes how the fruit, which is one of your favorites, is at its seasonal peak, and that the ice-cream maker has carefully se-lected the blend. It goes on in detail about the variety of fruit, where it is grown, how it is organic and healthy, and the ingredients and their preparation. The second item on the list is called chocolate mousse, made with fine chocolate and a delicious liqueur. The third is called toffee crisp, the fourth coconut sorbet, and so on. You feel exhausted just looking at the list and you're less than halfway done reading it when the person scooping ice cream asks what you want.

Since you have read about assembling preferences, you have some insight into what is going on. As you read about the fruit parfait, you recalled all the instances when you had that fruit when it was perfectly ripe, thought about how it looked, and imagined how it would taste in the ice cream. When you see the listing for chocolate mousse, very little came to mind. You might say, "They had me at 'parfait.'"

But what would happen if the mousse had been first? Your mind might dwell on the velvety mousse and the contrast between the sweet chocolate and the bracing flavor of the liqueur, and you would have a hard time thinking about the parfait.

These differences in how questions are asked, described earlier using query theory and inhibition, can cause changes in choice. When we make choices, we identify an option as the tentative best, or current first choice. As we consider other options, we compare them to this tentative first choice, and a fairly remarkable thing happens: we tend to distort the information that we see to favor this first choice. We look at the good aspects of the tentative options first and have a hard time remembering much about the other options. In the ice-cream example, our evaluation depended on order. This distortion seems quite common in research. Elke Weber and I call this *decision by distortion.*[5]

Jay Russo, a professor at Cornell University, is a bit of a gourmand. He and his colleagues Kurt Carlson and Margaret Meloy conducted a study in 2006 that used order to change choices among restaurants. They asked participants to choose between two restaurants, which were described by several attributes. Both were attractive options, but not equivalent. Restaurant A was preferred by 59 percent of the participants. Restaurant B was clearly better on one attribute that was important—dessert—but that was not enough to entice more people to choose it over A. In a week, the same people came back and were given the same choice, but the descriptions were disguised by changing the name and formatting. However, Russo and his colleagues made one important change: they changed the order in which the information was presented. Now the best attribute of the inferior restaurant (the desserts of Restaurant B, formerly known as the loser) was presented first. Leading with the weak restaurant's strength changed choices. The not-so-good restaurant went from being chosen 41 percent of the time to 62 percent. Simply changing the order presentation of the pair increased the market share of the initial runner-up by 43 percent. How? Russo and colleagues suggest that when people were thinking about the desserts of Restaurant B, they saw the other features of Restaurant A as less positive, relative to Restaurant B. They asked people to rate the attributes of the two restaurants and, as we would predict, when people saw the dessert first, they saw all the attributes of Restaurant B in a better light. People also rated the characteristics of the other restaurant as less attractive when compared to rating the exact same attributes a week earlier. The courteous service of the "better" restaurant now seemed less attractive. The dessert of Restaurant B shone at the end of the meal. Preferences were assembled differently merely based on presentation order.

Increasing the relative market share of a restaurant simply by changing the order in which its attributes are presented is pretty impressive. Russo and company saw that order made a big difference, so they asked choosers if they thought it influenced their choice. Almost all denied that order made a difference.

But when the list of options gets long, something else also happens that supports primacy. Life is full of choices that have many options. Remember Woodrow Wilson's hundreds of candidates? That may be an exaggeration, but long ballots do exist, like the twenty-five active major candidates in the 2020 Democratic presidential primary, or the seventeen Republican candidates running in the 2016 Republican presidential primary. In this book, we have seen other examples of long lists of options, from high schools to potential dates on dating apps. In these long lists, people may review only a handful of their options.

Primacy also occurs when people search too little and don't look very far down the list. Primacy will be stronger if the list is not fluent, and most ballots are not. The less fluent a list, the shorter the set of considered options becomes, and primacy becomes more powerful.

In chapter 6, we talked about people missing the best

option because they stop searching too soon. Here we are dealing with the same phenomenon and looking more carefully at the relationship between search and choice. When people stop searching too soon, they choose from a smaller set of options. If an option is not seen, it is not chosen. This driver of primacy helps explain when being first, or close to it, is best. If only primacy mattered, Wilson would be right: to get ahead in life, in lists sorted alphabetically, change your name—become Aaker or Aaron and be done with it.

Researchers love to calculate how much searching choosers *should* do. This is because the problem of when to stop is amenable to statistical optimization. Not surprisingly, there is a huge amount of literature on optimal stopping points in economics and applied math. Relevant studies look at how many suitors to consider before getting married and how many candidates to interview before filling a particular role. It's ironic then that an occupation preoccupied with optimal search should itself have fallen prey to order effects. As we shall see in the next section, one of the most important ways economists find one another's work has suffered from a huge order effect, one so large that it caused the field to change the choice architecture altogether.

Economists

Every Monday morning, the National Bureau of Economic Research (NBER) sends out an email describing new working papers to a mailing list of twenty-three thousand people.

The bureau is a private, nonprofit research organization best known for declaring the beginnings and ends of recessions, and its list of working papers is important, as papers in economics can take years to be published.

Each email lists that week's paper's title, its authors, a brief description, and a download link. Everyone gets a list that editors and readers believe is randomly ordered, and there is no editorial control over what papers are listed where. Order is a matter of happenstance. The list is usually lengthy—the most recent email I saw featured thirty-six working papers—and filled with exciting titles (to economists) like "Global Trade and Margins of Productivity in Agriculture" and "Deciphering the Macroeconomic Effects of Internal Devaluations in a Monetary Union."

Since everyone involved in making the list each week, from the submitting economists to the list's compilers, believes that the order of the list is random, order should be unimportant. There is absolutely no reason to expect the first paper in the list to be better, or the last paper to be worse. Order conveys no information.

But even for these economists, order has an effect because they also do not look at all the papers. Being listed first means that your paper's abstract will be read 33 percent more of the time and downloaded 29 percent more often than the second listed paper, and that trend continues down the list.[6]

One of the most important measures of success among academics is citations: the number of times other scholars mention your work in their own papers. Citation counts play an important role in earning tenure at most universities and attracting job offers from other universities, and they are, of course, a source of bragging rights. In fact, they are so important that one indicator of a researcher's citations, the *h-index*—a measure of the number of citations in one's career—is compared across scholars. When a well-known scholar walks by at a conference, other academics will mention their h-index ("I think George is a great scholar, but Sandra has a much higher h-index"). Citations really matter.

Does being first on a random list like this one help? You bet. Daniel Feenberg and colleagues looked at the effect of randomly appearing first by tracking how often those papers are referred to by other scholars in their papers over the course of the next two years. They found that being first in the NBER list resulted in 27 percent more citations. Since order contains no information, people could start reading anywhere on the list, and not necessarily at the top. It is also very easy to scan down the list. But the evidence is that economists read and cite the papers at the top more often, even though they are not the best papers on the list and are at the top by chance. The authors even controlled for the popularity of papers when they were listed in other places, and they still found that order itself made a large difference.

This is a good example of haphazard choice architecture. The NBER staff had made a selection of a choice-architecture tool—order—without considering its consequence. When they realized that their design had this effect, what did this group of sophisticated designers do? The economists started a new policy meant to minimize order effects. Each email listed the papers in a different random order, meaning that each reader received a unique random order. This certainly balanced any order effects. James Poterba, the president of the group, said that "choice architecture is an important and understudied dimension of economic choices." When asked why they randomized, he replied: "Once you recognize there might be a bias, it's almost a natural default to pursue." This is a natural way of minimizing order effects, but it might be not be the best way of presenting options. Imagine papers were grouped by interest area—say, microeconomics or game theory—and that each person could select the areas that interested them. The designer could use that information to order the papers by each person's interest, making order meaningful and helpful.

Expedia

The effect on working papers has real consequences for citations, and for academic egos. But economically, the effect of order on the internet means many more dollars. Expedia, the world's largest online travel agency, wanted to know what the best way was to arrange search results on its website. It thought perhaps a redesign would help profits. Seventy percent of its global revenue came from the sale of hotel rooms offered by chains like Holiday Inn or Marriott and by independent hotels. It was a much bigger revenue source than booking cars and airfares. Most of the time, the income came from a commission from the hotel, not advertising. If one ordering of search results helps someone find and book a room better than another order, Expedia would make more money. Leaving the site without booking means no commission.[7]

When a visitor to the site enters a location and dates of travel, Expedia returns a list of available hotel rooms (twenty-seven on average). To increase bookings, Expedia started using an algorithm to sort the list according to the relevance to the search. This rank was based on the amount of attention a hotel had gotten from other shoppers, and the match with the consumer's past purchases on features like price and quality. Then Expedia did an A/B experiment between that algorithm and randomly ordering the hotels to see the effect of order on sales.

Because Expedia now ordered the hotels at random, Raluca Ursu, a marketing professor at New York University, could identify how much a hotel's sales changed when it appeared in different positions in the list. Let's say many customers typed "Baltimore" and specified a weekend for the stay. All customers who did this saw the same hotels, but they appeared in different positions in the list. For one customer, a hotel might have been first; for another, it might have been twentieth, and so on. This allowed Ursu to study how the position alone affected sales. Thus, the best hotel for the customer could be anywhere in the list. Position in the list and the fit of the hotel to the customer were totally independent.

Since this list already had a fair amount of information about each hotel—like its name, price, location, and a star rating for quality—the logical thing to do would be to scan the list and click through to the hotel that looked most promising. Most of the information that consumers needed was right there in front of them. They should click on the link that seems to fit their needs best. Because scanning the list seems so easy, you might have expected order to have very little effect.

But the order of the hotels in the random list made a big difference: the first hotel was selected 50 percent more often than the second and almost twice as often as the fifth. People searched very little; 93 percent of them clicked on only one hotel. And this was a fairly expensive purchase, as the average hotel cost about $160 a night.

Ursu analyzed this data across 4.5 million Expedia searches. She used statistical models to see how this effect of order translated to cost. These models controlled for differences in hotels (such as distance from downtown, swimming pools, room quality, chain name, and the like), allowing her to look at whether people should search more and how much it cost them to search too little. She argues that people behave as if search costs are huge, even if it involves just one click. Customers could save money by searching more options. Ursu calculated, on average, that consumers give up about $2 by not clicking on another hotel, an act that would take only a few seconds. Let's look at this as an economist: if I could make $2 for, say, one minute more of work, by not searching I am turning down an opportunity to make $2 a minute— $120 an hour.

Ursu could use the model to see how choosers would do if Expedia replaced their algorithm with one that ranked options according to their predicted fit to the customer. The original Expedia rankings were much worse. According to Ursu's calculations, Expedia's order cost choosers more than

$30 a night. Not presenting rooms by their predicted fit effectively increased the price paid by consumers by 19 percent, compared to the improved algorithm. Expedia would be better off with Ursu's proposed algorithm, which would increase the number of rooms booked by 2.4 percent.

You might think that first is always best, and indeed that seems to be true for political candidates, academic papers, and hotels, but it's not the full story. These examples all have two things in common: they are all lists of mostly text, and the chooser is in full control of where they place their attention.

Losing Control: When Last Is Best

Say your partner comes home and offers to suggest five movies you might go to that evening. Since you find browsing the web to find nearby movies and reading reviews a chore, you are more than happy to listen to the list. Your partner lists all five options, giving you a sentence-long description of each. In this scenario, do you think the first movie would be the one most likely to be chosen? Since your partner is the designer, could they order the list to increase the odds that you choose the option they prefer? Should they put their favorite movie first?

Research suggests that first might not be best in this case. Think about the drivers here: the effects that drive primacy might be at work, but something is different. Imagine you are the listener in this marital conversation. You hear about the first movie, a sordid mystery, and quickly form an opinion. Your partner next tells you about a rom-com that just came out. You vaguely remember seeing a review, and as you listen, you quickly compare it to your impression of the mystery and decide which one wins: the mystery. The third is a documentary about your partner's favorite band (your partner has broad tastes). You know that you would like to avoid the documentary, so you try to remember which of the first two movies you liked best. The fourth is an action flick; it's a sequel and you both hated the first movie, so you quickly dismiss that. At this point you can't remember much about the first, just that you liked it better than the rom-com. Finally, your partner mentions the fifth film, another mystery, but this one is an old film noir playing at the classic movie house, and they mention that you can get a drink at the cute bar across the street. You both have said you wanted to try that bar sometime. You try to remember the other four movies, give up, and say, "Let's go to the last film," thinking as much about the drink as you are the movie.

You have lost control of your attention. Just like a waiter reciting the night's specials, your partner has taken control of the information presentation. This is different than looking at a ballot or a web list. With a webpage, you can go back if you forget something. You can't do that here. Your partner has changed the rules of the game. They have used a *sequential presentation* where the options are presented one at a time. Before, we were talking about *simultaneous presentations*, where you saw everything at once and you were in control. With a sequential presentation, you lose control.

Once you understand the difference in choice presentations, you will begin to notice sequential presentations all the time. Wine tastings. House hunting. Judging figure skating competitions. All of these are all sequential.

The Eurovision Song Contest pits pop performers from various member countries of the European Broadcasting Union against one another. ABBA won with what would become their first hit, "Waterloo." Celine Dion, the British singer Lulu, and the German singer Lena all received major career boosts from their wins. The Eurovision Song Contest is known for its combination of over-the-top performances of pop ballads with kitschy weirdness. First airing in 1956, it was the world's longest-running annual contest still in production until the pandemic forced the cancellation of the 2020 edition.

Eurovision presents its contestants sequentially: each country gets to submit one act with a single three-minute song. In the finals, twenty-six songs are presented over the course of two hours. The order of the presentation is determined at random. Judging is done by both professionals and the television audience watching throughout the world. One key rule is that you cannot vote for your own country's act.

Wändi Bruine de Bruin, a Dutch psychologist, has studied competitions like Eurovision closely. Unlike simultaneous-choice scenarios, where primacy is an advantage, she often finds a recency effect—that is, that later positions are better. Why is this different?

Think about your discussion about picking a movie with your partner. Given that you were not going to hear the information again, you evaluated each option as it came in and compared it to the best one so far. In these situations, it gets increasingly difficult to remember much about the earlier options. Even the one you liked the best so far, the current leader, becomes harder to recall. The option you heard most recently is very easy to remember. This means that options toward the end of the list have a better chance of being the winner. Indeed, Bruine de Bruin's research shows exactly that: in Eurovision contests, the later songs tend to win, despite the fact that order is determined randomly. Eurovision competitors understand this, at least intuitively, and try to stand out by providing memorable moments. In 2015, the Austrian entry, the Makemakes, seemed to set a piano on fire, and in 2016, the Belarus entry, Ivan, appeared with a holographic wolf howling at the moon—anything to be remembered through subsequent acts.

Bruine de Bruin finds the same recency effect in international figure skating contests. The ordering in the sport is particularly unfair: competitors enter the first round in a random order. As we have seen, the people at the end have an advantage. In the second round, the order is determined by who performed best in the first. This means that the advantage could be multiplied. To see this, imagine that every single skater was equally good. Now the very skaters who did better by chance, because they were last in the first round, would get a second boost by going last in the second round.

Again, it is important to realize that position in both cases is not informative. In figure skating, as in voting, we would prefer not to have the luck of the draw determine the winner. Similar effects show up in synchronized swimming contests and classical music competitions. Bruine de Bruin titles this series of papers describing recency effects beautifully, giving great advice to all contestants: "Save the Last Dance for Me."

There is a clever, if somewhat duplicitous, experiment in wine tasting done by psychologists that also makes this point. People choose a favorite from a series of wine tastings. Curious about the effect of the length of the list of wines, the researchers varied the length of the "flight." Participants tasted two, three, four, or five wines. Although they were told they were tasting a series of wines of the same varietal from different vineyards, they were actually tasting samples of the same wine. This bit of deception might make you think that this means their choices would be random, the equivalent of flipping a coin. The only thing that differed was the order, and yet order made all the difference.

Take a look at what happened. The figure on page 207 shows what people chose as their favorite wine as the length of the list increased from two samples to five.

These effects of order are large: In the two-wine sequence, the first wine was chosen 70 percent of the time, much more than the 50 percent we would expect by chance— meaning that the first wine was picked twice as often as the second, even though the wines were identical. In this limited list, the first position has an advantage. This is the primacy effect we described earlier and saw with ballots and restaurants. But notice what happens with longer flights: the advantage of being first decreases, and the last wine in the sequence starts to do better. This is the recency effect, where being last (or most recent) is best.[8]

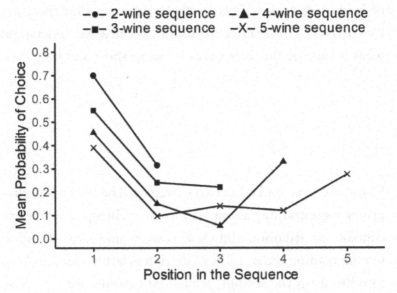

How often a wine was chosen by position,
with different numbers of possible choices

Why does this happen? Obviously being first in the tasting is an advantage, and because the wines are identical, this advantage is due only to order. We discussed the causes of primacy earlier, but here it cannot be due to stopping the search: you are forced to taste all the wines. It might, however, be due to palate desensitization or, as in other cases (such as voting), due to differences in preference assembly. But notice what happens when the list grows longer: there is a striking recency effect. The last wine has an advantage, becoming almost as popular at the first. Presumably, this is because it is difficult to remember the taste of the first.

This finding has an interesting implication: in sequential presentations, we should try to be in the first position if the list is short. As the list gets longer, however, the advantage of being last grows. This is where knowing that there are two drivers of order effects is useful, because we understand what is causing the differences between short and long lists.

Visuals

So far, we have looked at two extremes. The first is simultaneous presentation, as on ballots or webpages, where we control our attention and view as we would like, often following reading order. In English, that is left to right and top to bottom. In the second, sequential presentation, we have much less control over our attention. It might be your partner talking about movies, Eurovision, or a wine tasting, but here we lose control over the way information is presented to us. At times, it can feel like we are sipping from the metaphorical fire hose.

But reality is often in between. We might *think* we are in control, but our attention is not always ours to distribute. For example, walking in Tokyo while hungry might seem challenging, particularly if you don't speak Japanese. Fortunately for the language-challenged traveler, many restaurants have complete menus displayed as plastic or wax three-dimensional re-creations of the dishes on offer. The poor gaijin (foreigner) needs only to point to order.

With such rich visual (as opposed to text) displays, do you think you would simply read from left to right? Probably not. If the display is not too large, primacy will operate, but with a difference: it is not the first item on the list but instead the first item you look at. When you look at this display, your eye is naturally drawn to the center of a visual presentation. You are also probably drawn to brighter colors or more dramatic presentations. It is the item that draws the eye first that holds the advantage. Indeed, eye-tracking studies show that people tend to look more at the center of a display like this, and this gives the center items the advantage.[9]

Nowhere has this been studied more than in supermarkets. Supermarket shelves are choice environments where manufacturers like the American firm Proctor & Gamble or the German firm Henckel pay to have a choice architecture that benefits them. The placement of products on shelves is one of the most important features of modern retailing. The locations of products on the shelf is a decision made in a collaboration between two designers: the supermarket and the producer. Product location is so important that retailers charge producers for the privilege of using certain shelf positions. These are called *slotting allowances*. A retailer such as Kroger supermarkets might charge a producer like Nestlé a fee for the right to display a certain number of rows of its product on store shelves at a certain height and in a certain place in a row. The nature of these fees is a closely held secret: H. Armstrong Roberts, writing in *The Atlantic*, recounts how one witness in a congressional hearing examining slotting allowances testified hiding behind a screen, wearing a hood, and having her voice scrambled. We do have some idea of what is involved in these transactions, however. One ice-cream manufacturer reported paying $30,000 to appear in 350 stores, and in the early days of Whole Foods, that chain charged manufacturers $25,000 for a prime location on store shelves. When there is not an explicit fee for placement, many include placement as a part of the negotiations that determine the price that the manufacturer charges the supermarket chain for the product. While there are times that we may know what we are buying ahead of time, the positioning of packages at eye level will affect what we buy when we don't.[10]

The world of retail shelf design is a rich application of choice architecture. We know that having more *facings* (having eight Oreo packages in a row versus four, for example) will increase sales, and that lining up soup alphabetically actually hurts sales. Apparently hunting for the soup you want allows you to discover soups you didn't know you wanted. Moving choosers from an easy plausible path to one that is slower helps sales.

Retailers are very interested in plausible paths—particularly what people look at and how they move while shopping. In addition to studying sales, they put radio transmitters on carts, surveil shoppers with overhead cameras, and even watch participants in studies fitted with eye-tracking cameras on their heads. While the early versions of these devices were clumsy and looked like bike helmets with TV cameras attached, they have become quite sleek. Think of those Google glasses that never made it to market, but with a camera that tracks where your eyes look.

Much of what retailers know about shopper behavior is a trade secret, but we know, for instance, that fewer than 33 percent of shoppers look at nutritional labels. Even those who do look at them spend less than one second doing so on average. This study result was particularly interesting because it was done on the new labels that the Food and Drug Administration had introduced because they were supposed to be easier to understand. In general, what we do know can be summed up simply: the goal of allocating shelf space is all about attracting attention and being seen first.

Being at eye level and having many facings encourages being the first considered brand. This helps both because it affects the way a consumer assembles preferences and because it will be chosen by consumers who don't search much. While we may sense that a consumer has control of their attention in the supermarket, that is only partially true: packaging, facings, and end-of-aisle displays are all helping to guide your attention.[11] Primacy may be the relevant driver, but things like shelf facings determine what is looked at first.

Sorting Things Out

There is another example of order that you see all the time on the web: sorting options by an attribute, like from cheapest to most expensive. When we order things by an attribute, we make some paths easier to use, and that can make an attribute more important. In all the examples until now, we've been looking at how the order of options affects choices. Whether they are bands at Eurovision, wines at a tasting, or movies on the Netflix landing page, we considered the options as a whole. The designer is putting things in order in a way that they think makes sense, whether to maximize sales, as with Expedia, or alphabetically, for political candidates.

Sorting options by a particular attribute will also have an effect on choices. You see this kind of sorting every day online. For example, visit Google Flights and look for any set of flights, and the list that it returns will be ordered by one attribute: price. You, the chooser, can sort the options many different ways with just a click. But the designer sets the default sorting order: cheapest first.

Sorting by a single attribute makes that attribute more important to the chooser. If the options are sorted by price, you will be more likely to choose the cheapest flight. To use the technical term, you will appear more *price sensitive*. Sort cars by gas mileage, and people will be more sensitive to fuel economy. Sort restaurants by distance, and people will be more sensitive to the time it takes to get there.[12]

I was a consultant on a project that looked at how to design websites for school choice. The group, organized by the research and consulting firm Mathematica, found something rather striking. The previous chapter mentioned one trade-off between two key qualities of any school: its academic quality and its distance from the student's home. This group looked at what schools were chosen when the list was sorted either by academic performance or by distance. This is a challenging trade-off for families: Would you want your fourteen-year-old to commute an extra half mile to attend a better school? How much better does a school need to be to justify that lost time? This trade-off is a great example of having to assemble a preference. Since people make choices for a given school level rarely, usually once per kid, we might expect this to be an instance where preferences are constructed. If so, the effect of sorting might be large.

The Mathematica team gave different versions of the selection website to more than three thousand parents. They found that sorting made a difference in what families chose: even though parents could change the sort order with a click, the default sorting attribute mattered. When the list was sorted by academic performance, for example, families chose schools that were better (by 5 percentage points on a 100-point scale) and farther away (by 0.6 miles, which was a 30 percent increase from the average of 2.0 miles). Sorting by academic performance made parents make choices as if academic performance were more important and made the kids' commutes longer on average as a consequence; the reverse is true if we sort by distance. Sorting can have a significant effect on these important trade-offs.[13]

A paper by John Lynch and Dan Ariely illustrates the point nicely. They set up a website selling wine to their Duke University MBA students. Half of the students saw a site where wines were sorted by price, the other half by quality. The purchases were real decisions: people actually paid for the wines with their own money and took the wine home. As you might now expect, sorting determined how important the students considered price and quality. Sort by price and people buy cheaper wines. Sort by quality and people buy better wines. Lynch and Ariely then let people return to buy wine again, presumably after they drank either the cheap or tasty wine. The effect of sorting persisted. People who had their wines sorted by price the previous week tended to buy cheaper wines, even when the wines were no longer sorted that way. Let's emphasize this once more: the wines do not change because of how they are sorted, but the order changes what plausible paths are used to make the choice, and that effect lasted after drinking the bottles.

Making Menus

I was about to sit down at a restaurant I had heard good things about near a decision-making meeting I was attending. I was looking forward to having dinner and a drink with a friend I had not seen for a while. We were each handed a menu. It was typical of smaller restaurants, consisting of one sheet of paper folded over to make a booklet. The name of the restaurant was on the front, the back was blank, and the real business part of the menu was in the fold—the middle two pages.

Suddenly I realized that the menu is a great choice-architecture example and that it might be influencing my choice. Someone (the chef, perhaps?) had made, intentionally or by happenstance, many choice-architecture decisions. Having just been researching the effects of choice architecture, I realized that perhaps I could figure out how these decisions were made to influence what I would purchase that night. This was a particularly well-timed realization, since the friend I was eating with was Richard Thaler, one of the authors of *Nudge*.

Thaler talked to the waiter about the menu. The waiter had gone to the local culinary institute and explained that there is a course called *menu psychology* that is taught in these schools. Indeed, there are menu psychology consultants who help restaurants steer customers to more profitable entrees. Thaler felt proud that he had discovered a new area of choice architecture that I could research for my book, and I appreciated the idea. While menu psychology was indeed a concept, and taught in schools, much of what is taught is wrong.

The waiter later emailed me the name of the menu psychology text he had used for his class, so I ordered it, wondering what I could learn from that literature. There was lots of very specific advice, and clearly experts in this field think that the way restaurants present items in a menu is important, even if they don't call it choice architecture. One consultant said, "If you think customers decide on their own what to order, think again. A menu should tell a customer what you want them to buy."[14]

The advice can get very specific: "The placement of menu items, the graphics and the item descriptions all send messages about what you want customers to order. For example, in a four-page menu—including front and back covers . . . the 'power position' is on the inside right page above the center."[15]

That particular consultant argues that it should be simple for the restaurant owner to push more profitable items: since people start with the power position indicated by the number 1 in the figure on page 216, placing items in that power position will attract more attention and increase sales. I searched further and lots of consultants offered similar advice, but they often disagreed about where the power position might be.

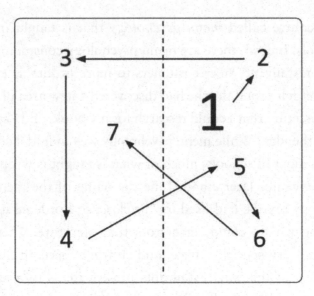

Consultants' notions of how menus are read

I became suspicious about this advice, and advice like it, given what I knew about order. Why would people start at the power position? It sounds like primacy, but why would a diner start on the second page? The menu psychology books don't actually have much psychology; they are based mainly on the intuitions of the consultants. It turns out the real lesson of reading this book, and others like it, is that consultants can be very wrong. The field that Richard Thaler and I hoped would be full of great examples, taught usefully in culinary schools and based on a strong set of studies, was instead a sad case where people created their choice architecture by intuition, devoid of solid theory or experiments.

One paper, called "Are Consultants Blowing Smoke? An Empirical Test of the Impact of Menu Layout on Item Sales," tested the effectiveness of similar design advice by another

The Elements of Choice

consultant. The researchers ran their experiments in a real restaurant, randomly switching the order of two pages in the menu. Over four months, they measured whether there was any difference in sales when using the order recommended by the consultant compared to the opposite order. They found no differences: the answer to the question "Are consultants blowing smoke?" was yes. There are many similar failures of menu psychology. It has not helped that some of the literature published has been retracted due to questionable research practices.[16]

Does this mean that menus are immune to the effects of choice architecture? No, but it might be that the consultants' advice is based on faulty assumptions about attention and search. Because the consultants and their suggestions sound sensible, they get a job, but since their advice is not usually tested, the restaurateur doesn't know whether it helps.

The problem is that the order suggested in the figure on page 216 is just wrong. It is based on an expert's opinion and on what people said in interviews long after they made the decision. Now simple eye trackers cost as little as $100, and researchers can empirically watch people make these decisions. How do people really allocate attention to menus? Sybil Yang, at the time at the Cornell School of Hotel Administration, recorded eye fixations while people chose meals from a two-page menu. The figure on page 218 shows the *actual* order of attention, called a scan path, for the two pages of a menu using eye tracking.[17] It is very different from what the expert said in the previous figure. It appears that people read the menu like a book, starting on the left, looking down that page, and then moving to the second page. After that scan, choosers pay the most attention to the location containing the entrees, and Yang suggests that people build around that choice.

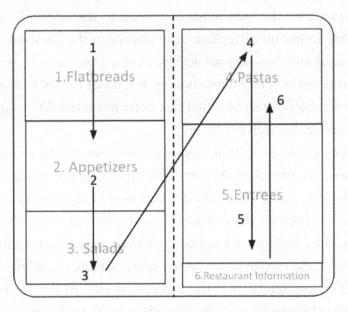

Actual average sequence of attention measured by eye movements. Pastas and entrees receive about the same amount of attention, and people seem to pick an entree and then go back to choose the rest of the meal (like a pasta) around that choice.

If this scan path is right, then the advice from "industry convention" is wrong: people don't start with the "power position." This suggests that with a brief ten-item menu, diners will look at the entire set of options, from the beginning to the end, and to do so from left to right, top to bottom. And we would expect order to give a boost to what is first on the list (primacy). If the menu is long enough, we may find a boost to what is last on the list (recency). Eran

Dayan and Maya Bar-Hillel tested this with students making choices from hypothetical menus, as well as with patrons of a real café in Tel Aviv. Apparently, they were quite persuasive, because the owner agreed to change menus daily over the course of a month in their experiment. It's important to note that for each menu category, the researchers manipulated the order in which items appeared: first, middle, or last. For example, croissants and brownies were the first and second desserts on some days and in the middle (fourth and fifth of ten) on others. And, indeed, they found that when items were moved to the front (primacy) or end (recency) of a menu category, they were more popular. In both the lab and field studies, the same product placed in the middle was chosen about 45 percent of the time, while it was chosen about 55 percent of the time when it was placed at the beginning or end.[18] This is exactly the opposite of what budding hospitality entrepreneurs are taught in their menu design classes.

But the overarching lesson here is that if we try to understand order effects by looking only at the position of an item on the menu, we might be asking the wrong question. What we need to understand are attention effects: the order that people look at items, not the order in which those items are presented. Lots of things on a menu can attract attention. Pictures draw our eye to certain areas. Headings and lines help us find the food we are looking for. Indeed, some menus might be looked at like a book. That would make designing choice architecture easier, since we know what customers look at first. But the truth, I suspect, is that attention is drawn by pictures and headings, particularly if they are colorful and vivid. This makes simple rules, like "Place expensive entrees in the power position," less useful. Consider, for example, how the "standard" advice might play in a restaurant whose menu looks more like a telephone directory. To understand order, we really have to understand what determines attention.

While we have mostly talked about ordering and sorting, the principal drivers of these effects are the paths that we pick and the role of memory. If you were a choice architect, you might be asked, "What is best: being first or last on the menu?" Before you answer, I hope that you now know the right thing to do would be to ask a question or two back: "Tell me about the menu—is it written or oral? How long and complex is it?" With answers to these questions, you can begin to give useful answers.

And speaking of recited menus, this brings us to an important feature we have missed: Where are the prices? The answer is that they are often not mentioned at all! One important attribute, the cost of the items, is usually not presented by default. By making you ask about the cost (and maybe making you feel a little like a cheapskate), the importance of the attribute in your decisions has diminished. This brings us to our next tool for choice architects to apply: How do we present the characteristics or attributes of the options?

8

Describing Options

Rani Cardona, an engineer from Los Angeles, gets 100 miles to the gallon in her car. Cardona is part of a community called *hypermilers* who try to get the best fuel economy possible. Just like some drivers brag about how quickly their cars accelerate from 0 to 60, hypermilers compete on fuel economy. There are thousands of adherents, and hypermilers congregate in online forums to trade tips and achievements. Hypermiling has grown to include electric cars, competing to see who can get the most out of a single charge, and there are even people who hypermile aircraft.

Cardona drives a car that most of us would consider pretty economical—a Honda Civic Hybrid that the Environmental Protection Agency (EPA) lists at 45 miles per gallon—but Cardona uses hypermiling techniques to do better. Cardona feels special stretching out extra miles:

When you see the gauge springing up toward 100 miles per gallon and you've got your foot just perfectly situated and you hold it there, you know, it's just a great feeling. . . . It's an indescribable feeling, like your car is almost defying the laws of physics and you're just kind of floating on air.

One hundred miles per gallon is pretty impressive. To achieve that, hypermilers change the pressure on the accelerator and touch the brake as little as possible. They cruise highways at speeds that are the most fuel efficient—usually about 50 miles per hour. At this speed you are passed by annoyed drivers who sometimes express their displeasure by honking or worse. Beyond the annoyances, hypermiling can also involve dangerous maneuvers, like coasting with the engine off, taking curves at higher speeds than recommended, or drafting behind large trucks. These tactics boost fuel economy but increase the chance of accidents. Trucks hit their brakes quickly, engines fail to restart, and exit turns can be slippery. I can only imagine what is involved in a hypermiling airplane.

What motivates hypermilers? Fuel efficiency is an attribute of a car, usually measured in miles per gallon (mpg). By driving to maximize fuel efficiency, hypermilers increase the value of that attribute. But maximizing fuel efficiency isn't really what motivates hypermilers; what motivates them is the goal it represents. This is an important distinction. The car may have attributes that can be maximized, but what choosers are seeking are ways to meet goals, and different people have different goals for the same attribute.

For some, the goal is to be the best. This might have been the case for participants in the Hybridfest MPG Challenge, in which participants drove a 20-mile course through the streets of Madison, Wisconsin. The winner often achieved fuel efficiency numbers far beyond 100 mpg. In 2006, the winner clocked 183 mpg.

Others, like Cardona, hypermile for sustainability: "I want to make this small effort of my own," she said. "It may not mean much in the whole macro scheme of things, but it's having an effect where I live and in my life. I see it as a positive thing, and it does rub off on others."

Wayne Gerdes, who coined the term *hypermiling* and is one of the movement's stars, has a different motivation: to limit the consumption of foreign oil. "The day after 9/11, I began changing my habits for the better, and ever since then I've looked for methods to improve fuel economy. We all have our trigger points—mine was global security."

This illustrates the important distinction between an attribute and the different goals it represents. Both Cardona and Gerdes want increased fuel efficiency, but this represents different goals for each of them. Cardona wants to limit greenhouse emissions, while Gerdes wants to limit the consumption of foreign oil. Gerdes talked about the different goals fuel efficiency might represent for hypermilers: "It doesn't matter if you're concerned with global warming, or smog, or government debt, or if you're worried about putting money in your pocketbook. All those reasons are good reasons to become a hypermiler."

A gauge showing miles per gallon is found on the dashboard of most fuel-efficient cars. It is typically a large, colorful display, updated in real time. A hypermiler might be watching the traffic ahead, anticipating when cars are slowing so that they can reduce their speed to avoid braking. They might look at the road for upcoming hills, up and down, so they can figure out when to accelerate and when to turn the engine off. They also anticipate curves, figuring out how fast they can take the bend without braking. But never far from their view is the center of their attention: the hybrid's fuel-consumption display, that bright LED screen. Wayne Gerdes said, "It's a running joke, but instead of a fuel-consumption display, a lot of us call them 'game gauges'"—a reference to the running score posted on video games—"because we're trying to beat our last score—our miles per gallon."

About the time that Gerdes was competing in Hybridfest, two Duke business school professors, Rick Larrick and Jack Soll, were carpooling together to the school. It was a twenty-minute, ten-mile drive in Soll's 2005 Camry Hybrid. In addition to talking about academic politics, the latest research papers, and, inevitably, Duke Blue Devils basketball, Larrick and Soll started talking about the mpg display. Soll, like Gerdes, watched this gauge: "I was feeling pretty good about my fuel efficiency, but sometimes I noticed it was pretty low." Rather than simply feel bad, Soll scrutinized the gauge more closely and realized something: "The display was really quite deceptive. . . . We realized that it was really counterintuitive." It turns out that mpg displays, and in fact, all discussions around mpg, are based on a misunderstanding.

To appreciate Larrick and Soll's insight, it's useful to work through an example. Wayne Gerdes was able to double the gas mileage of a Prius by practicing an extensive set of hypermiling techniques. There is a cost in comfort and safety associated with doing this. For example, when it's hot out, Gerdes wears a vest full of ice packs so he does not have to use the car's engine to power the car's air-conditioning. Now imagine that Gerdes makes a 1,000-mile trip home from Hybridfest using his best, if somewhat risky and uncomfortable, set of skills. His Prius goes from 50 to 100 miles per gallon.

Wayne's buddy, whom we will call Dwayne, makes a similar 1,000-mile trip, but has the choice of two cars to rent for the trip home: a Jeep Cherokee that gets 13 miles per gallon or a Toyota RAV4 that gets 27 miles per gallon. Dwayne chooses the RAV4 and drives the 1,000 miles normally with no hypermiling techniques. Both made a choice: Wayne, to hypermile, and Dwayne, to drive the RAV4. Which choice saved the most gas?

Larrick and Soll, bored during their commute, challenged each other with questions like this. Wayne and Dwayne both made a decision, but how much of a change in gas mileage did that decision entail? Take a second, before you read on, and answer for yourself. Like Larrick and Soll, you might be surprised by the answer.

If, like most people, you thought Wayne saved the most gas, you fell for what Larrick and Soll called the MPG illusion. It is an illusion because, until we do some calculations, it seems obvious that Wayne wins. It is true that he is using less gasoline, but he is making a much smaller dent in reducing gas usage. By increasing his mileage from 50 mpg to 100 mpg he is halving the amount of gas he is using. That must be a lot more than the 14 miles per gallon that Dwayne saves by renting the more fuel-efficient car, right? It isn't, and the reason you are fooled is that there's a common misunderstanding of how the attribute of fuel economy works.

To understand this, let's start with Wayne. He is driving 1,000 miles and will use 10 gallons (1,000 miles/100 mpg) of gas to make this trip. If he did not wear ice packs, draft trucks, and use other hypermiling strategies, the 1,000-mile trip would have used 20 gallons of gas (1,000 miles/50 mpg). By hypermiling, he has cut his fuel consumption in half, from 20 to 10 gallons of gas. He might have sweated a lot and risked his life, but at $3 a gallon for gas, he saved 10 gallons of gas and $30.

Now look at Dwayne: In the energy-inefficient Jeep, he would have used almost 77 gallons of gas (1,000 miles/ 13 mpg) to drive the 1,000 miles home. Using the slightly more efficient RAV4, Dwayne used 37 gallons of gas (1,000 miles/27 mpg). Wayne saved 10 gallons, but Dwayne saved 40 gallons (77 minus 37). By driving normally but changing cars, Dwayne's decision saved four times as much gas.

The same is true in dollars. When they compare notes, Wayne brags about his $30 saving. Dwayne calmly points out that by changing between the two cars, he saved $120. Dwayne's decision made a bigger difference, and this is true whether the goal was to save money, save gas, or reduce carbon emissions.

What happened here? It is actually quite simple: miles per gallon is the wrong metric. This figure shows the misleading

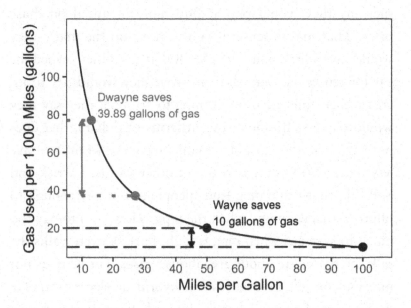

Miles per gallon vs. gallons per mile

relationship between fuel efficiency and mpg, and how it fools us into thinking Wayne reduced his gas usage more than Dwayne. If you look at the figure, you see that mpg is not linearly related to how much gas we use. As Larrick and Soll say, we really should be talking about how many gallons we use per mile (gpm) and not how many miles we can go per gallon (mpg). It is gallons that cost money, generate carbon emissions, and cause foreign oil imports.

Larrick and Soll published a now famous paper showing that most people think like Wayne. When asked to choose cars, respondents chose as if mpg was related linearly to fuel efficiency. Larrick and Soll show that people are willing to put their money behind this belief: if you ask them how much they would pay to increase their mileage from 20 to 30 mpg, they say they would pay $6,000 more in initial purchase price. That makes sense: if you were to do the math, they would save a little more than $6,000 in gas if they owned the car for ten years. But ask them what they would pay to increase their mileage from 40 mpg to 50 mpg, they say they would pay $4,600 more. But in terms of dollars, that does not pay back: they would actually be paying $4,600 to save less than $2,000 on gas costs. In other words, Larrick and Soll find that using mpg leads people to not pay enough to improve fuel economy when the mpg is low, and to pay too much to save gas when mpg is high. Larrick even walks the talk: he does care about greenhouse gases, but he does not max out on gas mileage with a hybrid or electric car. He drives cars that get 30 mpg. Instead, he puts the money he would have paid to increase gas mileage for the car into things like rooftop solar panels for his house, which make a bigger difference in carbon emissions per dollar.

So how do we solve the problem? Larrick and Soll suggest simply changing the metric: mpg is the number of miles that you get per gallon, or number of miles driven divided by the number of gallons consumed. If, instead, you were to use gallons per mile, or the number of gallons consumed divided by the number of miles driven, the metric has an easy-to-understand linear relationship to care about, be it operating costs or carbon emissions. When Larrick and Soll presented the same problem to people using gallons per mile instead of miles per gallon, potential car buyers thought about fuel efficiency correctly. To make the numbers more fluent, they suggest using gallons per 100 miles, so that if it takes 0.04

gallons to drive a mile, a car would display 4 gallons per 100 miles.[1]

This insight became one of the fastest examples of choice-architecture research moving from the lab to public policy. The research changed the way gas mileage was displayed on every car's energy label in just a couple of years. It also may have influenced the way the Obama administration designed a very popular program in 2009, the Cars Allowance Rebate System (CARS) or, as you probably know it, Cash for Clunkers.

Cash for Clunkers had two goals: first, to stimulate the economy by boosting sales of autos coming out of the 2008 recession, and second, to get "clunkers" (cars that consumed a lot of gas) off the road. You might think this involved trading in 25-mpg cars for 50-mpg hybrids. It didn't, which led to many complaints, but you may now appreciate why it concentrated only on swapping out the lowest-mileage cars. The program required the trade-in of cars that got less than 18 mpg for a vehicle that got at least 22 mpg. In practice, the Department of Transportation estimated that the average swap was a 15-mpg car for one that got 25 mpg. A trade-in like that would save 260 gallons of gas over 10,000 miles. The trade-in for the hybrid sounds good, but it would only save 200 gallons per 10,000 miles. In addition, the "clunkers" tended to be older and less well maintained, emitting higher quantities of pollutants.

Economists disagree whether the program was an effective stimulus policy, but it was undeniably popular: the initial budget of $1 billion was used up in the first month and

Congress allocated another $2 billion to it. It is not clear whether the architects of the program had read Larrick and Soll, but the program had a clear goal consistent with avoiding the MPG illusion: it would not help fuel-efficient Wayne, but it might get Dwayne into a much more fuel-efficient car.

When presenting choosers with options, designers must first figure out which attributes to display, and how to display them. The designers of a dating app might include concrete attributes like height and weight but exclude other attributes that are harder to discern in an online profile, like intelligence and charm. NFL draft books include attributes like an athlete's forty-yard-dash time, vertical leap, body-mass index, and even their Wonderlic (a kind of intelligence test) score.

Every choice architect must also select how to name the attributes. We have already seen in chapter 3 an example of the power of attribute names. When buying ground beef, *25 percent fat* seems much less desirable than *75 percent lean*. But there is more to learn about naming attributes.

Think of a table of options, like a list of flights on Expedia or a table of washing machines in *Consumer Reports*. When you build such a table, you, the designer, decide how many options to present, how to order them, and what the default option is, if there is one. As you have seen, we know a lot about these tools. However, what comes next, filling in the table, has been more neglected. Describing the options might seem less important, but it is not.

This chapter is a bit different from the others. Describing attributes has not been as deeply researched as such other

The Elements of Choice

tools as defaults and order. The studies we do have are mostly case studies in specific domains. This means that I'll be suggesting general principles, as I have in past chapters, but here they will be based more on logic and opinion than on extensive empirical results.

Names: Translating Attributes to Goals

As we've seen, attributes themselves are not very important. They are not *why* we choose things. We need to connect the attributes to the goals of the chooser—the goals are the reasons we choose things. We choose health insurance not to get a deductible of a specific amount, but rather to protect our health. We choose foods not because they contain ingredients like flour, tofu, or coriander but because they keep us healthy and taste good. I've often seen product development teams obsess over attributes while forgetting to communicate (or even think about) how those attributes apply to customers' goals. In the early days of personal computing, a team at Microsoft was in charge of accessories like computer mice. This team was obsessed by one attribute: the weight of the large rubber-covered metal sphere in the body of the mouse. In those days, the sphere rolled along the table and tracked the motion of the mouse. A heavier ball meant more accurate tracking. They told their marketing team that they wanted to advertise this property of the mouse. But the marketing team realized that this attribute, stated that way, had no meaning to consumers. The consumers' goal was smooth and accurate tracking, not the weight of a ball inside a mouse.

In 2013, the EPA introduced a radical change in its fuel-economy labels. The figures below show both a relatively old label (used from 1995 until 2008) and a new one (introduced in 2013). If you have gone car shopping, you have seen labels like this glued to every car window, as required by law. The old label below has only two numbers: the city and highway mpg. It presents these numbers, which we know can be misleading, and not much else. In fine print, it shows the range for cars that are similar, but you have to squint to see it.

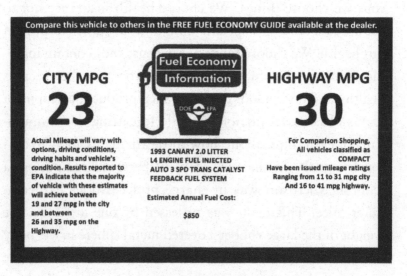

Pre-2008 gas mileage label[2]

Take a look and compare this label to the figure on page 233. Clearly, the new version includes more information: the EPA has added greenhouse gas and smog ratings as

EPA | DOT **Fuel Economy and Environment**

Fuel Economy

26 MPG
Small SUVs range from 16 to 32 MPG.
The best vehicle rates 99 MPGe.

22 city   32 highway

combined city/hwy

3.8 gallons per 100 miles

You **save**
$1,850
in fuel costs
over 5 years
compared to the
average new vehicle.

Annual fuel cost
$2,150

Fuel Economy & Greenhouse Gas Rating (tailpipe only)
7
1 10
Best

Smog Rating (tailpipe only)
6
1 10
Best

This vehicle emits 347 grams CO_2 per mile. The best emits 0 grams per mile (tailpipe only). Producing and distributing fuel also create emissions; learn more at fueleconomy.gov.

Actual results will vary for many reasons, including driving conditions and how you drive and maintain your vehicle. The average new vehicle gets 22 MPG and costs $12,600 to fuel over 5 years. Cost estimates are based on 15,000 miles per year at $3.70 per gallon. MPGe is miles per gasoline gallon equivalent. Vehicle emissions are a significant cause of climate change and smog.

fueleconomy.gov
Calculate personalized estimates and compare vehicles

Smartphone QR Code™

Gasoline Vehicle

Current gas mileage label

well as a listing of fuel costs over five years. And because of Larrick and Soll's research, there is a label for gallons per mile, although it is less conspicuous than the other statistics.

At first glance, this looks like quite a bit of information, but many of these numbers are actually redundant: fuel economy conveyed on different scales and by different names. Fuel cost is simply the gpm for 15,000 miles, multiplied by the cost of gas: $3.70. It even says that much in the fine print. The same is true for the greenhouse gas rating: a gallon of fuel burned will result in about 20 pounds of carbon dioxide released. So, this rating is simply the number of gallons burned multiplied by 20. That rating is then converted to a number on a 10-point scale. Since there is no carbon capture technology in cars, a gallon of gasoline used to power a Porsche results in the same carbon dioxide release as a gallon burned by a hybrid. The label takes one attribute, how much gas the car uses, and turns it into mpg, gpm, annual cost, five-year cost savings, and greenhouse gas rating. Even the smog rating is closely related to the car's gas consumption. Why does the EPA provide information that is redundant?

Initially, I thought it was probably a bad design formulated by a committee who could not come to an agreement. But I started talking to other psychologists who study environmental decisions and we became interested in the labels. Adrian Camilleri, Christoph Ungemach, Rick Larrick, Elke Weber, and I realized people want different things out of a high-fuel-economy car, just like our hypermilers. Some are motivated by wanting to save money; others, by wanting to lower their emissions. Gas mileage is relevant to both these goals, but choosers may not realize that. The team realized that it was not gas mileage that mattered, but its translation into goals. Miles per gallon could be translated to operating costs for those who were thrifty. Greenhouse gas ratings translated mpg for people interested in carbon emissions. For both types of people, the outcomes are similar—they buy fuel-efficient cars—but translated attributes remind them that this attribute is related to their goals. At the same time, each type of person is free to ignore the translation of attributes to goals they don't care about.

In our studies, we verified this using two groups of people who cared about different goals. One group cared the most about cost and the other cared most about the environment. We found each group made better decisions—meaning, they bought cars that were closer to their goals—when the right translations were presented. Displaying annual fuel costs helped people trying to cut operating costs, while the green car buyers did better when the greenhouse gas rating was present. They both chose cars closer to their goals when we gave them the right translation, even though it was easily calculated from gpm. When given only the irrelevant translation, people did not do better. In fact, without the translated attribute, they paid much more attention to other attributes, such as the purchasing costs, which we had ensured were less relevant to their goals. It wasn't bureaucratic redundancy, as I had thought, but the translation of the attribute into a format that gave the information most helpful to people with different goals that helped the two different groups of car buyers.[3]

Cars have other attributes with multiple possible names. People interested in speed aren't looking for an engine with a 347-cubic-inch displacement, they're looking for a car that accelerates quickly. Probabaly, 0-to-60 times are closer to those consumers' goals than engine size. Consider a Tesla Model S that sports a special software switch for Ludicrous+ Mode that allows it to go from 0 to 60 in less than 2.3 seconds, faster than any other production-line car. Because the car is electric, terms like *cubic inch displacement* do not represent how it does on the goal of acceleration. The central lesson of this section, then, is that attributes can do more than present technical specifications. From the chooser's perspective, an attribute is a means to achieving a goal, not an end in itself, and names help translate the attribute to the goal.

Here's another example of how attribute names have different associations. Imagine you are going to a website to buy round-trip, cross-country airplane tickets. There are two flights at the right time with good seats available, and you get frequent-flyer miles on both. But they differ in one way: one charges a small fee, $5, to help offset the carbon gases that the plane produces. Now think about two ways in which one might label this fee: it could be called a *carbon tax* or a *carbon offset*. Even if the revenue from this fee was used identically, say to plant trees, do you think the labels would have the same effect on your choice between flights?

David Hardisty, Elke Weber, and I did this study using respondents on the web, but with a twist. We had people type the thoughts they were having while they were making the decision. As you might guess, even though the fee and its end-use were the same, the label made all the difference, particularly for those who identified themselves as Republicans. Some of what this political group said when it was labeled "tax" cannot be printed here, but when it did not contain expletives it was mostly negative: "More money-grabbing fees wasted" and "It's all a hoax anyway" were just two examples. Overall, the term *tax*, like calling ground beef 25 percent fat, had strong negative associations, especially for Republicans.

Democrats' choices were less affected by the tax label: 62 percent of the Democrats picked the flight that had the tax, but only 26 percent of the Republicans chose that flight.

What happens when respondents saw the exact same flights but with the fee labeled a "carbon offset"? Some, but not all, of the objections of the Republicans disappeared. They were more likely to think of a benefit and, when they did, it appeared earlier in their decision. When we looked at what they chose, the differences between Democrats and Republicans disappeared: 64 percent of the Democrats chose the ticket with the fee, as did 58 percent Republicans.[4]

Turning back to dining choices, there is an increasing trend to list the number of calories in each food item on restaurant menus. The number of calories is, potentially, an important attribute, and it has a clear implication for the goal of controlling one's weight. The evidence on whether this helps people choose healthier meals, however, is mixed. One issue is understanding how to translate the attribute, calories, into its implications. The effect of eating a 250-calorie burger may be hard to understand. One proposal is to translate the number of calories into a physical activity—for example, saying "the burger you were about to eat is the equivalent of 2.6 miles of walking," as in the figure on page 238. This strategy was tried with the employees of a large state university. Half of the participating employees were asked to make hypothetical choices from a fast-food menu that included both total calories and an equivalent "walking miles" metric, while the other half were asked to make the choice without either metric. Including that meaningful metric reduced the number of calories ordered from 1020 to 826, about a 20 percent reduction. Unfortunately, attempts to reproduce this in other studies don't always replicate these results. The activity labels do reduce calorie consumption, but not more than simply listing the number of calories. There is some evidence, however, that individuals, even if they don't eat differently, do the next best thing: they walk more. But more research is needed.[5]

Because we know that attributes and goals are not the

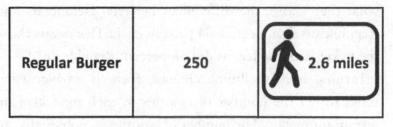

| Regular Burger | 250 | 2.6 miles |

An easy-to-understand calorie metric

same thing, we now have an insight into another important design question: How many attributes should we present to the chooser? To answer this, we first need to understand how many goals the chooser will have when making the decision. One attribute per goal, clearly named and labeled, would be a reasonable way to proceed.[6]

Making Metrics

After taking an Uber, you are always asked to rate your driver on a 5-point scale. At the fast-casual restaurant chain Chili's, you are asked to rate your server on a computer tablet using a similar 5-point scale: 4 is listed as "good," and 5 "excellent." These scales are all examples of metrics, or how we describe the alternatives on the attribute. You may not know it, but after you take an Uber, the driver rates you as well. Low ratings could mean that you will not get picked up. Ratings scales like this are all around us, and they determine outcomes for servers, drivers, and passengers.

The Elements of Choice

But do we really know what these scales mean? I teach for a living, which means that I have a fair amount of experience with one metric: the A, B, C scale used for grading. For some courses, I am even required to use a certain distribution of grades: a certain percentage of As, another percentage of Bs, etc. But when it comes to Uber or Lyft, I have no clue. Until recently, I thought it was fine to leave a 4 for any ride that was less than perfect. After all, I reasoned, the ratings of 1, 2, and 3 stars were for people who were really unhappy. Perhaps there is an age and expertise difference in how these ratings are perceived. A younger friend of mine recalled in horror how his mother defaulted to 3 for all Uber ratings, because they were "nothing exceptional." But a rating of 3 is not average on Uber, and for the driver, that rating is a disaster.

My friend's mom and I both misunderstood Uber's metric. According to Business Insider, the average rating for an Uber driver is 4.8 on the 5-point scale. Drivers whose ratings are less than 4.6 for their last one hundred rides are in danger of losing their access to driving for Uber. I had no idea that I was being such a harsh grader. This misunderstanding may cost the driver their job. Imagine a driver gets a 5 from each of four passengers and then runs into my friend's mother, who gives them her normal 3. That one clueless person puts them at the borderline rating of 4.6. Using a rating scale that is not understood has real consequences. It is feared by drivers and causes harm, unintentionally, when passengers don't know the norms.[7]

Choosing the metric is in the designer's control, and there

are many ways to do it. Think about describing the food at a new restaurant. You could say it's excellent. You could give it a 9 out of 10. You could say it is 4.5 stars, give it the famous movie critic's "two thumbs-up," or you could just say "delicious." All these metrics describe the same thing: how you thought the food tasted. If the chooser does not understand the metric, however, mistakes will be made.

It is important to realize that the metric can be objective but still be misunderstood by the consumer. The mpgs of cars are, for example, technically correct. The calorie count for food is objectively right. The problem is that these metrics are misunderstood by the chooser who does not know how to use the attributes to achieve their goals.

Straight Line Metrics

When I spent a few years as a scholar at the Consumer Financial Protection Bureau, I became involved in how lenders might disclose interest rates. Nowhere does nonlinearity create bigger mistakes, in dollars, than in consumer finance. We shop for credit cards and loans based on annual interest rates. We decide which investment to make depending upon the annual rate of return. But interest rates, as we all vaguely know, are exponential, compounding over time. This leads people to underweight interest rates.

Ask yourself this question, and try to answer it, like with most quick financial decisions, without the help of Google or a calculator:

What would be the value of a $10,000 gift you would give to a twenty-year-old young adult, invested in a security that would earn 10 percent yearly interest, and which they could not touch until they retired at sixty-five, assuming the earnings are not taxed (like in a IRA)?

What was your answer?

Most people are shocked when they learn that it would be worth $728,904. To see how well people could do, I gave this question to 509 participants on an online panel. Almost half guessed less than $100,000, and the average estimate was $270,000. Ninety percent of the respondents estimated less than the true amount.

Why are they wrong? Some people admit to just guessing, but most people use a simple plausible path to solve this problem. They first estimate the effect of interest for a year or two, and then try to adjust for compounding. In this question, the investment is worth $11,000 after one year. So, they reason, that after forty-five years, the investment might be worth $10,000 + 45 years of interest payment (45 times $1,000 = $45,000), or a total of $55,000. They try to adjust for compounding, but they adjust too little. For example, they might double the final sum to $110,000, underestimating the final amount by over $600,000. On average, the respondents to my survey see the investment to be 40 percent less than its true value. As a result, the investment looks much less attractive than it truly should.[8]

Underestimating the effect of compounding has a very real effect on both saving and borrowing. It makes saving look less attractive, because we underestimate what we will receive at the end of our investment. It also makes borrowing seem more attractive, because we underestimate the effect of compound interest on what we will owe. In fact, research shows that 98 percent of people underestimate the cost of borrowing, and that these effects are greater among those who are poorer, less educated, and worse at thinking about numbers.

While we all vaguely know that interest is compounded, the math is not easy or intuitive. The effects of compounding are larger if the time of the loan or investment is longer, or the interest rate is higher. These are exactly the cases where we need to think more carefully about the problem. Research has shown that the degree of misestimation is worse for longer terms and higher interest rates. Misunderstanding compounding also affects other important outcomes, such as discretionary savings, retirement savings, the perception of inflation, and credit card usage.

Here is an example of where not understanding compound interest hurts when we are borrowing money. It was used on large national surveys done by the Federal Reserve:

> Suppose you were buying a room of furniture for a list price of $1,000, and you were to repay this amount to the dealer in twelve monthly installments. How much do you think it would cost, in total, for the furniture after one year—including all finance and carrying charges?

This question asks them to estimate the cost, without giving them an explicit interest rate. The average response to this question is $1,350. Since we know the amount borrowed, and the time of the loan, we can calculate the annual interest rate implied from that response: 57 percent. This would be a very bad loan and the rate is so high that it would be banned in many states by usury laws, which limit interest rates to what regulators think is fair. The economists who analyzed this data, Victor Stango and Jonathan Zinman, found that when people were asked to name the implied interest rate, they said they thought that the interest rate for that loan would be 17 percent.

Not understanding compound interest is a form of a broader phenomenon called *exponential growth bias*. In general, people underestimate exponential growth. This bias happens in many different important areas: for example, people underestimate the long-term consequences of adding carbon to the atmosphere, as well as the growth of pandemics, both of which have exponential impacts. So it's clear that these problems go far beyond finance.

Interest rates (and exponential growth bias in general) are another case where the attributes of an option have a nonlinear relationship to the person's goal, which is having lots of money in retirement or minimizing borrowing costs. An interest rate is a precise concept—the rate of increase per time period—but if it involves more than one period, the math is not simple.

We could produce a metric closer to the goal by simply presenting the outcome instead. For the $10,000 investment we gave our twenty-year-old, we could just say it produces $728,904 over forty-five years at a 10 percent interest rate. For a furniture loan, we might simply disclose the total cost of borrowing: $350. This presents the outcomes in terms people care about. It also makes shopping for an investment or loan easier: all you would have to do is compare $1,000 loans to see whose cost is lowest.

This is not a universal solution. The challenge is that many financial arrangements don't have fixed time durations or fixed interest rates. Investments may average a certain rate of return, but stock returns vary with the ups and downs of markets. In the case of a mortgage, the contract says thirty years, but you can sell the house before then, and there are adjustable mortgages with varying terms. The best example of this complexity is credit cards, where not only do you need to track your payments of money you owe, but you also have to factor in what you add to that with new spending. People often make mistakes in estimating how much they spend, so knowing what they will pay on a credit card becomes difficult. Still, providing the costs a typical consumer may incur may be easier for prospective buyers to understand than the complex multipage contracts now used. A typical credit card contract from Bank of America is thirteen pages, single spaced, and has twenty different prices and fees. Because many of these contracts are not the same across banks, comparison shopping is close to impossible. No doubt people would argue that all the data is needed to figure out the cost, but I would argue that all that data prevents people from figuring out the cost of borrowing. They take the easier way out and compare interest rates and not total borrowing costs.[9]

Targets

Marathon runners often have target times. Fit friends of mine talk about finishing in 3 hours, while others are happy to finish in 5 or even 6 hours. Eliud Kipchoge had the most famous marathon target of all: 2 hours. He tried twice, and in 2019, on his second attempt, he became the first person to break the barrier. He ran 26.2 miles in 1:59:40. It was not an official world record because he had a lot of help. He followed an electric pace car. That car indicated the fastest path he could run with a green laser light shining on the ground. It also directed several sets of pacesetters, some of the world's best marathoners. Each set of seven runners formed a flying V in front of him to reduce drag. Kipchoge also wore an unreleased version of a Nike Vaporfly shoe (called the Alphafly) that increased his running efficiency by about 4 percent. But the amazing reality is that he ran 26.2 miles in the streets of Vienna in less than two hours.

His achievement received a lot of attention. One announcer compared it to the landing of men on the moon and called it a "Neil Armstrong moment." *The New York Times* called it "a sports milestone granted almost mythical status in the running world, breaking through a temporal barrier that many would have deemed untouchable only a few years ago."

But I wonder whether Kipchoge's achievement would have been seen as remarkable if that 2 hours were expressed differently, as a number of minutes. Would breaking the 120-minute barrier have gotten as much attention? There is something about round numbers that makes them appealing targets. Roger Bannister was world famous for breaking the 4-minute-mile barrier in 1954, but would it have been the same if it was the 240-second barrier? Choosing scales can make some numbers, like round numbers, appear to be obviously salient targets.[10]

Targets affect ordinary marathoners as well. They work harder to beat the target and slack off if they can't make it. Runners are choosers, deciding how hard to run in the race and how hard to train to meet their target. For them, targets matter.

A group of decision scientists and economists looked at almost 10 million marathon finishing times to test whether targets influenced runners' behavior. When asked, as suspected, people had goals that were round numbers: 4 hours was a common goal, with very few people having a goal of something like 4 hours 19 minutes. When the researchers looked at finishing times, there was a cluster just under these rounded times. The figure on page 247 shows the distribution of these millions of times. Look at 4 hours. Lots of people finish in just under 4:00, then there is a decrease, as if people who would have finished in 4:01 really push themselves to make their reference point. There is nothing magic about the number 4:00. The same thing happens at 3:00, 3:30, 4:30, and 5:00. Having a target and not making it also has an implication. If you don't make it, you might slack off. The big drops in the number of people finishing just over 4:00 (and 3:00, 3:30, 4:30 and 5:00) could also be partly explained by the number of people who slow down and finish even later when they miss their target time. Targets have implications for behavior.

Knowing this, designers could change behavior by changing the way we present attributes. Imagine that the big clock over the 20-mile checkpoint listed the time in minutes and not hours and seconds. Instead of saying 2:30, it says 150 minutes. They are the same amount of time, right? If the times were measured and displayed in minutes, we might have many more marathoners trying to break 200 minutes than if they were displayed in hours. Somehow 3:20 does not seem as attractive. Since the choice of scale is under the control of the designer, it can be used to focus the chooser on certain values, making them work harder to achieve them.

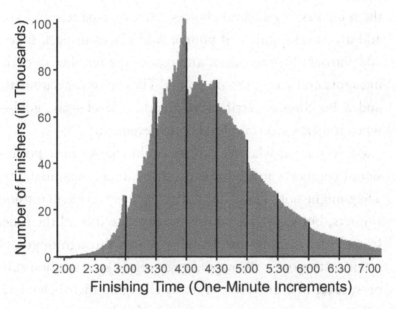

Distribution of almost 10 million marathon finishing times

Along with the engineers Tripp Shealy and Leidy Klotz, and the lawyer Ruth Greenspan Bell, Elke Weber and I explored whether a change in metrics would change choices by looking at systems used to assess the sustainability of new buildings. These days, anyone examining a new commercial building will ask if it was certified as environmentally friendly by an organization like LEED (Leadership in Energy and Environment Design). LEED uses levels starting at "certified," and going up through silver, gold, and platinum. More than one hundred thousand buildings have achieved one of these voluntary levels.

The certification process is determined by a computer system used by builders. The computer system presents the architect or engineer with a set of design decisions and gives the building points (LEED and similar organizations call them *credits*) for certain choices. Use solar panels and you add a certain number of points. Add places to park bikes, add showers for the riders, and reduce the number of parking spots and you get more points. These points accumulate and a building is certified as a certain level—say, gold—when it meets a certain level of achievement.

We wondered whether targets could change how professional engineers made these decisions about sustainability. They might not. These are not weekend-warrior marathon runners, but experts who use systems like this all the time. In real life, gaining sustainability points through upgrades often costs money. But would engineers, like marathon runners, react to a different target by changing their behavior?

There is another system, Envision, developed by the Institute for Sustainable Infrastructure that works much like LEED.[11] It uses points like LEED but assigns them based on the infrastructure and economic impacts of a new building. Envision's system starts by giving you 0 points for the standards that are usually adopted in the industry and awards more points only as you choose more sustainable options. There are dozens of questions, but let's look at one series that describes the impact of the building on the quality of life of the surrounding community. It contains the question "How will the project team develop local skills and capabilities?" If you do nothing different than usual, you get 0 points. If you hire locally, you get 1 point. The next level requires that you hire a substantial number of local firms and gives you 12 points. Finally, if you train minorities and disadvantaged groups with skills that they can use in future projects, you get 15 points. Thus, the scale runs from 0 to 15.

How could we adapt this metric to have a clearer target? We subtracted 12 from each level. The same outcomes now run from -12 to +3, with 0 being the second highest level of sustainability. This changed the metric from adding points for any sustainable action to subtracting points for doing anything but the top two levels. The options stayed the same, we just made the natural target, 0, the second highest level. None of the options were defaults, but before we made the change, 0, the status quo, reflected minimal effort. After the change, 0 reflected a fairly aggressive action. To get to each level, the building would still need to have the same set of answers to questions; they would just have a different number of points.

The changes in choices this caused was dramatic. The group that saw a reframed metric specified much more sustainable buildings. The best score possible was 181 points. To get that, the engineer would have to choose the most sustainable level, and get the highest total points, for each decision. When the options were presented with the old metric, the average building achieved 81 out of 181 points. With the new metric, they achieved the equivalent of 112 points on the original scale.

A designer can choose a metric to take advantage of targets and change the behavior of choosers. Whether it be marathons or sustainable buildings, equivalent numbers described differently can change choices.

Making Metrics Meaningful

One of the challenges of designing a metric for an attribute is that the chooser needs to understand not just what it means, but some basic things about the distribution. They need to understand which values are good, which are bad, and which are in the middle.

Remember when you were a student and you got a test back? What was the first thing you needed to know, particularly when it was from that wacky teacher who doesn't score everything on a 0-to-100 scale? They might score a test out of 35 one week, and 22 the next. Or the teacher would use 100 points, but the top score would be 73 one week, and 87 the next. The first thing you looked at was the score; next you wondered whether your score was good. It was only after you found out what the average was that you could judge how well you did. This is like Uber ratings: if they had told me that the average was 4.8, I might have rated drivers differently.

Making decisions requires us to understand the distribution underlying the metrics of the attribute. Imagine you are buying a refrigerator and you want one that does not cost too much up front but that is not going to bankrupt you when you use it. If you go shopping in the United States, the choice architecture for energy usage consists of a yellow label, required by law on many kinds of appliances. The label has one particularly important attribute: the estimated yearly cost. This is a translated attribute, based on estimates of how much electricity it will use and the cost of electricity, multiplied together to get an annual cost. With this attribute, we can compare the differences in the price of two refrigerators and judge whether we can make up the difference with the savings from lower utility bills. The translation helps us with our goal: saving money now and later. The label also tells us the range for operating costs. The one on page 252 is about average. We know how much money we could lose or save in operating costs by choosing another model.

There is another trick that designers can use to communicate ranges: they can map them into an existing scale that people already understand. People know traffic light colors. Red is bad, yellow is in between, and green is good. They also know grades. Despite grade inflation, we know that an A is the best, and isn't given to everyone; D is not good; and F is to be avoided at all costs. And there is even the famous "thumbs-up, thumbs-down" scale originating with Gene Siskel and Roger Ebert, the movie reviewers. Using these analogous metrics allows us to import our knowledge of the world to the attribute at hand.

In contrast to the United States, which uses dollars, the

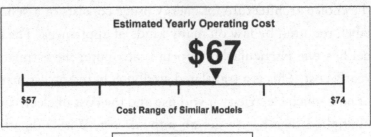

ENERGYGUIDE

Refrigerator-Freezer
- Automatic Defrost
- Side-mounted Freezer
- Through-the-Door Ice

XYZ Corporation
Model ABC.L
Capacity: 23 Cubic Feet

Estimated Yearly Operating Cost

$67

$57 $74

Cost Range of Similar Models

630 kWh

Estimated Yearly Electricity Use

Your cost will depend on your utility rates and use.

- Cost range based only on models of similar capacity with automatic defrost, side-mounted freezer, and through-the-door ice.
- Estimated operating cost based on a 2007 national average electricity cost of 10.65 cents per kWh.
- For more information, visit www.ftc.gov/appliances.

U.S. energy efficiency label

European Union uses grades and lights to display energy efficiency. Take a look at the figure on page 253, which shows the efficiency label for a clothes dryer available in Denmark. At first this scale seems quite appealing. It attempts to add meaning by putting the numbers into units we know from school—A, B, C, D—that relate to the energy usage of each clothes dryer. It uses traffic light colors to reinforce this: when displayed in full color, A+++, A++, and A+ are shades of green, an A is yellow, and B and C shade from orange to the bright red of D, reminding us that Ds are worse than Cs and Bs, which are not as good as As.

Most scales of this kind put numbers into categories. They take a number, like the 630-kilowatt hours of electricity consumed yearly and lump it into a group (the B for this dryer). Because a B is familiar, it makes the attribute easier to understand. And B implies a meaning: not great, but not terrible. Such categorical scales can make comprehending the metric easier for the user.

One aspect stands out, however. Apparently, the EU has had serious grade inflation: no dryer seems to have gotten an F, and the best don't get an A+, they get an A+++!

Energy efficiency label used in the European Union

Why A+++? The grade inflation stems from the fact that technology has been producing more efficient dryers. There were too many getting an A+, and consumers could not distinguish between a pretty efficient and a very efficient dryer. So, the EU's energy authority did something that the administration at a very easy college might be tempted to do: they added more top grades.[12]

This inflation demonstrates one drawback of using a categorical system: it limits the ability of the metric to change. After all, the alternative would be to rescale the grading system, which comes at a cost: people who had learned what a B was had to shift their understanding, and a manufacturer who had produced a dryer that was an A will not be pleased to be demoted to a B. Another example is the metric for restaurants given by the New York City Department of Health. Over 90 percent of the restaurants in Manhattan have a grade of A for cleanliness. That's good, but not of much use if someone wants to distinguish among restaurants.

This often happens when one technology supplants another. For example, as new, very efficient light-bulb technologies like LEDs appeared, people were puzzled. Would a 7-watt bulb replace the old 60-watt bulb? People were used to using a measure of the energy consumed, a watt, as a measure of brightness. But the new light bulbs consumed much less electricity for the same emitted light. A scale that had worked well with older technology no longer did. The standard scientific measure of brightness is not actually a watt: it's a lumen. A 60-watt incandescent bulb provides 800 lumens. For a CFL, that takes 14 watts, and for an LED, 10. But very few consumers know this. It is therefore no surprise that companies advertise both as "60-watt equivalents"; however, in 2010 the EU started requiring lumens to be the most prominent standard on the package.

The effort of having to learn a new metric helps explain

why we have, for centuries, used old units to describe new technologies. Candlepower was used to rate electric lights until 1948, and horsepower, which was coined in 1782 by James Watt to measure the energy output of a steam engine, is still used today to measure a car's energy output. (In case you are curious, 1 horsepower is about 742 watts.)

The second drawback to borrowing another metric is that it makes it difficult to compare differences between attributes. Imagine you are looking at two dryers. One has a B, the other an A in the EU labeling scheme. If the more efficient dryer costs more, is it worth it? Would you pay $50 to move from a B dryer to an A dryer? The consumer has no clue.

This suggests that simple categorical scales, like the grading scale, are not very useful when we want to encourage making trade-offs, particularly when there are important attributes expressed as numbers. On the other hand, they may be useful if we want to present an overall evaluation or if we want people to know which options are really bad. Like many choice-architecture tools, categorical scales make some plausible paths easy (screening) and others harder (making trade-offs).

A third strategy attempts to compromise by using a hybrid visual, combining the strengths of categorical and numeric scales. The Food Standards Agency in the United Kingdom does that with the label shown in the next figure. It uses three different metrics per attribute.

For people who do not want to do math, we have a categorical translation. This particular item has 353 calories, a

Each ½ pack serving contains

MED	LOW	MED	HIGH	MED
Calories	**Sugar**	**Fat**	**Sat Fat**	**Salt**
353	**0.9g**	**20.3g**	**10.8g**	**1.1g**
18%	**1%**	**29%**	**54%**	**18%**

Of your guideline daily amount

United Kingdom Food Standards Agency "hybrid" food label

medium rating compared to other products in its category. The label uses traffic light coloring for good measure (attributes in the low, medium, and high categories are colored green, yellow, and red, respectively). This food is not high in sugar, so that attribute is green. Another metric, in percentages, describes how much one serving contributes to your suggested daily intake for this attribute; note, for instance, that this item has a lot of saturated fat, also indicated by a red label for that attribute—two servings of this and you should be done for the day. Finally, if you already know the metric, you might be able to understand that 1.1 grams of salt is reasonable. Each of these metrics may serve choosers with different needs. The translations—from amount of salt in grams, to percentage, to color—might help different people. This approach seems particularly useful for things like nutritional labels, where many people do have different needs.

At the other end of the spectrum is a label for salt content, adopted in New York City, on the top of page 258. This is called a *warning label*. The idea is simple: put the black label next to any entree that contains more than 2,300 milligrams of sodium. That is the total recommended amount of sodium for the day, and here it would be consumed in one entree. Research shows that about a quarter of people's salt intake comes from restaurant foods, and that people underestimate the amount of salt in their restaurant orders by about 1,000 mg.

Even if you are sympathetic to the goal, this is a terrible label. It does not tell us how bad the food is, and I'm not sure people understand that the black triangle signifies hazard. I suspect that some people can't tell if it means the food has too much salt or that it needs salt.

This is not just my judgment. Experiments using decision simulators evaluated this label in contrast to the one below it. This label takes advantage of metrics borrowed from traffic lights, describing a food as getting a "Sodium Warning" in red, "High Sodium" in yellow, or "Low Sodium" in green. The label consists of the colored saltshaker and the text. In the study, people chose hypothetical food orders, seeing either the warning label, the traffic light label, or no label at all. When compared to a traffic light version, the warning label is less effective both in reducing the amount of sodium in the orders people chose and in imparting knowledge about the sodium in food.[13]

The example shows that even well-intentioned officials in New York can get labels wrong and that, if your goal is actually reducing sodium intake, testing through experimentation is important to getting it right. It also shows the

New York City (above) and traffic light (below) salt warning labels

Red: items > 2,300 mg sodium

 SODIUM WARNING

Yellow: items > 1,500 mg and ≤ 2,300 mg sodium

 HIGH SODIUM

Green: items ≤ 140 mg sodium per 100g (per FDA health claim regulations for "low sodium")

 LOW SODIUM

power of a borrowed scale: traffic light coding has been useful in nutrition in several studies. Finally, it illustrates a case where screening might be a reasonable goal: 2,300 mg of sodium is a lot, equal to the total recommended intake for a day, and knowing that you are consuming that in one sitting is probably useful. Finally, note that New York City is not banning such foods. If you want to order such an entree and eat your full day's sodium in one sitting, go right ahead.

Chile is a country with some of the world's highest obesity rates. Seventy-five percent of adults are overweight. In 2016, Chile took the warning sign approach to an extreme. It placed warning signs on food labels by using stop signs with the words *Alto en* (high in) if the item had too much salt, saturated fat, or sugar, or too many calories. Chileans have since changed their habits. There has been a 25 percent decrease in consumption of sugary drinks, for example. But it's hard to say it's all due to the label. At the same time the label was adopted many other things changed: television ads for unhealthy foods were limited to after 10:00 p.m., and a tax on sugary beverages was increased. So, while we know there was a change, we don't know how much of it was due to the labels.[14]

Nevertheless, one thing is clear: The use of a stop sign encourages screening, the plausible path we talked about in chapter 3. It is quite fluid to say, "Don't consider foods with a 'high in sugar' stop sign." Several food companies seem to know this: instead of posting the dreaded stop sign, they have reformulated the ingredients of the products to levels below the cutoffs.

Scaling Metrics

Many metrics can be scaled. We have talked about gallons per mile, but the reality is that gallons per hundred miles is used, because the designers believe that 3.8 gallons per 100 miles is easier to understand than the equivalent 0.038 gallons per mile. They are probably right. Multiplying by 100 makes the number easier to understand. Numeric metrics can usually be scaled this way. For example, we can take prices for services and scale them by years, months, or days. Famously, charities such as public radio stations change the units for donations, talking about how donations are only pennies a day: $0.28 a day is the same as a yearly donation of $100, but because it is a smaller number it seems much less impactful. The smaller amount changes the way we assemble our preference. We compare the $0.28 to trivial things, like a pack of gum, but the $100 to something serious, like a very nice dinner out or an expensive sweater. Changing the scale of numbers can change what is retrieved for comparison when making the decision.

While small numbers are easier to compare, large numbers are mind-boggling. This is particularly true of the kinds of numbers in the federal budget, a large document (typically more than 1,400 pages) of large numbers that are staggering and outside our normal experience. Richard Feynman, the twentieth-century physicist, observed, "There are 10^{11} stars in the galaxy. That used to be a huge number. But it's only a hundred billion. It's less than the national deficit! We used to call them astronomical numbers. Now we should call them economical numbers."

One way of coping with large numbers is to make them concrete and personal. Just like yearly public radio donations can be divided into pennies a day, budget changes can be framed as changes to either individual citizens or to the country as a whole. For example, a 2017 change in environmental policy, the America First Energy Plan, would, according to the Trump White House, "help American workers, increasing wages by more than $30 billion over the next seven years." That seems impressive, but hard to contemplate.

A little arithmetic translates the $30 billion for the country in seven years into the personal benefit for each of the approximately 150 million American workers: an average wage increase of about $29 a year. Are people's trade-offs influenced by changing the units used to describe the savings? One of these numbers ($30 billion) seems impressive and abstract, the other ($29 per year) seems far easier to understand because it is personal and concrete.

Elke Weber and I wondered if changing the units in this way would change people's minds. We asked a sample of Americans what they thought of the plan using either the large aggregate ($30 billion) or the smaller, more concrete number ($29). The figure on page 262 shows the percentage of people who wanted to keep the current policy (and forgo the wage increase), broken down by political affiliation and whether they saw the large or concrete number.

Clearly, breaking the number down to something smaller and more concrete changed choices: more people (an increase of 12 percent) wanted to keep current environmental regulations when removing them was described as yielding

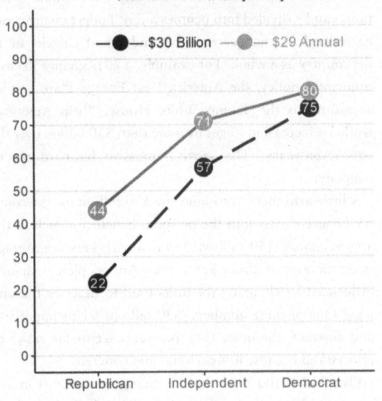

Percent Forgoing Salary Increase, Described as
$30 billion vs. $29 by Party

How changing the metric changes preferences

only a $29 change in average wages per year. The more striking finding, though, is that agreement between different parties increased when we used concrete numbers. Twice as many Republicans (44 percent) wanted to keep the policy as is when the benefits were described in smaller, concrete, and personal terms than when described as large, abstract billions (22 percent).[15]

While avoiding any claim that one position or the other is better, the data shows once again that how we present attributes—in this case the benefit of a governmental policy change—can significantly change people's choices.

Making Tough Trade-offs Easier

The scales we use when we ask people questions about their satisfaction have been studied quite a bit. Entire books have been written looking at the effects of the number of categories, the words used—and the *number* of words used—to describe the categories, or whether we should use pictures. Much less has been done with how we present information about options to people—and most of what *has* been done only took place in the last ten to fifteen years. Nevertheless, this is an important tool for designers. Our hypermilers from the beginning of the chapter were ingenious at figuring out ways of getting better gas mileage, but, in some ways, they were optimizing the wrong scale. Squeezing out the difference between 99 and 100 mpg, as we have seen, saves very little gas: about one-tenth of a gallon over 1,000 miles. If they had known this, perhaps they would not have drafted behind the truck or taken a 35-mile-per-hour turn at 55. We are really good at competing to get the best score on the game gauge, but not really as good at understanding what the gauge means.

Describing options, though, is the heart of designing choice architectures. A good designer might try really hard to make sure the information they present is accurate. But like choosers, they may not appreciate that what look like minor choices about a metric could have a greater impact on choices than the values themselves. One characteristic of hard-to-understand metrics is that they change not only what people choose, but *how* people choose—their plausible path. Many of the decisions in this chapter involve difficult trade-offs: good-tasting food versus eventual health, supporting taxation versus cutting back government spending, or paying now for later environmental benefits, both for builders and consumers. These decisions are hard enough, but when a designer gets the metric for an attribute wrong, choosers cannot make choices the way they would like and make worse choices. Describing options is the least appreciated tool of choice architecture, and the least explored by research, but one that has very important implications.

9

Building Choice Engines

C hoices are made in many different settings: on paper, on physical store shelves, on the web, or even on a smartphone. Moving from paper and physical stores to pixels and browsers lets the choice architect do things that are hard to do in the physical world. Stores cannot rearrange the shelves for each shopper or present the shopper with only their favorite brands, but websites can. It is difficult for a store shelf to instruct you on how to use a product, but a salesperson can. Because interactive environments are different, I will call these choice architectures *choice engines*, reflecting the fact that they can augment and react to the preferences of the chooser.

You can shop at Amazon, visit Netflix, decide to book a tour using TripAdvisor, search for a restaurant on Yelp, or find a movie to watch on IMDb. These choice engines are among the most visited websites in the United States.

Amazon, for example, gets more than 690 million visits in a month. The designers of these sites all influence what you choose.[1] Even small changes in how you use these sites to make decisions can have big consequences for the sites' profitability and the quality of people's choices. Because choice engines can transform themselves based on user input, they can do things that other kinds of choice architecture cannot.

Choice engines have three properties that distinguish them from other choice architecture.

- They are *customizable*. By using a model of the user, they can conform to the needs of the user. Remember the idea of a smart default, when we wanted to default to the option that was best for each user? Choice engines can make that a reality.

- They can give *control* to the chooser. We have talked about how choice architecture can encourage or discourage different plausible paths. But choice engines can change the choice architecture. Amazon allows me to sort options by price or average rating; I can be the designer *and* chooser. I can make the site conform to my desired plausible path.

- Finally, choice engines can help the chooser *comprehend* their choice. You see this often on websites where a little question mark may appear next to a box. If you click on it, you see a pop-up help screen. Providing more complex education is possible. For example, providing simulated experiences to see what the view would be like from any seat in the theater.

We will learn about all these special abilities of choice engines, looking at examples where they are done well and where they are done badly. Let's start with one of the most elaborate choice engines: the Netflix landing page.

Netflix

It's Friday night after a long week, and you're definitely going to relax and watch a movie. As you learned in an earlier chapter, asking your partner for movie recommendations does not work out so well. Somehow, when they present the choices, you always end up watching something that they like more than you do. They are obviously a very accomplished designer and perhaps they read this book before you, using these lessons to encourage you to pick the movies that they want to see. Whether this is a dark pattern, sludge, or just their knowing what you will really enjoy is for you to judge.

So instead, you turn to Netflix, the world's largest streaming service. It is also the prototypical choice engine: its goal is to help you find something to watch. It does not just passively present options, it tries to customize the set of things that you see, it gives you some control over what is presented, and it even helps you comprehend new options you might like. It does everything we associate with choice engines.

In fact, Netflix's entire existence depends on finding programs that you will want to watch from its large library of licensed content. Keeping you engaged and paying a monthly subscription is its major source of revenue. The Netflix stock price starkly reflects changes in the number of customers: announcing that it had lost 130,000 customers in 2019 (less than 0.2 percent of its total of 60 million) caused a 10 percent drop in the stock price in one day. Netflix needs to connect customers with content, so you think it will be able to find you something to watch.

You fire up Netflix on your streaming device. A simple question appears: Who is watching? You, your partner, your kids, or someone else? As soon as you answer, a webpage appears with a running trailer, including audio, for a show that seems potentially interesting. Some of the movies and shows are ones you might not have recalled, or that were unknown to you. The trailer automatically started and that annoys you, but soon the program captures your interest. When the trailer finishes, you notice two obvious buttons: one says "Play," and the other says "More info." As you scroll down the page, you see groups of movies and TV shows arranged in rows. The first row may be labeled "New Releases," the next "Trending Now," and then "Critically Acclaimed TV." Continue scrolling and a row of programs you have watched before appears. When your mouse scrolls over a program for more than a second, a trailer for that program starts, but it stops as soon as you mouse away. After a few minutes of this, you find yourself watching *Comedi-*

ans in Cars Getting Coffee, a show you did not know existed. It features Jerry Seinfeld, one of your favorites.

Not only has Netflix performed all three properties of a choice engine, but to do this, the landing page has used every choice-architecture tool in this book. Let's look at some of them:

> *Plausible Paths*: Netflix knows that decisions about how to make decisions, choosing a plausible path, happen quickly. Netflix does not keep the chooser waiting. It spends enormous effort preventing waiting, making the decision of what to watch very fluid. Netflix engineers brag about the technological innovations used to quickly load the landing page for customers, and how important preventing waiting is for keeping customers.

> *Defaults*: By default, when you go to Netflix, a trailer, complete with audio, starts playing. Until early 2020, there was no way to turn it off, despite many complaints on social media.

> *Number of Options*: Netflix has a catalog of almost 6,000 titles (about 4,000 movies and 2,000 TV series). They somehow reduce that flood of options to the 80 or so that they believe might be right for you to watch. This involves some serious AI magic, as we will see in a moment.

> *Ordering*: Netflix sets the order of the rows. Does "Trending Now" come first, or "New Releases"?

Once the order of rows is decided, Netflix needs to assign each program a position, at the beginning, middle, or end of the row. If you compare your landing page to anyone else's, you will see both orders are specific to each user. Films on the top left of the initial screen are watched more often than those elsewhere.

Describing Options: Each of the rows has a heading, like "Critically Acclaimed TV," "Trending Now" or "Witty TV Shows." Not only do the order of these differ for every customer, but different options appear for different people. Each program has a still image. Does Netflix pick pictures guaranteed to draw attention to all content, or is it more targeted, attempting to increase the popularity of some content?

Describing options also includes selecting which scenes are in the trailer that runs when you hover over the picture. How does Netflix decide which moments to show from the sixty-two episodes of *Breaking Bad*? For the introduction to the American version of *House of Cards*, it developed three different trailers for different audiences, based on what it knew of their past viewing. One was for fans of the British version of *House of Cards*. Another featuring Robin Wright (Claire Underwood) and other female characters ran for viewers who had watched *Thelma and Louise*. A third was aimed at serious film buffs, because the producer, David

Fincher, is well known in those circles for movies like *The Social Network* and *The Girl with the Dragon Tattoo*.[2]

Netflix presents an attribute predicting how much you will like each title, using a 0-to-100-percent scale. It also collects your ratings on a "thumbs-up, thumbs-down" scale. Why did Netflix make the two scales different? Netflix had used a 5-star scale for both, but it believed that people were confused by the scale. People found that the thumbs scale was easier to use, and changing to the thumbs doubled the number of ratings collected. It also found that people tended to only rate highbrow and serious movies with a 5, but they were happy to give a binge-watched situation comedy a thumbs-up. The response scale made raters, it seems, less pretentious and perhaps more honest.[3]

This entire set of tools is tuned through A/B tests, as many as a hundred a year, on every detail of the experience. With millions of viewers using the landing page each day, a lot can be learned.

Compare this to developing a choice architecture using paper. First, unlike Netflix, a piece of paper does not phone home every time you make an entry. It is also difficult for a paper form to adapt. To see this, think of a tax form. You might recall that these forms contain instructions like "If the total in column c is greater than the total in column d, divide by 5 and enter the number in row 8." This is cumbersome to say the least.

So how does Netflix do it? As I developed one of the first university courses on choice architecture, I tried hard to listen to my students. They live more of their life online than I do. At the end of the class, I always ask them about their most and least favorite choice architectures. Most years, the winner of both the best and worst award is Netflix. When I ask why, I hear the following:

> "I love Netflix because it finds me something to watch."

> "I despise Netflix because I can't find what I want to watch."

Listening to the conversation carefully reveals a disconnect between the goals of some choosers and those of Netflix. Netflix does not try to optimize customer satisfaction or, as they put it, "happiness." Netflix tries to maximize efficiency—that is, "maximum happiness per dollar spent" on content, as a vice president of product engineering there once put it. Some shows, such as *The Crown*, deliver happiness big-time but are expensive to make, costing over $10 million an episode. A menu full of such programs might make people happy, but the subscription would be prohibitively expensive, and Netflix would disappear. Instead, the goal of its choice architecture is to find things that will make you happy inexpensively. According to Jenny McCabe, director of global media relations at Netflix, "We look for those titles that deliver the biggest viewership relative to their licensing cost."[4]

Whether Netflix shares your goals depends, as my students' comments show, on what you are looking for. If you think of Netflix as a video Library of Congress, containing all the programs ever produced, you will be disappointed. If, instead, you are looking for an outlet that will entertain you, and provide that entertainment easily and efficiently, you have met your ideal video service.

But to do that, Netflix has to know you. Let's look at how sites like Netflix do that.

Customization and User Models

One of the things that can be done in an interactive choice engine is customizing the choice architecture. This can lead to happier customers and more productive firms. Netflix was producing more than 33 million versions of its site as early as 2013. To do that, Netflix has to know something useful about its customers. Some of that knowledge comes from Netflix's recommendation system. Some estimate that it adds $1 billion of value to the firm. We'll get to the topic of recommender systems, but first I want to talk about a broader and sometimes simpler concept: a user model.[5]

Whenever we customize a site to increase its usefulness to a chooser, it is because we believe we know something about that person. That knowledge, that picture of a person, drives the customization. While user models can sometimes be complex analytic systems, they can also be quite simple. Keep in mind the very first thing that Netflix asks when you log in—Who is watching?—alongside three buttons, typically your name, your partner's name, and "kids." Netflix ask this up front because the customization is different for each user.

Remember when we talked about GLAM, the German

car company? They presented many options to their customers (buyers chose from sixteen engines, for example) and unwisely, both for them and for their customers, had set the cheapest options as the defaults. Since the default engine was chosen more often, they became concerned that defaults might make some customers less happy, not to mention increase sales of the least-expensive engine.

We suggested that they customize defaults for different customers, something we call smart defaults. The managers liked the idea, but there was one small problem. They didn't want to invest in a complex recommender system to suggest defaults to each user. It would take a lot of effort to build such a system, and it might not be that useful. Cars are not purchased often and data about past purchases might not be that effective, given that people's needs change between purchases. A thirty-year-old whose last purchase was a sports car might now need a family sedan or SUV, having gotten married and had children since the last time they bought a car. And not everyone shopping on the site had been a GLAM customer or even bought a car before.

GLAM had a brilliant and simple idea: "Why don't we simply ask people what kind of car they are looking for?" So a landing page was built that asked that question, with options like these:

A family car

A sports car

An economy car

A car for off-roading

Knowing the response to this simple question was enough to set the defaults. Not only did the choice of a sports car default to an engine that had advanced performance, but it also set defaults for other attributes, like leather interior seats, a more expensive wooden steering wheel and gearshift, and high-performance chrome wheels and tires. Those looking for a family car got different defaults, like side airbags and harnesses for child seats. No expensive AI was necessary; a single question improved outcomes. We could call these *smart-enough defaults*, because they produced most of the benefit of smart defaults with much less modeling effort. According to GLAM, customers were satisfied. The smart-enough defaults also increased revenue: our research showed that compared to the mistake of their original policy (mass defaults using the cheapest option), the smart-enough defaults led to an increase in average revenue of €800 per car.

Smart-enough defaults can be based on something as simple as knowing a chooser's age. Recall from chapter 5, where we discussed target date funds, and how these funds lower the risk in retirement accounts as we get older by increasing the allocation to bonds relative to stocks. Simply asking the chooser's year of birth lets the funds default to the most appropriate mix of riskier stocks and safer bonds for your age. Even more important, the fund automatically changes the mix as you get older, something most people neglect to do. This shows that customization need not be hard: one number, reported by the chooser, improves the defaults. This particular smart default doesn't just offer benefits at the time of purchase but over the saver's whole life span.

More sophisticated methods exist, of course. A potentially

more powerful method is *collaborative filtering*. It gathers data about what users have bought in the past and uses AI to predict what people are likely to buy in the future. These methods can use both explicit information, like a customer's ratings of the options, and implicit information, like whether or not they finished a specific program on Netflix. Most famously, perhaps, collaborative filtering is used by Amazon in generating "People who bought this also bought . . ." listings. Collaborative filtering requires a large set of past user behavior to make predictions. This is the heart of suggestions made by Apple Music, "who to follow" suggestions on Twitter, and matches on Tinder. Yes, Tinder apparently changes the people it will show you based on your swipes. Swiping right will change who you see in the future.

It's important to realize that, in its pure form, collaborative filtering doesn't use in-depth information about the options themselves. When Apple Music recommends a tune, it knows nothing about the song's tempo, beat, lyrics, or instrumentation. It simply knows that people who are like you like that song too.

Compare that to *content-based filters*, which require knowing the attributes of the options. Sometimes that is easy—for example, if we were on a website that sells men's shirts. The description of a particular Oxford shirt contains a lot of information: its color, its material, the kind of collar it has, if it's no-iron, and so on. This is the same data that customers see when they make choices, and we can use it to predict choice. For other products, like music, knowing the product's attributes is really challenging. Companies that use content-based filters ask users to rate options on dimensions, like the sportiness of a shirt or the tempo of a song. They then write algorithms to decompose the song from its digitized representation (for example, the mp3 file) into its attributes. Content-based filtering is used by the online streaming service Pandora via its so-called Music Genome Project. A trained musicologist spends twenty to thirty minutes listening to each song, rating it on hundreds of dimensions, or "genes," as Pandora calls them. An algorithm uses those ratings to select similar songs. Here, unlike collaborative filtering, the algorithm knows much more about the song and less about the person. Pandora was purchased by SiriusXM in 2018 for $3.5 billion, and the technology is now used to select songs for some of SiriusXM's stations. As time went on, collaborative filtering and content-based algorithms were used together in ensembles. Since they have complementary strengths and weakness, this makes sense.[6]

It is important to note, however, that a user model is not synonymous with fancy AI. If we want to know something about the customer, we can often do important customization by asking a quick question, like "What kind of a car are you shopping for?" or "How old are you?"

Most of the buzz around recommender systems usually emphasizes replacing choice. Another view is that user models allow the designer to augment the choice architecture. Instead of AI for making choices, maybe we need to think about IA, intelligent augmentation, where choice architecture assists choices.

Control to the Customer

Visit almost any website and you are in control. You can, for example, visit Zappos, a shoe store run by Amazon, and see two main tools. The first tool lets the user, not the site's designer, decide how the options are sorted. Visitors can sort sandals by relevance, best for you, new arrivals, customer rating, bestsellers, price (high to low or low to high), and finally, brand name. This selection replaces the designer's decision about how to sort. The second tool lets you filter the shoes by size, gender, product type, brand, price, color, and other factors. This implements one of the plausible paths we talked about earlier in the book: screening. I can screen on any of these attributes. For example, by choosing color and style filters, someone can limit their results to beige pumps. This seems like a terrific idea, since it takes the design decisions away from the firm and lets the chooser do the choice architecture. This must make the chooser better off, right?

There are a couple of potential problems with this scheme. First, the designer still has a significant amount of control, although it may be hidden. There is, by default, a sort order selected by the designer. Even here, defaults are sticky. Remember our discussion of the websites that were used to make school choices? On these sites, parents could easily change the sort order, but they didn't do that very often. The default sort order is the most often used. Even if you try to change the sort order by using a drop-down box, the designer has still decided what order to present the different sorting options. It is not surprising that sorting by price (low to high) is not the first thing in the drop-down box on many sites, including Zappos. Giving choosers the ability to change the sort order is not the same as getting them to actually do so.

The same is true for screening. The designer chooses the order of possible attributes, like brand name, that can be used to screen. For brand, Zappos provides a list of more than one hundred options, from ABLE all the way to Zamberlan. Screening, too, has drawbacks. People can easily eliminate options they would actually like because they want to make the length of the list more manageable. In chapter 2 we talked about how screening could eliminate the best date ever. The same is true when screening is done by the website. The perfect shoe might be eliminated.

The real question is whether giving control over the choice architecture to the chooser improves their outcomes. This could be true: if people understand the impact of design upon their decisions, they may "self-design" environments that lead to better choices. Someone who is price sensitive might logically sort by price to make comparisons on that attribute easier. So will letting people choose the right architecture help them?

Unfortunately, there is not a lot of hard evidence one way or the other. We know that sorting can increase the importance of an attribute to the chooser, but we know less about what happens when choosers sort, and if it helps them make better decisions. But one case where adding control helps is in calculating attributes. Remember our story from chapter 6 about people struggling to buy medical insurance? People had difficulty accurately estimating the costs of the policies because costs occur in at least three ways: deductibles, out-of-pocket costs, and copays. These need to be combined to estimate the total cost of a policy. Early on, the people who ran the health care exchanges noticed that people were not paying enough attention to total costs. There were stories of people looking only at one component of the price, like the premium, and neglecting the others, like deductibles. Eventually, many exchanges added calculators to help, and by the fourth year of the Affordable Care Act, it was easy to see an estimated total cost in forty-five out of fifty states.

Does giving users a calculator make a difference in their choices? Researchers gave a sample of Americans a choice between three policies, a much smaller and therefore easier set to choose from. When choosers were given a calculator, they improved their decisions, increasing their purchases of the most cost-effective policy by 7 percent. Most important, these effects were larger for those who had lower incomes, were less educated, or had health needs that were unmet due to the cost of care. Not only does having a calculator help, it particularly helps the most vulnerable.[7]

But choosers can be given more help. The cost of insurance depends on how much health care you actually use. Most of the estimates provided by the calculators are based on the average number of doctor visits across all people, or across those who are similar to the user. But some people, because of their unique situation, will visit doctors far more often than others, use more prescription drugs, and have higher medical expenses. And others will have much less. You could improve the calculator by incorporating more accurate estimates. For example, if you had access to a large database of medical records, you could observe past usage and build a model that would estimate how much health care somebody would use. You could also give people an idea of the distribution of costs, telling them estimates of the minimum and maximum that they would spend between different policies. (I didn't pick the headline, but when I wrote about this idea for *Fortune*, they titled the piece: "What Affordable Care Can Learn from Netflix.")

One company that uses models to estimate usage is Picwell. Based in Philadelphia, it helps insurance companies guide choosers to the product that best fits their needs. Imagine you are asked, "How many times do you think you will go to the doctor this year?" You find yourself fumbling, trying to remember if that trip to the dermatologist was last January or maybe the previous December. Picwell does not rely on your memory, instead estimating how often you will go to the doctor by building statistical models based on the usage records of people similar to you.[8] Again, its system does not replace the chooser, but it augments their intelligence, letting them make decisions about what they want while aiding them in estimating the consequences of their choices.

It might be easy to see that we need help with our calculations, and that we can use computers and smartphones to help us. Less obvious, perhaps, is that choice engines can help increase our comprehension of the decisions we have to make.

Comprehension

A third thing that a choice engine can do is teach. It can be an infinitely patient instructor, never tiring of explaining a term to you. If you want to know what an insurance deductible is, the website might have an explanation if you hover over the term. Want to know the advantages of a certain color in your wardrobe? Some helpful shopper will tell you in a product review.

In theory, a good choice engine not only helps you make a decision but also helps you learn. But some domains are complex, like investing, and the instructor faces a challenge. Not only does actively trading securities present complexity, but the stakes can be large. If the instructor is not up to the job, the chooser can make big mistakes. In fact, a choice engine might make it faster and easier to make big mistakes, especially if you are a new investor operating in a complex and volatile market.

The advent of the pandemic and lockdown saw an enormous growth in retail investing. Whether people were bored at home or attracted by the volatility of the market, many retail brokers saw millions of new accounts opened in the first half of 2020. Traders on one such firm, Robinhood, drove many market trends in late 2020 and early 2021. In early 2020, Robinhood signed up over 3 million new users. Half of these were first-time traders. Although it was only founded in 2015, Robinhood had more daily average trades by June 2020 than two of the largest retail online brokers, Charles Schwab and E-Trade, combined. While you may know of the impact Robinhood traders had on market prices,

I'd like to concentrate on the company's role as a choice engine, servicing millions of new traders.

One new Robinhood customer was Alexander Kearns, a twenty-year-old rising senior at the University of Nebraska–Lincoln, majoring in management. Like many students, he went home to live with his parents in Naperville, Illinois, during the pandemic. There, Kearns opened a Robinhood account and started trading stocks. He seemed to enjoy it and started talking to relatives about stocks, the Federal Reserve, and the outlook for the economy. But this new interest ended tragically.

To understand how, we need to look at how smartphones have revolutionized and grown how stocks and options are traded and how Robinhood has handled the influx of new investors. Today, you can trade shares with less effort than it takes to order a food delivery. With as few as three taps on your smartphone, you can buy a share of any stock. The price is attractive as well: there is no fee. Trading was first revolutionized in the 1990s when discount brokerages lowered the price of a trade to $10. Now many retail brokers do not charge customers directly for trades.

Robinhood was founded by Vlad Tenev and Baiju Bhatt, who had great ambitions for the platform. A big part of their service's appeal was the lack of broker commissions. Tenev hoped, "When people hear the name Robinhood . . . they think they are getting a great deal."

As you might guess from the name, Robinhood aims to bring investing to those who have less money. Returns from stocks are, on average, much higher than from most other investments. It is a puzzle to some experts why people, particularly those who are less well off, do not invest in stocks. Along with companies like Acorn and Stash, Robinhood aimed to open up investing to more people.[9]

One way to do this is by lowering the amount needed to become involved in stocks. Firms do this by selling *fractional shares*. When the price of a single share of Tesla stock is more than $2,000, it's hard for a starting investor to buy one share, let alone invest in the broad range of different companies that would be needed for effective diversification. Fractional shares allow individuals to buy portions of individual shares for as little as a dollar.

Robinhood also uses customer education to bring investing to more new users. Its site says, "Our goal is to make investing in financial markets more affordable, more intuitive, and more fun, no matter how much experience you have (or don't have)."

Deciding which stock to purchase is not so easy. Developing a choice engine for investing, particularly for trading stocks and options, seems hard, especially on a smartphone. After all, stocks are complex, and screens are small. So how well does Robinhood educate these customers? Does it do a good job with comprehension? Its website has an educational section, learn.robinhood.com, that has definitions for terms, but many of the explanations there seem to fall short. For example, a fractional share is described as being like buying part of a rocket ship instead of buying the whole thing: it is like you are buying just the fins. This metaphor is all wrong because it suggests the parts are different—however, a fractional share still functions in that it gains or loses value with the stock. By contrast, a fin doesn't work without the rest of the rocket ship. Stock options, meanwhile, are "are like growing fruit. . . . You hope the seeds turn into something that can be picked at harvest. If the fruit is ruined and is inedible, then you lose the cost of the seeds. On the flip side, if the fruit is perfect and ripe, you have the option but not the obligation to pull the fruit off the tree." This is just confusing. Similarly, a section of the website tells us that "an option is like an umbrella. . . . It could be valuable for you, or it could end up having no value at all. The beauty with an option, and with an umbrella, is that you don't have to use it. You bought it, now it's your option whether to exercise it or not. You use the umbrella when it rains. You exercise the option if it's in the money. Options expire though, umbrellas don't (no analogy is perfect)."[10]

In addition to these subpar educational offerings, there is a sprawling ecosystem around Robinhood on social media, including a Reddit subgroup with about 360,000 members as of September 2020, and a sea of YouTube videos with titles like "How to Make a Minimum of $1000 a Month, in Only 30 Minutes a Day." Among the most viewed is a video on how to trade options for beginners; it has had 1.9 million views.

Robinhood may not attract the most sophisticated traders. Tesla and Apple both announced stock splits in early August 2020 that went into effect at the end of the month. The day of the split, Apple stock went up 3.3 percent and Tesla stock went up 12.5 percent. The volume traded on the day of the split was so great it caused a systems outage at Robinhood.

But nothing new had happened. A single share that cost $2,000 before the split simply became four shares that each cost $500. To use the analogy found on the Robinhood educational site, it is like cutting a pizza into twelve slices instead of eight. There are more slices, each costing less, but the total amount of pizza and the total value of the pizza remains the same. On the Reddit Robinhood board for the topic, you would have seen people asking why the price of Tesla had gone down so much and talking about what a great opportunity it was to buy the stock at this lower price.

Given its clientele, you might think that Robinhood would be dominated by simple transactions, like trading stocks. That was true once, but not now. Robinhood started offering free trades on options in December 2017, and just two years later, the majority of Robinhood's profits came from options. Although the concept of buying shares in a company is relatively straightforward, most people don't understand options. It is not a subject usually taught outside of finance classes, but it has an obvious appeal: an option is a small bet with a large potential upside (and downside).

An example might help: An option gives you the right to buy (or sell) a share of a stock at a given price. You can do that from now until when the option runs out. For instance, say it is April 1 and Apple is selling at $100 a share. You could buy an option to buy Apple at $100 at any time until, say, May 1. The option is exactly that: You could buy a share at $100 but are not obligated to make the purchase. You do not own the stock itself. If the price of Apple increases, say to $110 a share before May 1, you could still buy the share at $100 and sell it at $110.

This would give you a $10 profit, minus what you paid for the option.

This is not the simplest concept in the world, and options can quickly become quite complex. They are part of a large class of financial products called *derivatives*. If that sounds familiar, it is because very complex versions of derivatives based on mortgages were a major cause of the 2008 recession.

The appeal of options is that they are cheap. If you believed Apple was going to increase in value from $100 to $110, you could buy the stock right now for $100. The options let you act on that belief for much less of an investment, say for $1. Imagine you bought 100 options to buy shares of Apple for $100 at $1 each. Thus, the cost of the options would be the same as the cost of buying one actual share at $100. Now imagine the stock rose to $110. If you had bought one share, you would make a $10 profit. If you'd bought 100 options instead, you could buy 100 Apple shares for $10,000 and sell them for $11,000, walking away with $1,000 minus the $100 you paid for the options, or $900. You don't even need to buy the shares; the value of each option will have gone up by $10 and merely selling the options will net you the $1,000.

The disadvantage of buying options is what happens if you guess wrong. If Apple were to stay at $100 and you bought the stock, you would not have lost anything—you still own the stock. However, if you had bought the options, they would be worthless. While some people think that all investments in the stock market resemble gambling, stocks are more like choosing a favorite at the track or betting on red or black at roulette. Options are long shots. Like a ticket for the lottery or a trifecta at a racetrack, you are paying a small amount of money that you are very likely to lose for a small probability of a large payout.

Robinhood lets users buy options and trade stocks without paying any fees. You might be wondering how a company that offers no-fee trades on stocks and options even makes money. The secret is in how prices are displayed. Robinhood gets paid for every trade, but that money comes from the firms that actually perform the trades. These firms, called *market makers*, match people who want to sell a stock with those who want to buy it. But here's the thing: in many markets, the buying and selling prices are not the same. There is a small difference, termed the *spread*.[11] Market makers pay Robinhood (and all retail brokers offering free trades) a part of the spread as a commission for sending it the customers' trades. These trades may not be at the best prices for the customer.

The practice of no-fee trades has been controversial. In 2019 Robinhood was fined by an independent regulator, FINRA, for not ensuring that customers got the best possible execution of their trades. In late December 2020, Robinhood settled a Securities and Exchange Commission complaint for $65 million. The SEC contended that Robinhood steered trades to whomever gave them the highest fees and not those that gave their customers the best price, costing, it alleged, customers $34 million between 2015 and late 2018.[12]

If Robinhood makes money from stock trades, they make much more from option trading.[13] Perhaps because Robinhood has increased the volume of options trades, the market makers pay Robinhood three times more for options trades than for stocks. Options might not be an appropriate investment for a naive trader with limited funds—Robinhood's core customer—but they are ideal for maximizing Robinhood's profitability. In the second quarter of 2020, commissions for sending options to market makers provided $111 million of Robinhood's $180 million revenue.

It is easy to trade stocks on Robinhood. Some "hot" stocks, like Tesla may appear on the front page, and you only have to touch the name on your phone for a green button that says "buy" to appear. Options are not much harder; they require only one more screen to buy than a stock. But while Robinhood may have made options easy to trade, choice architecture did not make them easy to understand. At least one customer thought he had made a terrible mistake.

Alexander Kearns, the newly active trader, was known at the University of Nebraska–Lincoln as someone who always wanted to cheer up friends. He had been selected to be a teaching assistant in the introductory course Investing in Strengths at the university's business school.[14] Kearns's new options trading hobby went badly wrong, or so he thought. One day, he opened his Robinhood app and saw an apparent $730,000 loss, listed in red. The reality was that this was only one part of a complex option trade. There was another component, not displayed, that would have cancelled out almost all the loss when it completed. But he did not understand that.

The next day, his body was found on a nearby railroad track. His suicide note read: "If you are reading this, then I am dead. . . . How was a twenty-year-old with no income able to get assigned almost a million dollars' worth of leverage? The puts I bought/sold should have cancelled out, too, but I also have no clue what I was doing now in hindsight."

Kearns was right—they should have cancelled, but the app misled him. His cousin-in-law, Bill Brewster, a research analyst at Sullimar Capital Group, said, "Tragically, I don't even think he made that big of a mistake. This is an interface issue." We don't know the details, but Brewster showed that Kearns's account actually had a positive balance of $16,174. In response, Robinhood's executives promised changes to the interface and imposed stricter requirements before users could trade options.[15]

Choice engines can be powerful. We have replaced ticker tape and physical chairs with smartphone apps and notifications. We have talked about places where choice engines can help choosers better understand choice. But for all its attempts at increasing accessibility to investing, one wonders how effectively Robinhood is increasing comprehension. Kearns's suicide might not be attributable to Robinhood, but the greater tragedy is that new investors may be learning the wrong lesson. The vast majority of expert advice suggests that if an investor's goal is to accumulate wealth, they should not trade frequently. But investors behave differently on Robinhood. According to a *New York Times* analysis, in the first quarter of 2020, Robinhood users traded nine times as many shares per dollar as E-Trade customers and forty times as many as Schwab account holders. But options were traded eighty-eight times as often by Robinhood customers as Schwab customers, again, accounting for account size. The image of Robinhood is that it is an innovative platform dedicated to helping new investors who are not wealthy. Robinhood has made trading easy, but that does not, on average, mean it helps to build wealth. Trading frequently often leads to bad returns. For example, Robinhood traders are more likely to trade stocks featured on the Top Mover list, but those stocks lose on average almost 5 percent of their value in a month. There seems to be a disconnect between the image and what actually happens on its choice engine.[16]

Understanding Uncertainty

Decision-making is tough. You have to combine different attributes and consider many options. We have talked about how choice architecture can make this easier or harder, but there is one aspect of decision-making we have not discussed: uncertainty.

By their very definition, forecasts are uncertain. Whether it is stock prices, weather forecasts, election outcomes, or who wins the Super Bowl, no one knows in advance what will happen, but they have different degrees of certainty about their guess. For example, right before an election or the game, we may be more certain of the outcome than we would be weeks before. This is difficult to communicate, but there is evidence that choice engines can help people understand uncertainty.

Here are three ways of representing the possible outcomes of the 2016 election as predicted on election day.

You can give people a probability:

Donald Trump has a 0.36 chance of winning.

You can show a picture of the distribution of outcomes:

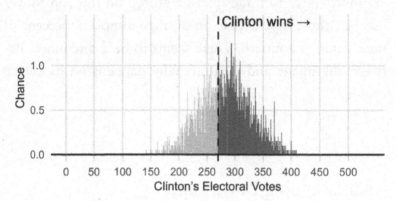

Distribution of possible outcomes of 2016
presidential election from FiveThirtyEight.com[17]

Or you can show a count of what would happen if the election was held 100 or 1000 times:

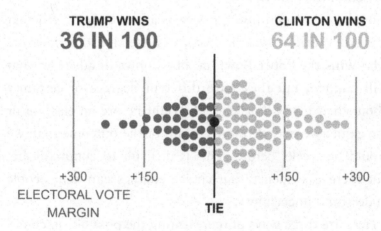

Dot plot of the distribution above[18]

All three methods present the same outcomes and are based on the forecasts from FiveThirtyEight.com, the well-known political prediction site run by Nate Silver. The two charts shown are in the style of that site; the next chart is in the style of a similar forecast done by *The Economist.*

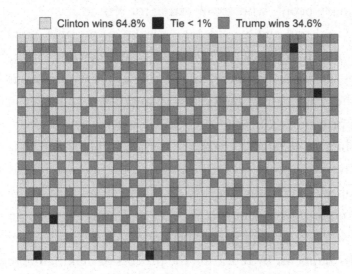

Similar data from *The Economist* forecast[19]

A fair amount of research in psychology shows that people use these three ways of presenting outcomes differently. The first one might be good if you are doing calculations, but for gathering a general impression, remembering outcomes, and making inferences, it appears that the last two representations are better.

Dan Goldstein from Microsoft Research, whom you met earlier when we discussed defaults, and William Sharpe, a Nobel Prize winner in economics, have tried to apply this idea to understanding financial outcomes. Those in finance might recognize "Sharpe ratios," a measure of the financial returns of a stock relative to its risk, based on Sharpe's research.[20]

There are numerical terms, like *beta*, that describe the volatility of an investment. These are useful for the technically trained, but Goldstein and Sharpe wanted to help ordinary people who are investing for retirement.

Goldstein and Sharpe use a display of possible outcomes, similar to the previous two charts, and then animate it, having each dot disappear, one at a time, until only one is left. The diagram can be reset, and another random set of disappearances can happen. While we normally glaze over when we see such a chart, the Goldstein-Sharpe charts come alive: you press a button and one by one the tokens disappear until only one is left. Of course, that animation simulates what happens with all investments: when you invest, there are many possible outcomes, but only one actually happens. By repeating the process of making the tokens disappear multiple times, Goldstein and Sharpe have shown that people can experience probability in a way that is much more involving and intuitive than staring at a static chart. These graphs belong to a class of graphs called *simulated outcome plots*, which let people experience outcomes rather than just passively look at a display.[21]

Hurricane tracks, like stock prices, are uncertain, and those paths have consequences. People need to decide to either evacuate their homes or stay and ride the storm out. To communicate uncertainty, forecasters use a map like the one on page 296. People don't do a very good job of estimating the potential threat by using traditional hurricane-tracking maps. The traditional hurricane map indicates a "cone of uncertainty" that naturally gets bigger the further out the forecast is in time. This is, of course, what happens with uncertainty. As the hurricane gets closer to landfall, its path is better known. There is a problem, however, with this illustration. Some people look at the expanding cone and think it means the storm will get bigger. This belief is so common, in fact, that the image includes a disclaimer. This seems like a natural conclusion since, on maps, area normally indicates size, not uncertainty.

Recent ways of presenting hurricane paths are, in reality, simulated outcome plots: they show a series of possible plots. These are called *spaghetti plots* because each path looks like a strand of spaghetti. The figure on the bottom of page 296 is a plot for the same storm at roughly the same time and forecast period. Each line is a possible outcome of the storm. You can see that many more of the paths end up on the Mississippi–Alabama border, but there are possible paths that strike as far west as Louisiana and as far east as Georgia. While each path also has information about the strength of the winds, what I really think would make the graph more effective would be to use Goldstein and Sharpe's idea of selecting a path randomly, animating it, and redoing this repeatedly, giving people a feel for the distribution.[22]

These plots seem to be very popular with the public. Mike Lowery, then of the Weather Channel, said that the National Hurricane Center reported more traffic to their website from a site that featured spaghetti plots than from their Twitter or Facebook pages.

Animating a hurricane chart brings us back to the key property of a choice engine. They are interactive, allowing the chooser the ability to control the choice architecture, customize the choice architecture, and, finally, to learn. They

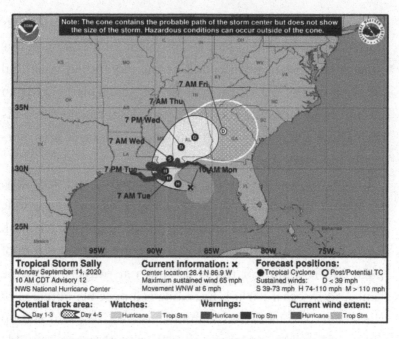

NOAA cone of uncertainty plot for Hurricane Sally

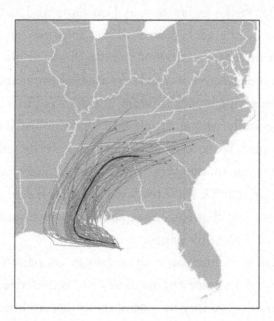

Spaghetti plot for the same storm and time period

can increase the impact of the designer, though. They give the designer many more tools to use and, potentially, more impact on what is chosen. The choice engine moves from a passive display of options and attributes to a more active partner in the choice.

Choice engines increase the power and possibilities of choice architecture, making designers more central than ever to choice. Designers have more responsibility when they can customize the environment for every chooser, deciding what options and attributes to show, how to describe attributes, and how to set defaults not just once, but uniquely for every chooser. Ignoring that responsibility is no longer an option. If it is ignored, as we will see in the next chapter, bad things might happen.

10

Becoming Better
Choice Architects

M any people, when first introduced to choice architecture, are uncomfortable with or even afraid of the idea. My students have told me they worry as both designers and as choosers. As choosers, they're afraid their choices might be influenced by something outside their control, without their awareness, and that they might be exploited. As designers, they worry about influencing others, unintentionally or in harmful ways. These are not new fears.

In 1957, James H. Vicary, a market researcher based in New York City, claimed he ran a six-week study in a movie theater just on the other side of the George Washington Bridge, in Fort Lee, New Jersey. He had flashed phrases like "Hungry? Eat Popcorn" and "Thirsty? Drink Coke" over a film for 1/3000 of a second at a time. The idea was that although people would not consciously perceive these words, they would be affected through *subliminal perception*. Psychologists will tell you that it is impossible that anyone could process these words—the words would need to be presented at least one hundred times longer (1/30 of a second) in order to have an effect. But Vicary asserted that the phrases increased people's consumption of Coke and popcorn. Popcorn sales in the theater, he reported, increased 58 percent, and Coke sales by 18 percent. News coverage of this claim generated what has been described as mass hysteria. The publicity surrounding his efforts led Vicary's firm to consulting contracts estimated to be worth $4.5 million.

Amplifying the fear, Vance Packard's bestselling book, *The Hidden Persuaders,* was published the same year and told stories about how marketers influenced consumers' choices of products and politicians without their awareness. Years later, in 1974, the Federal Communications Commission issued a warning that any broadcaster that used subliminal techniques would be in danger of losing its license.

There was only one problem: Vicary hadn't run the study. When confronted, he first claimed it was a pilot study with a sample size too small to be statistically significant. Later, he confessed that the study never happened. The manager of the theater was contacted and reported that there had never been a test of the sales of popcorn or Coke.[1]

The study was fake, but the fear was real and still is. We have a strong emotional reaction to feeling manipulated, particularly when we discover we weren't aware our behavior was being changed. It suggests that we are not the agents of our choices. This relates to a complex and contentious area of philosophy: the study of whether we have free will and agency. Some philosophers argue that free will is an illusion and all behavior is determined by external forces, while others contend that, despite the existence of external influences, we do in fact make our own choices. These two groups are termed, not very obviously, *incompatibilists* and *compatibilists*.

I am not all that interested in what philosophers believe, but I am interested in how ordinary people view their control over their choices. How do we think about the role of outside influences, particularly those that we don't know about? When do people feel that their choices have been influenced, and when do they resent it? To help us understand this, I turn to a relatively new area: empirical philosophy, in which philosophers, instead of pondering their own beliefs and intuitions, simply ask ordinary people what they believe. They study what psychologists call *lay theory* or *folk belief.*

It turns out that people mostly have two conflicting beliefs about free will. In some instances, people readily admit that, in the abstract, choices are determined by external forces: John may buy the red sports car because he is mad about something his friend said. At the same time, they strongly believe that their own behavior is determined by their own thoughts and beliefs: I decided to buy the sports car, and it was not related to my friend's snide remark about my hairline and paunch. Much as preferences are assembled, some of our beliefs about ourselves are not all that coherent. Other people's behavior can be determined by things outside their control, but we believe our own behavior is determined by our preferences, or agency. And when there are emotional consequences, we see free will as being more important.

One of the key reasons for this clash is that we have a strong experience that we are making choices. We are aware of the debate, the should-I-or-shouldn't-I, of our deliberations, and feel that this internal dialogue determines what we choose. But we don't know about the internal debate of others, so we feel comfortable saying that outside influences change *their* behavior.[2]

As odd as this sounds, it explains a couple of important facts. The first is why choice architecture can seem threatening: it gives the designer some control over what we choose. By setting a default, the car dealership is affecting what trim package you choose; by sorting wine, the online wine merchant may be making cheap, low-quality wine seem more attractive. Perhaps the reason that choice architecture provokes both fear and fascination is that it taps into our two incompatible beliefs. It matches our intuitive understanding that many of the choices of others are determined by their environment, and we feel comfortable with that. At the same time, it runs counter to our belief that we determine our choices. To better understand this awareness and fear, it's time to finally learn how Derren Brown, our mentalist from chapter 3, does one trick.

Do You Believe in Magic?

In chapter 3, we described the British mentalist Derren Brown as a mind writer. Psychologists have studied one trick popularized by Brown in depth, and it helps us understand not only how it works, but also what we mean by awareness.

This trick involves what magicians call *forcing*, covertly influencing a spectator's choices. *Covert* is the key word here. It means that while the choice may be influenced, the chooser does not connect the force with their choice. When asked, choosers maintain that they were free to choose any option. A study that looks carefully at one of Brown's forces goes like this.

You are sitting in a university cafeteria, sitting across from a young woman with auburn hair and a slight French accent. She says, "I'm going to try to transmit to you the identity of this card." She then holds up a playing card with its back to you. She says, "Don't try to guess what it is, but just wait until you get it." She pauses. "Make the color bright and vivid," she continues. "Imagine a screen in your mind, and on this screen, the little numbers low at the bottom of the card, in the corners, and at the top, and then the things in the middle in the center of the card." As she describes the card, she makes a rectangle with her fingers and then draws two squiggles with her index finger in the imaginary corners to indicate the position of the numbers. She then points to the center of the imaginary card with her thumb, index, and middle finger, saying, "The boom-boom-boom, the symbols, the suits, in the middle of the card," as she points to the middle of the card. She then says "Do you have it?" Chance alone says that you would pick one particular card a little less than 2 percent of the time, since it is one of fifty-two playing cards in a deck.

People in the experiment pick the 3 of diamonds about 18 percent of the time, nine times more frequently than by chance. They pick a card with the number 3 39 percent of the time, and a diamond 33 percent of the time, both exceeding what you would expect by chance. By now you know that I am suspicious of the data presented in any one paper, so I recently tried to replicate this result with two large groups of pretty sharp MBA students, using videos shared by the psychologists who did the initial research. My students showed an even stronger tendency to pick the 3 of diamonds. When I showed a version of the video where the woman does the exact same patter, minus certain key elements, there is no pattern to which card is chosen. Without these elements, people pick cards at random. With them, there is a strong pattern in the selection of cards.

Clearly the woman is influencing the spectators. She is the external force influencing, probabilistically, their choice of cards. How does that work? Derren Brown calls this the *mental priming force*, and it turns out that subtle primes, mostly gestures, change what is chosen. The hands that formed the screen were tilted to be a diamond, the squiggles in the air were drawn in the shape of the number 3. There were three fingers used to point, and "boom" was said three times. Finally, asking the spectator to make the color bright and vivid made red more accessible than black, since it is brighter and more vivid, and of course, all diamonds in a deck of cards are red.

That is how the trick worked, but were people aware of that? The researchers, Alice Pailhès and Gustav Kuhn, psychologists at Goldsmiths, part of the University of London, asked their respondents whether they noticed anything about the way the presenter asked the question. Pailhès and Kuhn found that 72 percent of the respondents detected at least one of the elements that the trick used, but they did not think it influenced their choice. Some people, for example, reported thinking the screen drawn by the woman was shaped like a diamond but did not connect that with their choice of cards.

But why should they see a connection? Most people are unaware of the effects of accessibility, and the term *mind writing* would seem mysterious to them. The magic here is that some concepts, like 3 and diamonds, became more accessible in memory and that choosers were unaware that this was happening.[3]

Since it doesn't work all the time, magicians never rely on this kind of force entirely. A good performer always has a way out. For example, they may start by saying, "Was it a diamond?" followed by "Was it a three?" followed by "Is it a three of diamonds?" When the participant says no, they might ask, "Was it a three of hearts?" This increases the probability that at least one of their guesses is right.

Choice architecture shares many characteristics with magic. Designers change something subtle in the design. Choosers may notice the change but remain unaware of how it affects their behavior. For the most part we don't know (unless you've read this book, of course) how choice architecture influences our choices.[4]

Do you think you are a generous person? Generosity feels like it would be part of our identity and not easily changed. Generosity is often studied in an experiment using what is called the dictator game. Imagine you were suddenly given $10 and asked if you would give some of the money you just received to a complete stranger. You could do what economists suggest and keep all the money, because, of course, more money is better than less. Also, in these studies, your identity is a secret and you don't confront the stranger. Still, most people actually give some of this "found" money to the stranger, usually just under $3 of the $10, keeping $7 for themselves. But that result is affected by choice architecture.

In a study run at the University of Pennsylvania, responses were collected on a webpage that listed different possible splits: $1 for them, $9 for you; $2 for them, $8 for you, et cetera. Some participants saw the selfish split ($0 for them, $10 for you) first, and it was prechecked. Others saw the most generous option ($10 for them, $0 for you) first and prechecked. In both cases the rest of the possible splits were listed randomly.

People given the selfish split first gave the other person only $1.47 on average, but those with the generous split first gave $3.14. The order and checklist changed people's generosity, doubling the amount given to strangers.[5] The change in choice architecture did change people's behavior, but they were unaware that it did. While 71 percent noticed that the first option was already checked, only 8 percent believed it had influenced their choice. Most (over 80 percent) of those who saw it said that it failed to change their choice.

In short, even when people notice choice architecture, they consider themselves basically immune.[6]

Does Disclosure Help?

If people are unaware of the influence of choice architecture, maybe we can just tell them that they are going to be influenced. Warnings accompany all sorts of products, from vacuum cleaners to cigarettes, so why not choice architecture?

Unfortunately, disclosing the presence and intent of choice architecture does not seem to work. Several studies have told people about what defaults do, in various ways, including saying that their goal is to change behavior. For example, researchers said that the purpose of a default was to increase donations to a climate protection fund. In fact, all that warning appears to do is to make the nudge seem more acceptable.[7]

It is not surprising that warning people about choice architecture does not work. People may know they are being influenced, but don't know how. Since they don't understand that accessibility can influence how preferences are assembled, they might not know a default can change their preferences. After all, thousands of people packed Broadway's Cort Theatre in 2019, paying large amounts of money knowing that Derren Brown was going trick them. That was not enough to keep them from being influenced.[8] If you don't know how the trick works, you are unable to stop the illusion. And in choice architecture, because you do not know how defaults, sorting, order, and the rest influence your choices, you are relatively helpless to resist, even when you are warned.

One final point about awareness: we might think, in the abstract, that a change in choice architecture is acceptable. In an extensive stream of research, Cass Sunstein and Lucia Reisch have done surveys asking people if they find certain interventions acceptable. For example, they ask people whether defaulting customers into green, sustainable energy suppliers is acceptable. The results show a fair amount of agreement about what people find to be acceptable interventions, and much of this consensus is worldwide. Even a slight majority of Republicans in the United States think that is okay. But their acceptance in the abstract may not predict their acceptance when they are told that they were personally affected by choice architecture. Instead they think, "When I'm fairly confident that this intervention won't influence me, I think it is fine."[9]

Choice-Architecture Neglect

Do designers appreciate the effects of choice architecture? In one study, designers were asked to set the default to present to choosers. It involved two hypothetical medicines. One was cheaper, costing $20 for a week's supply, but it needed to be taken six times during the week; the other cost $50, but had to be taken only once a week. There was a trade-off between cost and convenience. The researchers asked the designers to encourage the selection of one of the medicines using defaults—for example, the cheaper, less convenient drug.

The participants in this study should always use the default to encourage the choosers to select one of the two drugs. In fact, the designers selected the correct default only 51.9 percent of the time, about what you would expect by chance (remember there were two choices). There was some variability in the results—experts with experience posing decisions to others (practicing doctors and attorneys, for example) did better, but they were far from perfect. Other studies also show some degree of default neglect, even when designers are given a chance to learn.[10]

This is a very new area of research, and one limited, unfortunately, to defaults. But it suggests that designers don't always know the power of the tools that are at their disposal. As a result of their potential ignorance, a benevolent designer is not doing as good of a job as they could in presenting choices. When we look at the rest of the tools designers can use, there is very little reason to think that the effects of choice architecture are obvious. What happens if designers are sometimes clueless about the effects of what they are doing? They might be harming choosers unintentionally, making haphazard selections of tools.

Neglecting Choice Architecture Is Harmful

Neglecting choice architecture can lead to harm. In chapter 4, we talked about how many people should wait to claim Social Security retirement benefits. But the Social Security Administration inadvertently nudged people to do just the opposite. One piece of information provided by Social Security was called the *break-even age*. This is the age when the total amount of money you received from Social Security will be the same whether you claimed early, at sixty-two or later, say, at seventy. Experts argue that this piece of data is not particularly relevant to the decision of when to claim benefits. To the surprise of the Social Security Administration, providing this information backfired. Rather than making people claim later, it made them claim earlier—by about eighteen months.[11] This is not what the Social Security Administration thought was in retirees' best interests, and they removed the break-even age from the standard description of claiming benefits.

This kind of choice-architecture neglect assumes that people know how to make the right choice within the choice environment you've provided, ignoring that they really need help. This can have great consequences.

Consider end-of-life decisions. When people are gravely ill, they can choose interventions that could extend their lives, but these therapies are intrusive and unpleasant, and the time added to your life often comes with the price of being put on a ventilator or having a feeding tube inserted. Grouped together, these treatments are called *life-extension care*. The alternative is called *comfort care*. The latter in-

The Elements of Choice

volves declining many invasive interventions and focusing on managing pain and ensuring comfort.

Ideally, these decisions should involve the patient and be made in advance, in the form of a living will, or what doctors call an *advance directive*. But more often than not, patients do not have advance directives—only about a third of all patients have one when they need it.

If you have had major surgery, you may have been asked to complete an advance directive. Giving you this form assumes that you can specify your preferences. But what if you haven't given much thought to the kind of care you would want? For most people, this is a decision they have not made, and do not want to make. The choice of options for terminal care is often a preference that needs to be assembled. The advance directive, like every choice, has an architecture. Could that influence this important choice?

In a remarkable study by Scott Halpern and colleagues, patients with terminal illnesses made choices about end-of-life care that actually determined their treatment. The advance directive given to them by the researchers first asked what their goal for care was: life extension or comfort care. For a third of the patients, the directive had a comfort-care default, indicated by a prechecked box. A second group had no preselection, and the third group had the life-extension goal already checked. Comfort care was selected 77 percent of the time when it was the default, 66 percent of them time when no option was preselected, and only 43 percent of the time when life extension was the default. Similar results were seen for choices involving specific interventions, like having a feeding tube. It is remarkable that the default had such a large effect on such an important decision. But what happened next is even more informative.

Being ethical scientists, the investigators later explained to all the patients (at least those that were still living) that they had been randomly assigned to those defaults, told them about the influence of default effects, and most important, offered the respondents the chance to change their minds. If patients had preferences, this was their chance to express them. Yet, of the 132 terminal respondents, only 2 changed their choices. Even when they were told what the defaults were, that the defaults had been determined randomly, and the way defaults influence choice, the effect of defaults persisted.

This is strong evidence that preferences for end-of-life care are assembled, and that people do not have preexisting preferences for these options. This is an incredibly difficult decision, and most patients have not experienced intubation, the insertion of a feeding tube, or dialysis before making these choices, and these aren't decisions anyone enjoys thinking about in advance. When the time comes, the primary decision-maker may not be conscious, and the family members who inherit the decisions are overwhelmed.

Making sure that people have a choice is laudable, but if they are overwhelmed, they are even more likely to take the default. This is a problem: there is a major disconnect between what people say they want when they are forced to make a choice and what happens when they are not forced. Comfort care, which emphasizes minimizing pain and invasive procedures, was selected by the majority of patients in the Halpern-led study when there was no default. But if you don't make a choice, that is not what happens in reality. Unless the patient or their immediate family says otherwise, the patient will be treated as if they had chosen life extension. In other words, it is the default option, and they will receive those treatments. The design of most of the commonly used advance directives seems to bias people toward life extension. For example, "I want to have life support" is the first option on one commonly used document.

Assuming patient autonomy and ignoring the influence of choice architecture has a significant impact on suffering, cost, and dignity. Doctors may be loath to influence end-of-life care choices, but then patients are loath to make these decisions, and this reluctance increases the importance of defaults.

One simple piece of advice might be to set defaults to the option most people want: comfort care. If people avoid the choice, that is what they will receive, but of course, they could choose life-extension therapies if they do have that preference.[12]

Not only is end-of-life choice an important topic, but it also illustrates when choice architecture might have its largest effects. These are the situations when preferences have not been assembled before the choice is posed, and when people lack prior experience in choosing a plausible path. Knowing this, we can understand when it is particularly dangerous to ignore choice architecture.

Most choices are mundane and repetitive, but there are choices that are both important and rare. When people must make them, they lack clear ideas of what they want or how to proceed. Choosing a school, buying a house, selecting a pension plan, and settling on a type of end-of life care are all examples of infrequent decisions with big consequences. Particularly if the decision-maker has conflicting goals, choice architecture will play a larger role.

Deliberately Bad Choice Architecture

Not all bad choice architecture results from ignorance or naivete. Neglecting choice architecture might be common but it is not universal. Some designers experiment to see what works—for example, in direct mail campaigns or by conducting A/B tests on the internet. These designers could use this knowledge to advance their interests, and not those of the choosers. The result may be malevolent choice architecture. What happens when choice architecture goes bad?

Let's start with several examples, of increasing severity.

Some evil choice architecture takes advantage of fluency, people's initial judgments of effort. As we know, choosers are very sensitive to initial costs, in terms of both money and effort. Badly intentioned designers can exploit that. We have all made the decision to start or stop a subscription service—say, a newspaper or a streaming service like Spotify or Hulu. Fluency can be used to construct a subscription trap, where the designer has made it is easy to start and hard to stop. Newspapers are a mild example. It is very easy to start a subscription with a few clicks on most newspapers' websites for a low initial rate, like $1 a week for fifty-two weeks. But once you have started, it is more difficult to stop—say, when the early rate increases to almost $5 a week. To cancel, you must call an 800 number. For some firms that use subscription traps, that call involves a long wait on hold.

Researchers who study dark patterns give this a name all its own: *asymmetries*; more colorfully, this is known as the roach motel of human-computer interfaces. Paraphrasing the famous commercial for the pest trap, customers check in, but they don't check out. Asymmetry describes the difference in the effort required to decide to start consuming the service and the greater effort to register your decision to stop the plan.[13]

Designers can also use fluency to inhibit choices and maintain the status quo. Several years ago, I was interviewed by National Public Radio's *Marketplace*. The interviewer and I sat together as he tried to change his privacy settings. By default, Verizon could track his phone calls and potentially sell that information. Another reporter had interviewed a Verizon representative who described a very easy system for opting out of such tracking. The reality was different: after a long robotic message that suggested that the interviewer could "restrict or change options to his telecommunications service information," he was given a long menu of options. After pressing 1, indicating that he wanted to change his privacy options, he was asked whether he wanted to place a restriction on his account. This seemed scary, like he would be giving up something rather than just changing his privacy settings. He was then asked to type in his ten-digit telephone number as it appears on his bill, followed by pound. The robotic voice read it back, very slowly, digit by digit, and then asked him to enter it again. It then asked for the first thirteen digits of the account number from his bill, then asked him to speak his first and last name, remembering to press pound each time, speak his address, then his town, state, and zip code, and finally his first and last name again to confirm that he is the decision-maker. I suspect the phone company already knew his phone number. Not surprisingly, Verizon reported that the number of people opting out was in the single digits.

Of course, many privacy agreements have exactly this structure: we are presented with long and complex terms of service that seem designed to restrict comprehension. It's estimated that over 90 percent of website users do not read terms-of-service documentation. This can lead to bad decisions. In one study, 98 percent of users agreed to a privacy policy that explicitly said it would share all information with the National Security Agency and their employer, and required them to provide their first-born child as payment. Fortunately, this was an experiment, but bad choice architecture does lead to mistakes in understanding what we are giving up.[14]

Perhaps the most egregious example of malicious choice architecture involves electronic health records (EHRs). In chapter 1, we saw how large hospital systems used a change to the interface to increase the prescribing of generic drugs. Because it delivered the same care for less money, this change in choice architecture increased the welfare of patients, and because it was faster, it benefited physicians.

Smaller practices and single-physician practices don't have the resources to develop and tune EHRs of their own. Many

The Elements of Choice

adopted a free system, provided by a successful start-up called Practice Fusion. Heralded as "the Facebook of health" by *TechCrunch*, the company provided the EHRs and in turn sold advertising targeted to the physicians.[15]

But that was not all it did. Practice Fusion also received payments from pharmaceutical companies in return for changes in their EHR's choice architecture. One particularly nefarious example was an agreement between Practice Fusion and a company known in a court settlement as "Pharma X." In exchange for $1 million, in 2016 Practice Fusion added an alert that reminded physicians to ask patients about their pain and then provided options. The alert was presented to doctors 230 million times in a three-year period, and Pharma X estimated that the alert would add three thousand customers and as much as $11 million in sales. This was happening at the same time that concern was rising about overprescribing of pain medicines, specifically extended-release opioids. The Centers for Disease Control and Prevention produced guidelines emphasizing nonpharmaceutical and nonopioid treatments. If opioids were required, doctors were advised to avoid time-release drugs, since those were more likely to lead to long-term use, and to limit the number of pills provided. But Practice Fusion's EHR system included an option for extended-use opioids, even where the guidelines warned against them.

Pharma X was later revealed to be Purdue Pharma, the maker of OxyContin, which in 2020 settled a suit for misleading marketing of opioids with fines and payments estimated to be $8 billion. Meanwhile, Practice Fusion admitted to the payments it had received to change the EHR choice architecture, settling the charges brought by the state of Vermont for $145 million.[16] Practice Fusion and Purdue were the designers of a choice architecture that caused harm to patients by providing inappropriate options to doctors.

This illustrates that the designers' decisions had an influence and there is no neutral version of the EHR: either Oxy-Contin will be listed, increasing its sales, or it will not be listed. It is particularly ironic that studies now show the choice architecture of EHRs can reduce opioid prescribing. For example, changing the default to reduce the number of pills or changing the calculator used to determine the number of pills prescribed can make prescriptions come closer to the guidelines.[17]

Choice architecture can have an enormous impact on people's welfare. It can make it harder or easier to maintain control over our privacy and personal information. It can increase savings for retirement and help students find better schools. It can increase or decrease prescriptions for potentially addictive drugs. Choice design can make a difference, and ignoring it is not an option.

This is particularly true when we look at who is most affected by choice architecture. It has a greater impact, positive or negative, on the people who are the most vulnerable: those with lower incomes, less education, and challenging social circumstances. Put another way, choice architecture could be a particularly potent tool for addressing income disparity and social justice. On the flip side, this means that malevolent choice architecture, like the examples we have just discussed, are particularly harmful to those who are the most disadvantaged.[18]

What Is One to Do?

Having looked, throughout this book and in this chapter, at choice architecture, both good and bad, there are three things that we should consider going forward:

1. Choosers are unaware of the effects of choice architecture and do not respond to warning.

2. Designers can underestimate the effects of choice architecture.

3. Choice architecture has a larger effect on the most vulnerable.

If these three statements are true, what should we do? One place to start is educating designers and choosers. The education I have in mind is not just pointing out choice architecture and its effects, but also providing an understanding how it works.

I have argued here that choice architecture works largely in two ways: changing plausible paths and changing how preferences are assembled. These processes are very much automatic. Psychologists call these *System 1 processes* and show that they largely operate without our awareness. Just as you cannot explain how it is you read text, or the decisions involved in brushing your teeth, you do not have access to how you choose plausible paths or how you assemble preferences. It is not surprising that people are unable to resist choice architecture, even when informed about its consequences. Even disclosing the intent to use choice architecture is less helpful, since people's understanding of how choice architecture works is incomplete at best. We may know that the designer is trying to change our choice, but we don't know how to prevent that from happening.

The story might be different if we know how the influence works. While there is very little research about this, here is an intuition: I have now taught you how the mental priming force works. In the example we saw, it involved repeatedly invoking the number 3 in symbols written in the air and saying "boom" three times, invoking the color red by asking us to think of vivid colors, and invoking the shape of a diamond by making the screen into a diamond. You now know that the performer uses this to make the number 3 and the suit of diamonds more accessible in memory. You know not only the intent but the process as well. You could watch out for similar tricks in the future, noticing the diamond shape of the performer's hands, seeing the number 3 being drawn in the air, and realizing that the mention of vivid colors makes you think about red instead of black. If you wanted to prevent the influence of the trick, you could think of other numbers, close your eyes, or, knowing you are being manipulated, pick at random any card other than the 3 of diamonds. Knowing how it works, you are more likely to understand the trick's impact.[19] In fact, if you know all this, and see the video, you might try to do the trick yourself.

Just as knowing how the trick works makes it less effective, a detailed knowledge of how choice-architecture tools work may make them less effective. For example, we know that defaults work, in part, by focusing your initial attention on the default option. You could then decide to look at other options first. This may be enough to overcome the effect. This has worked in my lab for other biases: we can make people more patient or prevent the endowment effect by changing their focus.[20] Warning people that they are about to be exposed to choice architecture may not be enough, but teaching them how the tools work and how to avoid those effects may allow them to overcome the intention of the designer. Now that you have read this book, I hope that you are in a better position to be both a more effective designer and a wiser chooser. Perhaps this is the start of your choice architecture self-defense training.

I also hope that anyone reading this book aspires to lead others to better, more beneficial choices. While a deeper understanding of how choice architecture works may tempt some to manipulate others for their own ends, I hope they will be very much in the minority. Overall, a more widespread understanding of how our design choices affect others should result in more intentional and constructive choice architectures from which we can all benefit.

Designing choice architecture is like picking a path on a map. Many paths are possible, but some are much better for the chooser. Defaults can be selected in choosers' best interests. Good alternatives can be made easy to see, and not obscured by many bad or irrelevant options. Benefit programs can be made easy to access instead of more difficult. And when we do know what we want, a good choice architecture can make it either easy to find or difficult. But how you use your newfound skill is, of course, up to you.

Becoming Better Choice Architects

The idea of choice architecture may be new, but it has existed for as long as we have had to make choices. Designers may underestimate choice architecture in the abstract, but through observation as well as trial and error, they can't help but stumble onto designs that advance their goals.

What is new is a better understanding of how choice architecture affects decisions and the reality that it has become much easier to change the choice environment. Altering a website requires much less work than redesigning a store, and it can be customized to change the choices of each visitor in unique ways, and controlled experiments and A/B testing can discover what leads to better choices.

What is also new is the idea that choice architecture is not optional. All choices have some elements that can influence the chooser. What this book adds, I hope, is an understanding of the scope of the tools available and how they fundamentally work.

While some have questioned whether choice architecture is ethical, I believe the opposite: ignoring choice architecture is ethically wrong. The designer will inevitably influence the chooser. Pretending otherwise leads to outcomes that neither the designer nor the chooser wants, and worse outcomes for both.

The ethical imperative is even stronger if we think that choice architecture will have a greater influence on important but rarely made decisions or have a greater influence on more vulnerable populations. Here, choice-architecture neglect has even greater negative consequences.

While I have argued that ignoring choice architecture is not ethical, I would also argue that it would be unwise. We face many problems that may not be easily solved with the two major tools of standard economics, information and incentives. I'll offer three examples: climate change, inequity, and polarization and fake news. Choice architecture can be an impressively efficient addition to the other tools we have to address these issues.

- *Climate change*: We have seen how defaults can affect choices between green and gray electricity, and how it can make trade-offs between short-term savings and long-term efficiency gains more apparent. It can do more, and these changes are cheap.

- *Inequity*: In chapter 1, we talked about how changing the interfaces in cabs and services like Uber and Lyft can increase the tips given to drivers. We also saw how choice architecture can improve schools and increase the uptake of social benefits, like a program to increase kids' cognitive development. These all are steps to reducing inequity, and they can be less expensive, more efficient, and less controversial than some alternatives.

- *Polarization and fake news*: We saw in chapter 9 that describing policies in numbers that are easily understood in context can reduce the disagreement between those on the left and right, for both tax cuts and carbon fees. Recently Twitter started an innovation: before you retweeted an article, Twitter would ask if you had read it. No choice was removed, but an upfront cost was imposed on retweeting without reading. Similar changes to the interface are being made to increase what Twitter calls the *conversation quality*: "humanization" prompts that remind you of similarities you have with someone, and warnings when you retweet something that has been labeled as false. We await data on the effectiveness of these changes, but they share two important characteristics that makes choice architecture so appealing: they are relatively cheap to implement, and we can do experiments, so we can evaluate their effects.

These are big problems, and solutions will involve much more than choice architecture.

These are pretty important applications for a field that was named just twelve years ago. But like a twelve-year-old, the field is much closer to its beginning than its end, and somewhat oblivious to what it does not know, but it shows promise. Some of the hard work will be understanding what tools work and when, inventing new tools, and finding new applications in the future. We need better ideas of how to incorporate these ideas into organizations and institutions, and to better understand how they affect individuals.

Finally, consider how you might be a designer for the chooser you know the best: yourself. You might think that choice architecture is only useful for large institutions. Yet we often structure our own choices, whether they're about jobs, mates, moves, or other important life choices. The tools in this book might help you to understand when to search more and when to stop, how to label attributes, and in general how to select good plausible paths and assemble helpful preferences. As you do that, you might realize that the designer, you, has a great deal of influence on the chooser—in this case, also you. It suggests one ultimate observation on how to use choice architecture, a paraphrase of the golden rule: Design for others as you would like them to design for you.

Acknowledgments

The German composer Helmut Lachenmann has said that the process of writing a composition produces a different composer. The process of writing this book has certainly changed me. During the four serious years of writing, I have learned much, thought intensely about some of the issues raised by applying choice architecture, and, I hope, developed a way of communicating these exciting possibilities to people who do not know they are designers.

Changes have also happened to the study of decision-making. I did not know that I was studying choice architecture for most of the time I was doing research in the area. My friends Richard Thaler and Cass Sunstein coined the term *choice architecture* in *Nudge*, and this gave much of my research a great descriptive name. There have been many influences during my career, but this acknowledgment focuses on those most related to the book. I want to thank mentors who have helped change the field, because they might not be acknowledged elsewhere. These include J. Edward Russo,

Herbert Simon, Hillel Einhorn, and Amos Tversky. Colin Camerer has been a very influential and inspiring friend, as has Robert J. Meyer.

This book's initial ideas resulted from a working group that I organized at the Triennial Invitational Choice Symposium, an event that sounds much more like an art fair than a wonky conference. Here a bunch of academics sit around writing a chapter describing the state of the field. The resulting highly cited article, "Beyond Nudges: Tools of a Choice Architecture," encouraged the idea of writing a book. Important contributors to that effort not thanked elsewhere include Suzanne Shu, Benedict Dellaert, Craig Fox, Ellen Peters, and David Schkade.

Early versions of chapters of the book were taught in the "Becoming Better Choice Architects" course at Columbia Business School that I developed. I want to thank students in the sections of that class for their comments, input, and patience. The Business School also supported the book and I'm very appreciative for their support. At Columbia, Amanda Eckler edited versions of early chapters and Chung Ho was a wizard at producing graphics. Also helping with research for the book were Simon Xu, Inez Ajimi, Erica Shah, and Wanja Waweru, and especially Shannon Duncan.

Linnea Gandhi, now a PhD student at the Wharton School of the University of Pennsylvania, helped immensely and convinced me that this book was worth the effort. I hope she was right; the book would not exist without her early support. I also benefited from a monthlong residency at the Bellagio Center of the Rockefeller Foundation. I like to pace when I write, and it was particularly refreshing to pace down the paths of the estate. I would go back anytime.

Early comments on the book idea and on very early drafts came from Bob Cialdini, Cass Sunstein, Chip Heath, and Daniel Kahneman. Their comments were very helpful, and they have all served as inspirations.

The last two years of more serious work started with the counsel of Max Brockman, my agent, and the great oversight and editing of Courtney Young at Riverhead Books, who was masterful at helping me navigate the process of turning my wordy wandering prose into a tighter final product. Jacqueline Shost helped shepherd the book through production and David Moldawer of Bookitect also helped shape many chapters during development.

Several friends deserve thanks for reading parts of this book. A particular shout-out to Gregory Murphy for detailed comments on the entire book, rendered with wit. Daniel G. Goldstein, Kellen Mrkva, and Nathaniel Posner provided comments on several chapters. Many thanks to all those researchers whose work I cite and who tactfully pointed out errors or better ways of saying things. This includes Jessica Anker, Jack Soll, Maya Bar-Hillel, Wändi Bruine de Bruin, Raluca Ursu, and Jay Russo. And thanks to Richard Thaler for many discussions and comments on organ donation.

I have done interviews by phone and email with several researchers for background and to test out ideas. These include Irwin Levin, Gerald Häubl, Rick Larrick, Al Roth, and Scott Halpern. These conversations added clarity and color.

I have tried to highlight the contributions of co-authors of my prior work throughout the book and won't repeat my thanks here, but I'm appreciative of all the ideas, fun, patience, and friendship.

Finally, there is always the perfunctory acknowledgment to the long-suffering spouse. In this case that spouse, Elke Weber, has been patient with my half-baked ideas expressed over many lunches, dinners, and walks, but her additional contribution to the book has been as a co-author and co-creator of many of the research projects. Thank you.

Notes

1. Shaping Choices

1. For the speech, see "House of Commons Rebuilding: HC Deb 28 October 1943 Vol 393 Cc403-73." The history is discussed in "Bomb Damage" and "Churchill and Commons Chamber." The importance of a full house was clearly evident when social distancing limited attendance. Lindsay Hoyle, the speaker of the House, said, "There is no greater day than seeing a packed chamber with everybody jostling to be in there. That's what brings this House alive, that's what makes this House. But that won't happen until we know it's safe." Elgot, "Commons May Never Return to Packed Chamber Debates, Says Speaker."

2. Health outcomes are documented in Shrank et al., "The Implications of Choice: Prescribing Generic or Preferred Pharmaceuticals Improves Medication Adherence for Chronic Conditions." The failure of incentives is in O'Malley et al., "Impact of Alternative Interventions on Changes in Generic Dispensing Rates."

3. Malhotra et al., "Effects of an E-Prescribing Interface Redesign on Rates of Generic Drug Prescribing: Exploiting Default Options"; Meeker et al., "Effect of Behavioral Interventions on Inappropriate Antibiotic Prescribing among Primary Care Practices: A Randomized Clinical Trial."

4. Haggag and Paci, "Default Tips"; Hoover, "Default Tip Suggestions in NYC Taxi Cabs."

5. On the exchanges established under the Affordable Care Act, different states differ quite a bit: for instance, Alaska and Alabama offer

six options or fewer in total. Ohio offers seventy-three. This count is based on visiting the exchanges from a location (for example, Juneau, Alaska or Columbus, Ohio) and seeing the options for a forty-year-old male with a spouse and child and no dental coverage in October 2020. Thanks to Benedict Dellaert of the Erasmus School of Economics, Erasmus University Rotterdam.

6. Rosenblatt "Ad Tracking 'Blocker' Comes to iOS6."

7. Brignull, "Dark Patterns: Inside the Interfaces Designed to Trick You." Data comes from a study conducted by the consulting company Tune, reported in Kaye, "Use of Limit Ad Tracking Drops as Ad Blocking Grows."

8. Auxier et al., "2. Americans Concerned, Feel Lack of Control over Personal Data Collected by Both Companies and the Government."

9. Leswig, "Apple Makes Billions from Google's Dominance in Search—and It's a Bigger Business than iCloud or Apple Music"; Wakabayashi and Nicas, "Apple, Google and a Deal That Controls the Internet." Apple has more recently tried to promote privacy as a core value in competition with social media companies.

2. Plausible Paths

1. Kenneth P. Byrnes, chairman of the flight training department at Embry-Riddle Aeronautical University, in Wichter and Maidenberg, "More Jobs Will Be Cleared for Takeoff. Aspiring Pilots Are Ready."

2. Wodtke, "Sully Speaks Out."

3. See Croft, "Connectivity, Human Factors Drive Next-Gen Cockpit."

4. Adapted from figure 3 in National Transportation Safety Board, "Loss of Thrust in Both Engines after Encountering a Flock of Birds and Subsequent Ditching on the Hudson River, US Airways Flight 1549 Airbus A320–214, N106US Weehawken, New Jersey, January 15, 2009."

5. See Langewiesche, "Anatomy of a Miracle"; National Transportation Safety Board, "Loss of Thrust in Both Engines after Encountering a Flock of Birds." The figure and statistics about performance and transcripts come from the NTSB report.

6. In fact, Sullenberger thought he had been right on the green dot speed and above the stall speed throughout the descent. The flight data recorder indicated that he was in fact flying slower (and therefore descending faster) than the green dot speed, and below the suggested stall speed at the end. The NTSB understandably attributes this to the "tunnel vision" that accompanies this high-stress situation. But, as

will be a theme throughout this book, this illustrates how decision-makers' self-reports can be misleading.

7. Two common names in the decision-making literature for these decisions are *choice strategies* or *choice heuristics*. I'm not using those terms to avoid confusing the reader. Kahneman and others have made famous a set of judgmental heuristics, but the choice heuristics that I talk about are different in several ways. Most important, they are not automatic processes: once chosen, they usually occur with awareness. People can talk about them, and they can be interrupted. As we will see, the process of choosing a strategy tends to be automatic, what Kahneman calls *System 1 thinking*. For an in-depth dive into choice heuristics, see Johnson and Payne, "Effort and Accuracy in Choice"; Payne, Bettman, and Johnson, *The Adaptive Decision Maker*.

8. Adapted from figures 1 and 2 in Hulgaard et al., "Nudging Passenger Flow in CPH Airports."

9. Hulgaard et al., "Nudging Passenger Flow in CPH Airports."

10. Evidence that people are not calculating interest rates come from studies that supply the interest rate. When supplied with the interest rate, people become more patient. For a discussion, see Read, Frederick, and Scholten, "DRIFT: An Analysis of Outcome Framing in Intertemporal Choice."

11. For more complex decisions, decisions to shift plausible paths are more common and made more frequently. See Shi, Wedel, and Pieters, "Information Acquisition During Online Decision Making: A Model-Based Exploration Using Eye-Tracking Data," for a nice example of using eye tracking.

12. Early on, research on how people selected plausible paths discussed a trade-off between accuracy and effort. More recently, there has been a lot of work in economics suggesting that the decision about expending effort is present-biased: see Augenblick, Niederle, and Sprenger, "Working over Time: Dynamic Inconsistency in Real Effort Tasks"; Augenblick and Rabin, "An Experiment on Time Preference and Misprediction in Unpleasant Tasks." This stands in contrast with other work in economics, usually labeled as *rational inattention*, that assumes that people select strategies consistent with standard economic theory, accounting for the effort involved in making the choice. For example, these models suggest that biases will diminish because people work harder when the stakes are higher.

13. There is a large and somewhat disjointed literature on fluency effects in judgment. Alter and Oppenheimer, "Uniting the Tribes of Fluency to Form a Metacognitive Nation," provides a good review. See also Oppenheimer, "The Secret Life of Fluency." The idea that fluency is

computed quickly and without awareness, and that it includes many features of the object under consideration, is found in Reber, Wurtz, and Zimmermann, "Exploring 'Fringe' Consciousness: The Subjective Experience of Perceptual Fluency and Its Objective Bases"; Wurtz, Reber, and Zimmermann, "The Feeling of Fluent Perception: A Single Experience from Multiple Asynchronous Sources." Its influence in choice is documented in Novemsky, "Preference Fluency in Choice." Marewski and Schooler, "Cognitive Niches: An Ecological Model of Strategy Selection," describes a very similar idea applied to inference. It is part of a larger literature on meta-cognition, or what we think about our thinking. I do not mean to review this extensive literature, and its controversies, but think that the concept is a useful label for the subjective feeling we have about the process of making a choice.

14. Undorf and Zimdahl, "Metamemory and Memory for a Wide Range of Font Sizes: What Is the Contribution of Perceptual Fluency?" is one paper that is relevant. If you think about this, it could happen both because the big words feel easier to read, and because we believe that the big fonts are easier to read (even if we don't feel that). While this is an important theoretical distinction, what is central to our discussion is that it affects how easy we think something is to remember, even when there is no difference.

15. Rosenfeld, Thomas, and Hausen, "Disintermediating Your Friends: How Online Dating in the United States Displaces Other Ways of Meeting."

16. BernieSingles has since become loveawake.com. See Cesar, "Of Love and Money: The Rise of the Online Dating Industry."

17. Etherington, "Daily Dating Site Coffee Meets Bagel Lands $600K from Lightbank, Match.Com Co-Founder."

18. Bruch et al., "Extracting Multistage Screening Rules from Online Dating Activity Data."

3. Assembled Preferences

1. Green, "How Derren Brown Remade Mind Reading for Skeptics."

2. For example, see Levin and Johnson, "Estimating Price-Quality Tradeoffs Using Comparative Judgments."

3. So far, Small World of Words has data for over 12,000 words, representing 3.6 million responses. You can visit the site and see what comes to mind for your favorite words, while also seeing how others have replied. Small World of Words. https:// smallworldofwords.org.

4. Kristensen, "8 E-Commerce A/B Testing Examples You Can Learn From."

5. Of course, Mandel used other products and wallpapers in addition to the couches. See Mandel and Johnson, "When Web Pages Influence Choice: Effects of Visual Primes on Experts and Novices."

6. Scientists were quick to point out that small-scale weather variation in one city for a short period had practically nothing to do with climate change.

7. One reason that this is a causal statement, and not just correlational, is the use of an econometric technique called *instrumental variable regression*. See also Zaval et al., "How Warm Days Increase Belief in Global Warming." The experiments that vary temperature are described in Risen and Critcher, "Visceral Fit: While in a Visceral State, Associated States of the World Seem More Likely." Other studies show the correlational result: Egan and Mullin, "Turning Personal Experience into Political Attitudes: The Effect of Local Weather on Americans' Perceptions about Global Warming"; Hamilton and Stampone, "Blowin' in the Wind: Short-Term Weather and Belief in Anthropogenic Climate Change."

8. Busse et al., "The Psychological Effect of Weather on Car Purchases," conducted the car study. Busse and company have a slightly different explanation, termed *projection bias*. Our story about accessibility is closer to another explanation they consider, *salience*, and as they note, their data cannot distinguish between the two effects.

9. See Conlin, O'Donoghue, and Vogelsang, "Projection Bias in Catalog Orders," for details.

10. There is another surprising way of increasing inhibition and reducing recall in this test: show participants a blank map of the fifty states. Most people, including myself, would have bet this would be a helpful aid. In reality, the blank map reduced the number of states the study participants recalled. If they have to put the states names into the map, people typically "lost" nine states, recalling only thirty-one, instead of the 40 recalled without the map. See Brown, "Reciprocal Facilitation and Impairment of Free Recall" and Karchmer and Winograd, "Effects of Studying a Subset of Familiar Items on Recall of the Remaining Items: The John Brown Effect."

11. Laberee and Bell, eds., *Mr. Franklin: A Selection from His Personal Letters.*

12. We will use query theory later in the book, but if you want to read more, you might want to look at Johnson, Häubl, and Keinan,

"Aspects of Endowment: A Query Theory of Value Construction";
Weber et al., "Asymmetric Discounting in Intertemporal Choice."

13. Payne et al., "Life Expectancy as a Constructed Belief: Evidence of a
Live-to or Die-by Framing Effect." Annuities use the payments of
those who die young to pay for the benefits of those who die old. You
need to be a good actuary to sell annuities.

14. Partners Advantage, "Getting Your Prospect to Think About Longevity, and Longevity Calculators."

4. Goals of Choice Architecture

1. "Apple COVID-19."

2. The success of the COVID-19 tracker is documented in Menni et al.,
"Real-Time Tracking of Self-Reported Symptoms to Predict Potential
COVID-19."

3. This is true whether the decision concerns Social Security retirement
benefits or other similarly structured public benefits or employer program benefits. Other countries' public pension plans (Germany's, for
example) have a similar structure.

4. This discussion is based on Knoll et al., "Time to Retire: Why Americans Claim Benefits Early and How to Encourage Delay"; Muldoon
and Kopcke, "Are People Claiming Social Security Benefits Later?";
Song and Manchester, "Have People Delayed Claiming Retirement
Benefits? Responses to Changes in Social Security Rules."

5. While the treatment in Thaler and Sunstein's book is much more nu-
anced, the common meaning of *nudge* has evolved to mean any ma-
nipulation that changes behavior toward a predefined outcome,
dropping the important caveat that that outcome should be in the
decision-makers' best interests.

6. Other suggestions have been made about how to increase the claiming age for Social Security. For example, we might use the term *full
retirement age* to refer to claiming at seventy instead of the current
age of sixty-six for people retiring now.

7. See the pages "Retirement Benefits" and "How the Retirement Estimator Works." The pages still exist as of March 2021, but a more
fluent set of pages has been added.

8. There is too little research on this important topic, but see Novemsky,
"Preference Fluency in Choice," for more details.

9. MacDonald, "How Long Do Workers Consider Retirement Decision?" See Helman, Copeland, and VanDerhei, "The 2015 Retirement Confidence Survey: Having a Retirement Savings Plan a Key Factor in Americans' Retirement Confidence," for recent facts about time spent and feelings about retirement.

10. In the case of Social Security, there is an additional benefit that most people do not appreciate: it pays out, in principle, for as long as you live. If you have a lump sum saved for retirement—say, the $76,000 that the average American has—you can run out of cash if you live long enough. With Social Security, you do not have that risk. It is known in the industry as an *annuity* or *longevity insurance*: it covers you if you live too long. Clearly that is worth something; we have not included that in our monetary calculations, but it could be done.

    Should you think this changes the idea that most people are making a mistake, there have been studies of people who have annuities *and* claim Social Security early: see Bronshtein et al., "Leaving Big Money on the Table: Arbitrage Opportunities in Delaying Social Security." These researchers find that this costs these households up to $250,000 and that there may be millions of households making this mistake.

11. Much of the history is described in Lichtenstein and Slovic, "The Construction of Preference."

12. Another way of using decision simulators is to measure what the chooser is looking for. In the example of the dating website, we might try to figure out your ideal type. To do this, researchers use techniques that model your preferences. Fortunately, there are ways of measuring these trade-offs, which are often used in developing new products.

    There are two challenges with this approach. First, when preferences are indeed assembled, it is impossible to accurately model them in a way that is stable over time and situations. Second, models end up making assumptions that may not hold. (This is a technical argument that I will not describe in detail here, but you can explore in the referenced paper if interested.) These are described in Meyer and Johnson, "Empirical Generalizations in the Modeling of Consumer Choice."

13. See Mullainathan, Sendhil et al., "The Market for Financial Advice."

5. Decisions by Default

1. Johnson and Goldstein, "Do Defaults Save Lives?"

2. Thaler and Sunstein, *Nudge*.

3. Abadie and Gay, "The Impact of Presumed Consent Legislation on Cadaveric Organ Donation: A Cross-Country Study."

4. Abadie and Gay's study uses a more sophisticated technique and a larger set of countries than in the original Johnson and Goldstein paper. A systematic review was done in Britain just before the British considered changing the policy: see Rithalia et al., "Impact of Presumed Consent for Organ Donation on Donation Rates: A Systematic Review." This report looked at studies that compared countries and those that changed and concluded that defaults increased donations in cases. They repeat the caution that countries that change defaults might also increase publicity and advertising.

   Shepherd, O'Carroll, and Ferguson, "An International Comparison of Deceased and Living Organ Donation/Transplant Rates in Opt-In and Opt-Out Systems: A Panel Study," looks at the joint effect of defaults on deceased and living donation, what economists call *crowding out*: people, knowing the default has changed, might not donate. These researchers find some evidence of this, but the effect is not large enough to overcome the effect of defaults. Bilgel, "The Impact of Presumed Consent Laws and Institutions on Deceased Organ Donation," argues that the effects of defaults depend upon these other factors.

   A challenge in this entire literature is that it's impossible to randomly assign countries to a default. But some advanced econometric techniques try to infer causality using instrumental variable regression and argue that the effect of defaults actually causes the increase in transplants, but this is weaker evidence than a causal demonstration.

5. Steffel, Williams, and Tannenbaum, "Does Changing Defaults Save Lives? Effects of Presumed Consent Organ Donation Policies."

6. The original Singapore law applied only to kidneys available after accidental deaths for non-Muslims. For example, the number of kidney transplants rose from about five per year before the original 1987 law to over forty-nine after the 2004 revision: see Low et al., "Impact of New Legislation on Presumed Consent on Organ Donation on Liver Transplant in Singapore: A Preliminary Analysis." The Chilean experience is documented in Zúñiga-Fajuri, "Increasing Organ Donation by Presumed Consent and Allocation Priority: Chile." The Welsh experience followed a long study by the United Kingdom; see "Wales' Organ Donation Opt-Out Law Has Not Increased Donors." The French set up a National Rejection Registry; see Eleftheriou-Smith, "All French Citizens Are Now Organ Donors Unless They Opt Out." Nova Scotia's change is documented in "Changes to Organ and Tissue Donation."

7. Obviously, the medical infrastructure must be in place. In most places, the family must be consulted, even if the potential donor has actively agreed to donate. The Spanish model is discussed in an

interview in Badcock, "How Spain Became the World Leader in Organ Donations," and in Matesanz, "Factors Influencing the Adaptation of the Spanish Model of Organ Donation." Interestingly, in some hospitals, doctors are paid for high agreement rates. This of course raises ethical issues, which we have written about in Smith, Goldstein, and Johnson, "Choice Without Awareness: Ethical and Policy Implications of Defaults," and in Chapter 10.

8. Fabre, Murphy, and Matesanz, "Presumed Consent: A Distraction in the Quest for Increasing Rates of Organ Donation."

9. Zink and Wertlieb, "A Study of the Presumptive Approach to Consent for Organ Donation."

10. See Glazier and Mone, "Success of Opt-In Organ Donation Policy in the United States."

11. In 2019, surveys showed that 56 percent of Americans support opt-out policies, an increase of 5.2 percent from 2012, although there is concern that web respondents were responsible for the increase. Nonetheless, about 50 percent support the opt-out scheme, with younger people being more likely to support an opt-out policy. About 30 percent of respondents said they would opt out if such a scheme was adopted. See "2019 National Survey of Organ Donation." The impact of such a possible change is discussed in DeRoos et al., "Estimated Association Between Organ Availability and Presumed Consent in Solid Organ Transplant."

12. "Organ Trafficking: The Unseen Form of Human Trafficking"; May, "Transnational Crime and the Developing World."

13. Becker and Elias, "Introducing Incentives in the Market for Live and Cadaveric Organ Donations." This does not have to be an explicitly cash payment. Even in the case of donation after death, the family can be compensated. Economists have suggested, for example, that the family of donors receive payments for funeral expenses.

14. However, simply forcing people to respond is not likely to work. In 2012, New York State adopted Lauren's Law, a form of active choice. People are asked if they want to be a donor or are given the option to skip this question. New York's efforts do not seem to have been effective, with only 28 percent of its citizens willing to be donors, ranking forty-eighth among the fifty states. In contrast, in Montana, 89 percent of adults are registered.

15. Johnson, "Apple, AT&T Shares Fall on Fewer-than-Expected iPhone Subscriptions"; Posner and Snyder, "Attention and Cognitive Control."

16. The video is available at Ezarik, "iPhone Bill," while details of the reaction are documented at Hafner, "AT&T's Overstuffed iPhone

Bills Annoy Customers," which includes the photo of Ezarik's bill. The *Computerworld* article is Haskin, "Technology's 10 Most Mortifying Moments." AT&T's reaction is documented in Perenson, "The 300-Page iPhone Bill to Disappear."

17. Benartzi and Thaler, "Behavioral Economics and the Retirement Savings Crisis."

18. For details see Johnson et al., "Framing, Probability Distortions, and Insurance Decisions."

19. Earlier work had looked at the more general phenomenon called the *status quo bias*, meaning that one option was preselected somehow, including by past decisions of the chooser: Samuelson and Zeckhauser, "Status Quo Bias in Decision Making," is the classic paper.

20. Dinner et al., "Partitioning Default Effects: Why People Choose Not to Choose"; see also McKenzie, Liersch, and Finkelstein, "Recommendations Implicit in Policy Defaults." The railroad example in the following paragraph is from Goldstein et al., "Nudge Your Customers Toward Better Choices."

21. Pichert and Katsikopoulos, "Green Defaults: Information Presentation and Pro-environmental Behaviour"; Ebeling and Lotz, "Domestic Uptake of Green Energy Promoted by Opt-out Tariffs."

22. For a review of subsequent studies, see Kaiser et al., "The Power of Green Defaults: The Impact of Regional Variation of Opt-Out Tariffs on Green Energy Demand in Germany."

23. We checked that ease and endorsement didn't influence the decisions, by asking people whether they thought the contractor wanted them to make one decision or the other, and we checked ease by measuring how long it took them to make a decision. None of this affected their choices.

24. This research is from Dinner et al., "Partitioning Default Effects: Why People Choose Not to Choose."

25. For example, see Sunstein and Reisch, "Automatically Green: Behavioral Economics and Environmental Protection."

26. See Hedlin and Sunstein, "Does Active Choosing Promote Green Energy Use: Experimental Evidence"; Pichert and Katsikopoulos, "Green Defaults: Information Presentation and Pro-environmental Behaviour"; Sunstein and Reisch, "Green by Default," for a discussion and similar results.

27. Kahneman, Knetsch, and Thaler, "Experimental Tests of the Endowment Effect and the Coase Theorem," is the original demonstration

of the endowment effect. Johnson, Häubl, and Keinan, "Aspects of Endowment: A Query Theory of Value Construction," explored the query theory explanation.

28. This differs from the standard forest plot. I turned the plot in ways that I think are good choice architecture: higher here means a more positive effect. Forest plots are normally presented rotated so that effects go from right to left. I also plotted the distribution of the confidence interval, and not simply the 95 percent confidence interval, since that emphasized that the outcomes are likely to be closer to the mean and portrays the variability continuously. In the full analysis, there is one study that has a small significant and negative effect, but the average that I report includes all the studies.

29. Forest plots are not the whole story. We need to worry about two additional things at least. First, how did we select the studies to put in the plot? If we look only at published studies, it is likely that we will not plot studies that did not "work"—that is, have results that are not different from zero. Why? Because of publication bias: researchers submit, and journals accept, mostly those papers that do not fail. Researchers overcome this by searching all the online databases for results and by systematically asking people to share these studies.

   The second caution about forest plots is that they won't necessarily detect which experiments have inflated their results, and/or shrunk their confidence intervals by what is called *p-hacking*—essentially doing many possible analyses and reporting only those that worked best.

   There are plots and analyses that can help detect this called *funnel plots* and *p-curves*.

30. See Jachimowicz et al., "When and Why Defaults Influence Decisions: A Meta-Analysis of Default Effects."

31. For a review of this and related work, see Goldstein et al., "Nudge Your Customers Toward Better Choices." In particular, we discuss at length the conditions that favor the choice of one default over the other.

32. "Characteristics of U.S. Mutual Fund Owners."

33. See Smith, Goldstein, and Johnson, "Choice Without Awareness: Ethical and Policy Implications of Defaults"; Johnson and Goldstein, "Decisions by Default."

34. Peters, "Zoom Adds New Security and Privacy Measures to Prevent Zoombombing"; Garber, "A Company Called Zoom Technologies Is Surging Because People Think It's Zoom Video Communications (ZOOM, ZM)."

35. "Automatic Voter Registration"; Brater, "Automatic Voter Registration in Oregon a Huge Success."

6. How Many Options?

1. Robbins, "Lost in the School Choice Maze."

2. Other examples include the matching of residents to hospitals and kidneys to potential donors.

3. Nathanson, Corcoran, and Baker-Smith, "High School Choice in New York City: A Report on the School Choices and Placements of Low-Achieving Students."

4. "The Tyranny of Choice: You Choose."

5. Scheibehenne, Todd, and Greifeneder, "What Moderates the Too-Much-Choice Effect?"

6. Scheibehenne, Greifeneder, and Todd, "Can There Ever Be Too Many Options? A Meta-Analytic Review of Choice Overload"; Chernev, Böckenholt, and Goodman, "Choice Overload: A Conceptual Review and Meta-Analysis."

7. Schwartz, *The Paradox of Choice: Why More Is Less.*

8. We could also look at the probability of presenting one of the top two, three, four, etc., or the quality of the best options in the set. The math gets much more complicated than this simple example, but the basic point holds: having more options that are considered carefully increases the quality of the best option in the set. We also are assuming that none of the options are dominated or dominant in the sense that we talked about in chapter 4.

9. Bhargava, Loewenstein, and Sydnor, "Choose to Lose: Health Plan Choices from a Menu with Dominated Option."

10. Johnson et al., "Can Consumers Make Affordable Care Affordable? The Value of Choice Architecture." This discussion is based mostly on experiment 6 in this paper.

11. Compared to cases where we did not pay people, having real money on the table made people work about 30 percent longer, but, interestingly, they did not make better decisions.

12. Barnes et al., "Moving Beyond Blind Men and Elephants: Providing Total Estimated Annual Costs Improves Health Insurance Decision Making"; Johnson et al., "Can Consumers Make Affordable Care Affordable? The Value of Choice Architecture."

13. LoGiurato, "Meet the 16-Year-Old Kid Who Got to Introduce President Obama in Brooklyn"; Saddler, "The Day I Introduced Barack Obama"; Zazulia, "Early College High School a Strong Path for IBM's Radcliffe Saddler."

7. Putting Things in Order

1. This discussion and the Wilson quote are from Krosnick, Miller, and Tichy, "An Unrecognized Need for Ballot Reform: Effects of Candidate Name Order."

2. Grant, "The Ballot Order Effect Is Huge: Evidence from Texas."

3. Most studies find support for this notion: see Miller and Krosnick, "The Impact of Candidate Name Order on Election Outcomes"; Koppell and Steen, "The Effects of Ballot Position on Election Outcomes"; Meredith and Salant, "On the Causes and Consequences of Ballot Order Effects"; King and Leigh, "Are Ballot Order Effects Heterogeneous?"; Krosnick, Miller, and Tichy, "An Unrecognized Need for Ballot Reform: The Effects of Candidate Name Order on Election Outcomes." But also see Ho and Imai, "Estimating Causal Effects of Ballot Order from a Randomized Natural Experiment: The California Alphabet Lottery, 1978–2002." Krosnick, Miller, and Tichy, "An Unrecognized Need for Ballot Reform," speculate the reason the effect was so large in 2000 is that people were more ambivalent between the two presidential candidates.

   There is also experimental evidence that demonstrates these effects: see Kim, Krosnick, and Casasanto, "Moderators of Candidate Name-Order Effects in Elections: An Experiment." This is one area that needs a meta-analysis.

   The effects of order permeate even further into politics. Krosnick has found that differences due to order can partially explain why polling and voting results can be different. Pollsters carefully randomize the order of candidates' names when they ask for preferences. See Adams, "How the Pollsters Got It So Wrong in New Hampshire." In 2008, Barack Obama was predicted to win the New Hampshire primary, leading the polls by 3 to 13 percent. Then Hillary Clinton surprised everyone by winning by 3 percent. Krosnick says: "I'll bet that Clinton got at least 3 percent more votes than Obama simply because she was listed close to the top."

4. "Did Trump Win Because His Name Came First in Key States?"; Kam, "No, Donald Trump's Name Will Not Appear Automatically at the Top of Your Ballot"; Saunders, "Court Refuses to Reconsider Ballot Order Ruling."

5. Many papers discuss this effect: see Brownstein, "Biased Predecision Processing"; Carlson, Meloy, and Lieb, "Benefits Leader Reversion: How a Once-Preferred Product Recaptures Its Standing"; Blanchard, Carlson, and Meloy, "Biased Predecisional Processing of Leading and Nonleading Alternatives"; Russo et al., "Choosing an Inferior Alternative"; Simon, Krawczyk, and Holyoak, "Construction of Preferences by Constraint Satisfaction"; Simon and Holyoak, "Structural Dynamics of Cognition: From Consistency Theories to Constraint Satisfaction"; Simon et al., "The Emergence of Coherence over the Course of Decision Making."

6. The original research is by Feenberg et al., "It's Good to Be First: Order Bias in Reading and Citing NBER Working Papers"; see also Irwin, "How Economists Can Be Just as Irrational as the Rest of Us."

7. This work is described in Ursu, "The Power of Rankings: Quantifying the Effect of Rankings on Online Consumer Search and Purchase Decisions."

8. We have just been talking about order effects in choice. For a more ambitious effort to talk about a greater range of order effects, see Bar-Hillel, "Position Effects in Choice from Simultaneous Displays," who developed some of the arguments I use here.

   There is other evidence for recency effects: see Bruine de Bruin and Keren, "Order Effects in Sequentially Judged Options Due to the Direction of Comparison"; Bruine de Bruin, "Save the Last Dance for Me: Unwanted Serial Position Effects in Jury Evaluations"; Bruine de Bruin, "Save the Last Dance II: Unwanted Serial Position Effects in Figure Skating Judgments."

   Finally, we should note that the terms *primacy* and *recency* have their origins in work that seems similar on memory. Here, researchers have studied how well people learn a list of words or digits given to them one at a time and are then asked to recall them. While the terms are similar, the results of that literature are not relevant. These decisions are based on information (and tastes) that are right in front of the decision-maker and are not directly dependent on memory. The work with wine tasting is described in and the figure adapted from Matonakis et al., "Order in Choice Effects of Serial Position on Preferences."

9. Atalay, Bodur, and Rasolofoarison, "Shining in the Center: Central Gaze Cascade Effect on Product Choice." This effect appears to be stronger for vertical than for horizontal displays: see Kim et al., "Position Effects of Menu Item Displays in Consumer Choices: Comparisons of Horizontal Versus Vertical Displays." Strong primacy effects are shown in Nguyen et al., "Examining Ordering Effects in Discrete Choice Experiments: A Case Study in Vietnam"; Raghubir

and Valenzuela, "Center-of-Inattention: Position Biases in Decision-Making." See also Li and Epley, "When the Best Appears to Be Saved for Last: Serial Position Effects on Choice," for effects of primacy.

10. See Drèze, Hoch, and Purk, "Shelf Management and Space Elasticity."

11. To better understand what is salient, the designer can observe eye tracking or employ algorithms that analyze a digital version of an image. See Bartels, "How Eye Tracking Can Unlock Consumer Insights"; Chandon, Hutchinson, and Bradlow, "Does In-Store Marketing Work? Effects of the Number and Position of Shelf Facings on Brand Attention and Evaluation at the Point of Purchase."

12. Lynch and Ariely, "Wine Online: Search Costs Affect Competition on Price, Quality, and Distribution"; Diehl, "When Two Rights Make a Wrong: Searching Too Much in Ordered Environments"; Diehl, Kornish, and Lynch, "Smart Agents: When Lower Search Costs for Quality Information Increase Price Sensitivity."

13. Details are in Glazerman, "The Choice Architecture of School Choice Websites."

14. Steve Miller, who teaches a menu-design seminar and is president of the Miller Resource Group, in Grafton, Massachusetts, quoted in Panitz, "Does Your Menu Attract or Repel Diners?"

15. From Reynolds, Merritt, and Pinckney, "Understanding Menu Psychology." Another, more contemporary example is "Meet the 'Menu Engineers' Who Optimize Restaurant Revenue."

Menu designer William Doerfler identified power position as an optimum position in the November 1978 issue of *Cornell Hotel and Restaurant Administration Quarterly*. For years, menu designers have operated on the premise that menu layout affects sales directly. The supporting research in this area has, however, been sparse. To evaluate this relationship empirically, an experiment was conducted in an independent, casual-dining restaurant located at a large, northeastern university. The first treatment integrated manipulations of price location on menus but did not result in significantly different average-check totals. The second tested the effects of displaying specific items more prominently on the menu. Again, contrary to the hypothesis, this failed to affect the probability that guests would purchase either of the selected items. See Doerfler, "Menu Design for Effective Merchandising."

16. Kincaid and Corsun, "Are Consultants Blowing Smoke? An Empirical Test of the Impact of Menu Layout on Item Sales." One retracted paper is Wansink and Love, "Slim by Design: Menu Strategies for Promoting High-Margin, Healthy Foods."

17. Both figures are from Yang, "Eye Movements on Restaurant Menus: A Revisitation on Gaze Motion and Consumer Scanpaths."

18. Dayan and Bar-Hillel, "Nudge to Nobesity II: Menu Positions Influence Food Orders—ProQuest." But remember that these effects depend on the way people allocate attention. A menu is not like a salad bar. Making things hard to reach will also make them less popular. Rozin and colleagues show that changing the "accessibility" of different foods in a pay-by-weight-of-food salad bar in a cafeteria serving adults for the lunch period changes the choice of foods. Making a food slightly more difficult to reach (by varying its proximity by about 10 inches) or changing the serving utensil (spoon or tongs) modestly but reliably reduces intake, in the range of 8 to 16 percent: see Rozin, Dingley, and Urbanek, "Nudge to Nobesity I: Minor Changes in Accessibility Decrease Food Intake." See Cadario and Chandon, "Which Healthy Eating Nudges Work Best? A Meta-Analysis of Behavioral Interventions in Field Experiments," for a recent review of how nudges affect eating.

8. Describing Options

1. For information on hypermiling, see Gaffney, "This Guy Can Get 59 MPG in a Plain Old Accord. Beat That, Punk"; Moskowitz, "Hypermiling: Driving Tricks Stretch Miles Per Gallon." The mileage for Cardona's Honda is from U.S. Department of Energy, "Gas Mileage of 2008 Honda Civic." Research is described in, and figure based on, Larrick and Soll, "The MPG Illusion."

2. Adapted from https://www.epa.gov/sites/production/files/styles/large/public/2016-08/label_pre2008_650_0.gif

3. This is demonstrated in Ungemach et al., "Translated Attributes: Aligning Consumers' Choices and Goals Through Signposts."

4. This example comes from Hardisty, Johnson, and Weber, "A Dirty Word or a Dirty World?," study 2. These differences are usually described as loss aversion, the observation that people dislike losses more than equivalent gains. However, loss aversion is more of a label for the observation than an explanation. Query theory adds to the traditional explanation of loss aversion by involving memory retrieval as an essential process: see Wall et al., "Risky Choice Frames Shift the Structure and Emotional Valence of Internal Arguments: A Query Theory Account of the Unusual Disease Problem."

5. The figure and results are from Dowray et al., "Potential Effect of Physical Activity Based Menu Labels on the Calorie Content of Selected Fast Food Meals." I first became aware of this stream of

research from an entry in *Decision Science News*. See Antonelli and Viera, "Potential Effect of Physical Activity Calorie Equivalent (PACE) Labeling on Adult Fast Food Ordering and Exercise"; Deery et al., "Physical Activity Calorie Expenditure (PACE) Labels in Worksite Cafeterias: Effects on Physical Activity"; Long et al., "Systematic Review and Meta-Analysis of the Impact of Restaurant Menu Calorie Labeling."

6. Many utility bills (like cable, internet, electricity, and phone) do the opposite, providing many attributes for a single goal: the chooser cares about the eventual total price of a month of service, but along with that price there are many components, like franchise fees for cable TV or required maintenance fees. Since they don't serve a different goal, the chooser would rather just see the total price. The provider may have the reasonable goal of communicating the size of such fees, but adding them makes the total less obvious, and unless the chooser realizes that all these fees are identical, the listed fees discourage the chooser from comparing. See Thaler and Johnson, "Gambling with the House Money and Trying to Break Even—The Effects of Prior Outcomes on Risky Choice"; Read, Loewenstein, and Rabin, "Choice Bracketing"; Gabaix and Laibson, "Shrouded Attributes, Consumer Myopia, and Information Suppression in Competitive Markets"; Morwitz, Greenleaf, and Johnson, "Divide and Prosper: Consumers' Reactions to Partitioned Prices"; Greenleaf et al., "The Price Does Not Include Additional Taxes, Fees, and Surcharges: A Review of Research on Partitioned Pricing."

7. See O'Donovan, "An Invisible Rating System at Your Favorite Chain Restaurant Is Costing Your Server"; DeShong, "Do Drivers Think You're a 'Ridezilla'? Better Check Your Uber Rating"; Shaban, "Uber Will Ban Passengers with Low Ratings"; Cook, "Uber's Internal Charts Show How Its Driver-Rating System Actually Works."

8. The actual way of calculating this is given by the formula (log(2)/log(1 +(interest rate)/100), which I am sure you can do in your head. But there is a trick that gets you very close, called *the rule of 72*. To find out how long it takes to double an amount at interest rate *r*, 10 percent in the example, simply divide 72 by *r*. So 72/10 in our example means that the money doubles in 7.2 years. In 7.2 years, you will have $20,000. That means that in forty-five years, the money will double 6.2 times, or total $760,000, a close approximation. When I give this item to my MBA students, about 10 percent who get it right use this rule of 72.

9. This is a well-explored area, but it does not mean that people have changed how borrowing costs are presented. One of the first experimental papers, Einsenstien and Hoch, "Intuitive Compounding:

Framing, Temporal Perspective, and Expertise," was followed by an analysis of governmental survey data (the Survey of Consumer Finances), Stango and Zinman, "Exponential Growth Bias and Household Finance," that has a representative sample *and* a picture of the demographic and financial "balance sheet" of the household. It provides a nice history of this topic as well. The inability to understand interest rates matters. All these relationships are correlational, but worrisome. Households that make bigger mistakes tend to hold fewer stocks (which means less growth of their assets, according to economic theory in the long term) and have more short-term debt. The bias is also larger for African Americans and women, even when controlling for obvious things like education and current wealth.

Other relevant papers include Soll, Keeney, and Larrick, "Consumer Misunderstanding of Credit Card Use, Payments, and Debt: Causes and Solutions"; Song, "Financial Illiteracy and Pension Contributions: A Field Experiment on Compound Interest in China"; McKenzie and Liersch, "Misunderstanding Savings Growth: Implications for Retirement Savings Behavior."

10. Description of Kipchoge's achievement is from Keh, "Eliud Kipchoge Breaks Two-Hour Marathon Barrier"; Pope and Simonsohn, "Round Numbers as Goals"; Heath, Larrick, and Wu, "Goals as Reference Points." Figure and marathon results are from Allen et al., "Reference-Dependent Preferences: Evidence from Marathon Runners."

11. "Envision Version 2.0: A Rating System for Sustainable Infrastructure"; Shealy et al., "Using Framing Effects to Inform More Sustainable Infrastructure Design Decisions."

12. Beko, "Freestanding 7kg Condenser Tumble Dryer DCX71100." The picture describes a Freestanding 7kg Condenser Tumble Dryer DCX71100.

13. Musicus et al., "Online Randomized Controlled Trials of Restaurant Sodium Warning Labels."

14. See Reyes et al., "Development of the Chilean Front-of-Package Food Warning Label" and Taillie et al., "An Evaluation of Chile's Law of Food Labeling and Advertising on Sugar-Sweetened Beverage Purchases from 2015 to 2017."

15. "President Trump's Energy Independence Policy." For a discussion, see Peters et al., "Numeracy and Decision Making," and Johnson et al., "Beyond Nudges: Tools of a Choice Architecture." See also Peters, *Innumeracy in the Wild: Misunderstanding and Misusing Numbers.*

9. Building Choice Engines

1. Hardwick, "Top 100 Most Visited Websites by Search Traffic (as of 2020)."

2. Carr, "Giving Viewers What They Want."

3. McAlone, "The Exec Who Replaced Netflix's 5-Star Rating System with 'Thumbs Up, Thumbs Down' Explains Why."

4. Ciancutti, "Does Netflix Add Content Based on Your Searches?"; Netflix, "Netflix Quick Guide: How Does Netflix Decide What's on Netflix."

5. Gomez-Uribe and Hunt, "The Netflix Recommender System"; Carr, "Giving Viewers What They Want."

6. You do need, for example, large databases of user behavior for collaborative filtering, as well as a large database describing the characteristics of the options for content-based filters. A new enterprise may have one of these databases, but not the other; nevertheless, it can develop new kinds of data as the business grows.

7. Giovanelli and Curran, "Efforts to Support Consumer Enrollment Decisions Using Total Cost Estimators: Lessons from the Affordable Care Act's Marketplaces"; Barnes et al., "Moving Beyond Blind Men and Elephants: Providing Total Estimated Annual Costs Improves Health Insurance Decision Making."

8. "Picwell." Full disclosure: I currently have no affiliation with Picwell but was an adviser when it was founded. I have no financial interest in the company.

9. Chien and Morris, "Household Participation in Stock Market Varies Widely by State," and many others document the difference in returns and the lack of participation. It seems to vary systematically. In addition to the effects of wealth, people with fewer social connections invest less in stocks, and some states are systematically worse than others, even when controlling for factors like income and wealth. Nevadans, for example, are much less likely to hold stocks than people in Vermont.

10. These webpages were edited on June 17 and June 30, 2020, according to the site and retrieved on September 12, 2020. The dates are important. In the aftermath of the suicide of Kearns, and the controversy surrounding the events of early 2021, the webpages were radically changed to be more complete and complex.

11. The mechanics of how the trades are made is very complex. The market maker may sell the stock for a slightly higher price, say $100.01 and buy at a slightly lower price, say $99.99. Here the spread is $.02. It seems like small potatoes, but over 200 million shares may change hands over a day and if the spread was $.02, the market makers could receive $4 million that day alone. That money is split among the maker, the retailer (like Robinhood), and the customer. What this means to customers is complex, but what is clear is that this arrangement means that Robinhood (and potentially other commission-free brokers) makes more money if you trade more, and even more if you trade options.

    Not everyone takes a payment for order flow. Fidelity Investments passes all its share of the spread to its customers, and in the United Kingdom, payments for order flow are banned by the Financial Conduct Authority.

12. Popper and Merced, "Robinhood Pays $65 Million Fine to Settle Charges of Misleading Customers."

13. You need to be certified by Robinhood, like in many financial services firms, to trade some kinds of options, but simply stating you have experience in trading options is often enough to get certified, and approval can happen in as little as ten minutes.

14. Holladay, "Alexander Kearns Remembered by UNL Community as Positive, Always Willing to Help."

15. Alexander Kearns took his own life on June 12, 2020. Robinhood executives explained that they were personally distraught by the death, made a $250,000 contribution to a suicide prevention fund, and said they were "considering additional criteria and education for users seeking level 3 options authorization to help ensure customers understand more sophisticated options trading." They also said they would improve education, expand their educational content related to options, and are "working on changes to the user interface."

16. This has been well reported in Popper, "Robinhood Has Lured Young Traders, Sometimes with Devastating Results." See also Barber et al., "The Cross-Section of Speculator Skill: Evidence from Day Trading"; Choy, "Retail Clientele and Option Returns," for studies linking trading and outcomes. The effect of top movers is documented in Barber et al., "Attention Induced Trading and Returns: Evidence from Robinhood Users."

17. Adapted from "2016 Election Forecast."

18. Same data as in the previous figure replotted as a dot density plot, a form adopted by FiveThirtyEight.com for the 2020 election.

19. Graph adapted from simulated outcomes for 2016 using graphs in "President—Forecasting the US 2020 Elections."

20. I was lucky enough to be involved in one aspect of this work. In Goldstein, Johnson, and Sharpe, "Distribution Builder: A Tool for Measuring Preferences for Investment Risk," we showed that the estimates of risk generated from this technique are reliable and did a better job of predicting people's stock holdings.

    Perhaps the most important part of Goldstein and Sharpe's idea was that people could build distributions of outcomes as a way of expressing their preferences for risk. I focus here on the second phase: experiencing the outcomes. See also Hofman, Goldstein, and Hullman, "How Visualizing Inferential Uncertainty Can Mislead Readers about Treatment Effects in Scientific Results"; Kaufmann, Weber, and Haisley, "The Role of Experience Sampling and Graphical Displays on One's Investment Risk Appetite"; Goldstein and Rothschild, "Lay Understanding of Probability Distributions"; Sharpe, Goldstein, and Blythe, "The Distribution Builder: A Tool for Inferring Investor Preferences," for other tests and applications.

21. See Hofman, Goldstein, and Hullman, "How Visualizing Inferential Uncertainty Can Mislead Readers about Treatment Effects in Scientific Results"; Kaufmann, Weber, and Haisley, "The Role of Experience Sampling and Graphical Displays on One's Investment Risk Appetite"; Hullman, Resnick, and Adar, "Hypothetical Outcome Plots Outperform Error Bars and Violin Plots for Inferences about Reliability of Variable Ordering."

22. Ruginski et al., "Non-expert Interpretations of Hurricane Forecast Uncertainty Visualizations"; Meyer et al., "Dynamic Simulation as an Approach to Understanding Hurricane Risk Response: Insights from the Stormview Lab"; Meyer et al., "The Dynamics of Hurricane Risk Perception: Real-Time Evidence from the 2012 Atlantic Hurricane Season." The spaghetti plot is adapted from https://www.weather nerds.org/tc_guidance/images/AL19_2020091318_ECENS_0-120h _large.png available from Weathernerds.org.

10. Becoming Better Choice Architects

1. Rogers, "How a Publicity Blitz Caused the Myth of Subliminal Advertising"; Salsa, "Subliminal Advertising Doesn't Exist"; Smith, Goldstein, and Johnson, "Choice Without Awareness: Ethical and Policy Implications of Defaults."

2. Nichols, "Experimental Philosophy and the Problem of Free Will"; Nichols and Knobe, "Moral Responsibility and Determinism: The Cognitive Science of Folk Intuitions."

3. You can see the primed video and the one without the prime in the supplementary materials of Pailhès and Kuhn, "Influencing Choices with Conversational Primes: How a Magic Trick Unconsciously Influences Card Choices." These are Pailhès, "Mental Priming Force."

4. There is no formal meta-analysis yet, but there are many studies consistent with this idea.

5. Dhingra et al., "The Default Pull: An Experimental Demonstration of Subtle Default Effects on Preferences." For an introduction to using games to study preferences, see Henrich et al., *Foundations of Human Sociality: Economic Experiments and Ethnographic Evidence from Fifteen Small-Scale Societies.* In the Penn study, respondents made four divisions. I am talking about the effect of the first default, but the rest of the trials showed similar effects.

6. Bang, Shu, and Weber, "The Role of Perceived Effectiveness on the Acceptability of Choice Architecture." These researchers actually had people experience the effects. For example, people rated the ground beef twice, once seeing it described as a percent of fat and again as a percent of lean. Even when they saw both labels and saw that the effect occurred for themselves, they thought that others would be more affected.

7. Bruns et al., "Can Nudges Be Transparent and Yet Effective?" See also Loewenstein et al., "Warning: You Are about to Be Nudged." The House of Lords report is "Behavior Change (Second Report)."

8. Not everyone is unaware. I went to Derren Brown's most recent show on Broadway with Elke Weber, and two friends who are very sophisticated about magic, Barbara Mellers and Phil Tetlock. Barbara is a magician herself and a member of the Brotherhood of Magicians. She knows how magic is done. Elke and I were spellbound by Brown, and we had at best a glimmer of how the trick is done. Phil and Barbara were less impressed, since they knew how the magic happened. It is no wonder that the Brotherhood of Magicians has a strict nonsharing code.

9. Reisch and Sunstein, "Do Europeans Like Nudges?"; Sunstein et al., "A World-Wide Consensus on Nudging? Not Quite, but Almost."

10. The experiments were done by a group at Stanford and Hong Kong: see Zlatev et al., "Default Neglect in Attempts at Social Influence." Additional work, using other contexts, did not show total default neglect; about 69 percent of respondents chose the default: Jung, Sun, and Nelson, "People Can Recognize, Learn, and Apply Default Effects in Social Influence." See also McKenzie, Leong, and Sher, "Default Sensitivity in Attempts at Social Influence."

For other examples of default neglect, see Robinson et al., "Some Middle School Students Want Behavior Commitment Devices (but Take-Up Does Not Affect Their Behavior)"; Bergman, Lasky-Fink, and Rogers, "Simplification and Defaults Affect Adoption and Impact of Technology, but Decision Makers Do Not Realize It."

11. This result is described in Brown, Kapteyn, and Mitchell, "Framing Effects and Social Security Claiming Behavior."

12. The original study is Halpern et al., "Default Options in Advance Directives Influence How Patients Set Goals for End-Of-Life Care." The result was largely replicated in Halpern et al., "Effect of Default Options in Advance Directives on Hospital-Free Days and Care Choices among Seriously Ill Patients." Yadav et al., "Approximately One in Three U.S. Adults Completes Any Type of Advance Directive for End-Of-Life Care," is the source of statistics about the frequency of advance directives. Evidence for the desire for comfort care comes from Fried et al., "Understanding the Treatment Preferences of Seriously Ill Patients."

13. Mathur et al., "Dark Patterns at Scale: Findings from a Crawl of 11K Shopping Websites"; Valentino-DeVries, "How E-Commerce Sites Manipulate You into Buying Things You May Not Want"; Brignull, "Dark Patterns: Inside the Interfaces Designed to Trick You."

14. Obar and Oeldorf-Hirsch, "The Biggest Lie on the Internet: Ignoring the Privacy Policies and Terms of Service Policies of Social Networking Services."

15. Empson, "Practice Fusion Continues to Reach beyond Digital Health Records, Adds Free Expense Tracking to New Booking Engine"; United States of America v. Practice Fusion, Inc.

16. United States of America v. Practice Fusion, Inc; U.S. Department of Health and Human Services, Centers for Disease Control and Prevention, "Checklist for Prescribing Opioids for Chronic Pain"; Court, "Health-Records Company Pushed Opioids to Doctors in Secret Deal with Drugmaker"; Lopez, "Purdue Pharma Pleads Guilty to Criminal Charges in $8 Billion Settlement with the Justice Department"; Empson, "Practice Fusion Continues to Reach beyond Digital Health Records, Adds Free Expense Tracking to New Booking Engine"; Farzan, "A Tech Company Gave Doctors Free Software—Rigged to Encourage Them to Prescribe Opioids, Prosecutors Say."

17. Santistevan et al., "By Default: The Effect of Prepopulated Prescription Quantities on Opioid Prescribing in the Emergency Department"; Delgado et al., "Association Between Electronic Medical Record Implementation of Default Opioid Prescription Quantities and Prescribing Behavior in Two Emergency Departments"; Crothers

et al., "Evaluating the Impact of Auto-Calculation Settings on Opioid Prescribing at an Academic Medical Center"; Jena, Barnett, and Goldman, "How Health Care Providers Can Help End the Overprescription of Opioids"; Zwank et al., "Removing Default Dispense Quantity from Opioid Prescriptions in the Electronic Medical Record."

18. Data about financial literacy is from Fernandes, Lynch, and Netemeyer, "Financial Literacy, Financial Education, and Downstream Financial Behaviors." The results from Mrkva and others is in Mrkva et al., "Do Nudges Reduce Disparities? Choice Architecture Compensates for Low Consumer Knowledge."

19. As Pailhès and Kuhn say, "First, participants' feeling of freedom is one of the key elements of a successful forcing technique. If the magician manages to force a card but this person feels constrain[ed] and not free for their choice, the trick does no longer work": see "Influencing Choices with Conversational Primes: How a Magic Trick Unconsciously Influences Card Choices."

20. Weber et al., "Asymmetric Discounting in Intertemporal Choice"; Dinner et al., "Partitioning Default Effects: Why People Choose Not to Choose."

Bibliography

Abadie, Alberto, and Sebastien Gay. "The Impact of Presumed Consent Legislation on Cadaveric Organ Donation: A Cross-Country Study." *Journal of Health Economics* 25, no. 4 (July 2006): 599–620. doi:10.1016/j.jhealeco.2006.01.003.

Adams, Richard. "How the Pollsters Got It So Wrong in New Hampshire." *Guardian*, January 9, 2008. https://www.theguardian.com/world/2008/jan/10/uselections2008.richardadams.

Allen, Eric J, Patricia M. Dechow, Devin G. Pope, and George Wu. "Reference-Dependent Preferences: Evidence from Marathon Runners." *Management Science* 63, no. 6 (2016): 1657–72. doi:10.1287/mnsc.2015.2417.

Alter, Adam L., and Daniel M. Oppenheimer. "Uniting the Tribes of Fluency to Form a Metacognitive Nation." *Personality and Social Psychology Review* 13, no. 3 (July 28, 2009): 219–35. doi:10.1177/1088868309341564.

Antonelli, Ray, and Anthony J. Viera. "Potential Effect of Physical Activity Calorie Equivalent (PACE) Labeling on Adult Fast Food Ordering and Exercise." *PloS One* 10, no. 7 (July 29, 2015): e0134289. doi:10.1371/journal.pone.0134289.

"Apple COVID-19." App Annie. Accessed April 3, 2020. https://www.appannie.com/apps/ios/app/1504132184/ratings/?countries=US.

Atalay, A. Selin, H. Onur Bodur, and Dina Rasolofoarison. "Shining in the Center: Central Gaze Cascade Effect on Product Choice." *Journal of Consumer Research* 39, no. 4 (June 3, 2012): 848–66. doi:10.1086/665984.

Augenblick, Ned, Muriel Niederle, and Charles Sprenger. "Working over Time: Dynamic Inconsistency in Real Effort Tasks." *Quarterly Journal of Economics* 130, no. 3 (May 6, 2015): 1067–1115. doi:10.1093 /qje/qjv020/-/dc1.

Augenblick, Ned, and Matthew Rabin. "An Experiment on Time Preference and Misprediction in Unpleasant Tasks." *Review of Economic Studies* 86, no. 3 (May 14, 2018): 941–75. doi:10.1093/restud/rdy019.

"Automatic Voter Registration." Ballotpedia, December 23, 2020. https:// ballotpedia.org/Automatic_voter_registration.

Auxier, Brooke, Lee Rainie, Monica Anderson, Andrew Perrin, Madhu Kumar, and Erica Turner. "2. Americans Concerned, Feel Lack of Control over Personal Data Collected by Both Companies and the Government." Pew Research Center, November 15, 2019. https:// www.pewresearch.org/internet/2019/11/15/americans-concerned-feel -lack-of-control-over-personal-data-collected-by-both-companies-and -the-government/.

Badcock, James. "How Spain Became the World Leader in Organ Donations." *Newsweek*, February 11, 2015. https://www.newsweek.com /2015/02/20/spain-has-become-world-leader-organ-donations -305841.html.

Bang, H. Min, Suzanne B. Shu, and Elke U. Weber. "The Role of Perceived Effectiveness on the Acceptability of Choice Architecture." *Behavioural Public Policy* 4, no. 1 (2020): 50–70. doi:10.1017/bpp.2018.1.

Barber, Brad M., Xing Huang, Terrance Odean, and Christopher Schwarz. 2020. "Attention Induced Trading and Returns: Evidence from Robinhood Users." SSRN Electronic Journal. https://papers.ssrn.com /sol3/papers.cfm?abstract_id=3715077.

Barber, Brad M., Yi-Tsung Lee, Yu-Jane Liu, and Terrance Odean. "The Cross-Section of Speculator Skill: Evidence from Day Trading." *Journal of Financial Markets* 18 (2014): 1–24. doi:10.1016/j.finmar.2013 .05.006.

Bar-Hillel, Maya. "Position Effects in Choice from Simultaneous Displays." *Perspectives on Psychological Science* 10, no. 4 (July 14, 2015): 419–33. doi:10.1177/1745691615588092.

Barnes, Andrew J., Yaniv Hanoch, Thomas Rice, and Sharon K. Long. "Moving Beyond Blind Men and Elephants: Providing Total Estimated Annual Costs Improves Health Insurance Decision Making." *Medical Care Research and Review* 74, no. 5 (July 8, 2016): 625–35. doi:10.1177/1077558716669210.

Bartels, Mike. "How Eye Tracking Can Unlock Consumer Insights." *Progressive Grocer*, December 6, 2018. https://progressivegrocer.com/how -eye-tracking-can-unlock-consumer-insights.

Becker, Gary S., and Julio Jorge Elias. "Introducing Incentives in the Market for Live and Cadaveric Organ Donations." *Journal of Economic Perspectives* 21 (2007): 3–24.

Beko. "Freestanding 7kg Condenser Tumble Dryer DCX71100." 2020. https://www.beko.co.uk/7kg-condenser-tumble-dryer-dcx71100 -silver-white.

Benartzi, Slomo, and Richard H. Thaler. "Behavioral Economics and the Retirement Savings Crisis." *Science* 339, no. 6124 (March 7, 2013): 1152–53. doi:10.1126/science.1231320.

Bergman, Peter, Jessica Lasky-Fink, and Todd Rogers. "Simplification and Defaults Affect Adoption and Impact of Technology, but Decision Makers Do Not Realize It." *Organizational Behavior and Human Decision Processes* 158 (May 1, 2020): 66–79. doi:10.1016/j.obhdp .2019.04.001.

Bhargava, Saurabh, George Loewenstein, and Justin Sydnor. "Choose to Lose: Health Plan Choices from a Menu with Dominated Option." *Quarterly Journal of Economics* 132, no. 3 (2017): 1319–72. doi: https://doi.org/10.1093/qje/qjx011.

Bilgel, Fırat. "The Impact of Presumed Consent Laws and Institutions on Deceased Organ Donation." *European Journal of Health Economics* 13, no. 1 (September 17, 2010): 29–38. doi:10.1007/s10198-010-0277-8.

Blanchard, Simon J., Kurt A. Carlson, and Margaret G. Meloy. "Biased Predecisional Processing of Leading and Nonleading Alternatives." *Psychological Science* 25, no. 3 (February 8, 2014): 812–16. doi:10 .1177/0956797613512663.

"Bomb Damage." UK Parliament. Accessed December 30, 2020. https:// www.parliament.uk/about/living-heritage/building/palace/architec ture/palacestructure/bomb-damage.

Brater, Jonathan. "Automatic Voter Registration in Oregon a Huge Success." Brennan Center for Justice, April 8, 2016. https://www.bren nancenter.org/our-work/analysis-opinion/automatic-voter-registration -oregon-huge-success.

Brignull, Harry. "Dark Patterns: Inside the Interfaces Designed to Trick You." *Verge*, August 29, 2013. https://www.theverge.com/2013/8/29 /4640308/dark-patterns-inside-the-interfaces-designed-to-trick -you.

Bronshtein, Gila, Jason Scott, John B. Shoven, and Sita N. Slavov. "Leaving Big Money on the Table: Arbitrage Opportunities in Delaying Social Security." *Quarterly Review of Economics and Finance* 78 (March 25, 2020): 261–72. doi:https://doi.org/10.1016/j.qref.2020 .03.006.

Brown, Jeffrey R., Arie Kapteyn, and Olivia S. Mitchell. "Framing Effects and Social Security Claiming Behavior." National Bureau of Economic Research, 2011. doi:10.3386/w17018.

Brown, John. "Reciprocal Facilitation and Impairment of Free Recall." *Psychonomic Science* 10, no. 2 (1968): 41–42. doi:10.3758/bf03331397.

Brownstein, Aaron L. "Biased Predecision Processing." *Psychological Bulletin* 129, no. 4 (July 2003): 545–68. doi:10.1037/0033-2909 .129.4.545.

Bruch, Elizabeth, Fred Feinberg, and Kee Yeun Lee. "Extracting Multistage Screening Rules from Online Dating Activity Data." *Proceedings of the National Academy of Sciences* 113, no. 38 (2016): 10530–35. doi:10.1073/pnas.1522494113.

Bruine de Bruin, Wändi. "Save the Last Dance for Me: Unwanted Serial Position Effects in Jury Evaluations." *Acta Psychologica* 118 (2005): 245–60. doi:10.1016/j.actpsy.2004.08.005.

———. "Save the Last Dance II: Unwanted Serial Position Effects in Figure Skating Judgments." *Acta Psychologica* 123, no. 3 (January 25, 2006): 299–311. doi:10.1016/j.actpsy.2006.01.009.

Bruine de Bruin, Wändi, and Gideon Keren. "Order Effects in Sequentially Judged Options Due to the Direction of Comparison." *Organizational Behavior and Human Decision Processes* 92, no. 1–2 (September 2003): 91–101. doi:10.1016/s0749-5978(03)00080-3.

Bruns, Hendrik, Elena Kantorowicz-Reznichenko, Katharina Klement, Marijane Luistro Jonsson, and Bilel Rahali. "Can Nudges Be Transparent and Yet Effective?" *Journal of Economic Psychology* 65 (April 2, 2018): 41–59. doi:10.1016/j.joep.2018.02.002.

Busse, Meghan R., Devin G. Pope, Jaren C. Pope, and Jorge Silva-Risso. "The Psychological Effect of Weather on Car Purchases." *Quarterly Journal of Economics* 130, no. 1 (February 26, 2015): 371–414. doi:10.1093/qje/qju033.

Cadario, Romain, and Pierre Chandon. "Which Healthy Eating Nudges Work Best? A Meta-Analysis of Behavioral Interventions in Field Experiments." *Marketing Science* 39, no. 3 (2020): 465–86. doi:10.1287/ mksc.2018.1128.

Carlson, Kurt A., Margaret G. Meloy, and Daniel Lieb. "Benefits Leader Reversion: How a Once-Preferred Product Recaptures Its Standing." *Journal of Marketing Research* 46, no. 6 (May 14, 2013): 788–97. doi:10.1509/jmkr.46.6.788.

Carr, David. "Giving Viewers What They Want." *New York Times*, February 24, 2013. https://www.nytimes.com/2013/02/25/business/me dia/for-house-of-cards-using-big-data-to-guarantee-its-popularity .html.

Cesar, Mary-Lynn. "Of Love and Money: The Rise of the Online Dating Industry." Nasdaq, February 13, 2016. https://www.nasdaq.com/articles/love-and-money-rise-online-dating-industry-2016-02-13.

Chandon, Pierre, J. Wesley Hutchinson, Eric T. Bradlow, and Scott H. Young. "Does In-Store Marketing Work? Effects of the Number and Position of Shelf Facings on Brand Attention and Evaluation at the Point of Purchase." *Journal of Marketing* 73, no. 6 (2009): 1–17. doi:10.1509/jmkg.73.6.1.

"Changes to Organ and Tissue Donation." Province of Nova Scotia. Accessed December 30, 2020. https://novascotia.ca/organ-and-tissue-donation-changes/.

"Characteristics of U.S. Mutual Fund Owners." Investment Company Fact Book: A Review of Trends and Activities in the Investment Company Industry. Investment Company Institute, 2020. https://www.icifactbook.org/ch7/20_fb_ch7.

Chernev, Alexander, Ulf Böckenholt, and Joseph Goodman. "Choice Overload: A Conceptual Review and Meta-Analysis." *Journal of Consumer Psychology* 25, no. 2 (April 1, 2015): 333–58. doi:10.1016/j.jcps.2014.08.002.

Chien, YiLi, and Paul Morris. "Household Participation in Stock Market Varies Widely by State." *Regional Economist*, 2017. https://www.stlouisfed.org/~/media/publications/regional-economist/2017/third_quarter_2017/stock_market.pdf.

Choy, Siu-Kai. "Retail Clientele and Option Returns." *Journal of Banking and Finance* 51 (2015): 26–42. doi:10.1016/j.jbankfin.2014.11.004.

"Churchill and Commons Chamber." UK Parliament. Accessed December 30, 2020. https://www.parliament.uk/about/living-heritage/building/palace/architecture/palacestructure/churchill/.

Ciancutti, John. "Does Netflix Add Content Based on Your Searches?" Quora, March 14, 2012. https://www.quora.com/Netflix-product/Does-Netflix-add-content-based-on-your-searches/answer/John-Ciancutti.

Conlin, Michael, Ted O'Donoghue, and Timothy J. Vogelsang. "Projection Bias in Catalog Orders." *American Economic Review* 97, no. 4 (September 1, 2007): 1217–49. doi:10.1257/aer.97.4.1217.

Cook, James. "Uber's Internal Charts Show How Its Driver-Rating System Actually Works." *Business Insider*, February 11, 2015. https://www.businessinsider.com/leaked-charts-show-how-ubers-driver-rating-system-works-2015-2?op=1.

Court, Emma. "Health-Records Company Pushed Opioids to Doctors in Secret Deal with Drugmaker." Bloomberg, January 29, 2020. https://www.bloomberg.com/news/articles/2020-01-29/health-records-company-pushed-opioids-to-doctors-in-secret-deal.

Croft, John. "Connectivity, Human Factors Drive Next-Gen Cockpit." *Aviation Week Network*, April 22, 2013. https://aviationweek.com/connectivity-human-factors-drive-next-gen-cockpit.

Crothers, Garrett, David A. Edwards, Jesse M. Ehrenfeld, Edward Woo, Lauren McCluggage, and Bob Lobo. "Evaluating the Impact of Auto-Calculation Settings on Opioid Prescribing at an Academic Medical Center." *Joint Commission Journal on Quality and Patient Safety* 45, no. 6 (March 2019): 416–22. doi:10.1016/j.jcjq.2019.02.010.

Dayan, Eran, and Maya Bar-Hillel. "Nudge to Nobesity II: Menu Positions Influence Food Orders—ProQuest." *Judgment and Decision Making* 6, no. 4 (June 2011): 333–42.

Deery, Christopher B., Derek Hales, Laura Viera, Feng-Chang Lin, Zhao-pei Liu, Emily Olsson, Julie Gras-Najjar et al. "Physical Activity Calorie Expenditure (PACE) Labels in Worksite Cafeterias: Effects on Physical Activity." *BMC Public Health* 19, no. 1 (November 29, 2019). doi:10.1186/s12889-019-7960-1.

Delgado, M. Kit, Frances S. Shofer, Mitesh S. Patel, Scott Halpern, Christopher Edwards, Zachary F. Meisel, and Jeanmarie Perrone. "Association Between Electronic Medical Record Implementation of Default Opioid Prescription Quantities and Prescribing Behavior in Two Emergency Departments." *Journal of General Internal Medicine* 33, no. 4 (January 6, 2018): 1–3. doi:10.1007/s11606-017-4286-5.

DeRoos, Luke J. et al. "Estimated Association Between Organ Availability and Presumed Consent in Solid Organ Transplant." *Jama Network Open* 2, no. 10 (October 2, 2019): e1912431. doi:10.1001/jamanetworkopen.2019.12431.

DeShong, Travis. "Do Drivers Think You're a 'Ridezilla'? Better Check Your Uber Rating." *Washington Post*, July 18, 2019. https://www.washingtonpost.com/lifestyle/do-drivers-think-youre-a-ridezilla-better-check-your-uber-rating/2019/07/18/8b441588-a291-11e9-b732-41a79c2551bf_story.html.

Dhingra, Nikhil, Zach Gorn, Andrew Kerner, and Jason Dana. "The Default Pull: An Experimental Demonstration of Subtle Default Effects on Preferences." *Judgment and Decision Making* 7, no. 1 (2012): 69.

"Did Trump Win Because His Name Came First in Key States?" BBC News, February 25, 2017. https://www.bbc.com/news/magazine-39082465.

Diehl, Kristin. "When Two Rights Make a Wrong: Searching Too Much in Ordered Environments." *Journal of Marketing Research* 42, no. 3 (2005): 313–22. doi:10.1509/jmkr.2005.42.3.313.

Diehl, Kristin, Laura J. Kornish, and John G. Lynch. "Smart Agents: When Lower Search Costs for Quality Information Increase Price

Sensitivity." *Journal of Consumer Research* 30, no. 1 (June 1, 2003): 56–71. doi:10.1086/374698.

Dinner, Isaac, Eric J. Johnson, Daniel G. Goldstein, and Kaiya Liu. "Partitioning Default Effects: Why People Choose Not to Choose." *Journal of Experimental Psychology: Applied* 17, no. 4 (December 2011): 332–41. doi:10.1037/a0024354.

Doerfler, W. "Menu Design for Effective Merchandising." *Cornell Hotel and Restaurant Administration Quarterly* 19, no. 3 (1978): 38–46.

Dowray, Sunaina, Jonas J. Swartz, Danielle Braxton, and Anthony J. Viera. "Potential Effect of Physical Activity Based Menu Labels on the Calorie Content of Selected Fast Food Meals." *Appetite* 62 (March 2013): 173–81. doi:10.1016/j.appet.2012.11.013.

Drèze, Xavier, Stephen J. Hoch, and Mary E. Purk. "Shelf Management and Space Elasticity." *Journal of Retailing* 70, no. 4 (1994): 301–26. doi:10.1016/0022-4359(94)90002-7.

Ebeling, Felix, and Sebastian Lotz. "Domestic Uptake of Green Energy Promoted by Opt-out Tariffs." *Nature Climate Change* 5, no. 9 (2015): 868–71. doi:10.1038/nclimate2681.

Egan, Patrick J., and Megan Mullin. "Turning Personal Experience into Political Attitudes: The Effect of Local Weather on Americans' Perceptions about Global Warming." *Journal of Politics* 74, no. 3 (July 2012): 796–809. doi:10.1017/s0022381612000448.

Eisenstein, Eric M., and Stephen J. Hoch. "Intuitive Compounding: Framing, Temporal Perspective, and Expertise." 2008. http://www.eric-eisenstein.com/papers/Eisenstein%26Hoch-Compounding.pdf.

Eleftheriou-Smith, Loulla-Mae. "All French Citizens Are Now Organ Donors Unless They Opt Out." *Independent*, January 4, 2017. https://www.independent.co.uk/news/world/europe/french-citizens-organ-donors-france-opt-out-donation-hospital-healthcare-doctors-a7508576.html.

Elgot, Jessica. "Commons May Never Return to Packed Chamber Debates, Says Speaker." *Guardian*, July 26, 2020. https://www.theguardian.com/politics/2020/jul/26/lindsay-hoyle-commons-may-never-return-to-packed-chamber-debates-says-speaker-coronavirus.

Empson, Rip. "Practice Fusion Continues to Reach Beyond Digital Health Records, Adds Free Expense Tracking to New Booking Engine." *TechCrunch*, May 22, 2013. https://techcrunch.com/2013/05/22/practice-fusion-continues-to-reach-beyond-digital-health-records-adds-free-expense-tracking-to-new-booking-engine.

"Envision Version 2.0: A Rating System for Sustainable Infrastructure." Institute for Sustainable Infrastructure, 2012. https://sustainable-infrastructure-tools.org/tools/envision-rating-system.

Etherington, Darrell. "Daily Dating Site Coffee Meets Bagel Lands $600K from Lightbank, Match.Com Co-Founder." *TechCrunch*, September 26, 2012. https://techcrunch.com/2012/09/26/daily-dating-site-coffee-meets-bagel-lands-600k-from-lightbank-match-com-co-founder.

Ezarik, Justine. "iPhone Bill." YouTube, August 13, 2007. https://youtu.be/UdULhkh6yeA.

Fabre, John, Paul Murphy, and Rafael Matesanz. "Presumed Consent: A Distraction in the Quest for Increasing Rates of Organ Donation." *BMJ* 341, no. 2 (October 18, 2010): c4973. doi:10.1136/bmj.c4973.

Farzan, Antonia Noori. "A Tech Company Gave Doctors Free Software—Rigged to Encourage Them to Prescribe Opioids, Prosecutors Say." *Washington Post*, January 28, 2020. https://www.washingtonpost.com/nation/2020/01/28/opioid-kickback-software/.

Feenberg, Daniel, Ina Ganguli, Patrick Gaulé, and Jonathan Gruber. "It's Good to Be First: Order Bias in Reading and Citing NBER Working Papers." *Review of Economics and Statistics* 99 (March 2017): 32–39. doi:10.3386/w21141.

Fernandes, Daniel, John G. Lynch Jr., and Richard G. Netemeyer. "Financial Literacy, Financial Education, and Downstream Financial Behaviors." *Management Science* 60, no. 8 (2014): 1861–83. doi:10.1287/mnsc.2013.1849.

Fried, Terri R., Elizabeth H. Bradley, Virginia R. Towle, and Heather Allore. "Understanding the Treatment Preferences of Seriously Ill Patients." *New England Journal of Medicine* 346, no. 14 (2002): 1061–66. doi:10.1056/nejmsa012528.

Gabaix, Xavier, and David Laibson. "Shrouded Attributes, Consumer Myopia, and Information Suppression in Competitive Markets." *Quarterly Journal of Economics* 121 (June 1, 2006): 505–40.

Gaffney, Dennis. "This Guy Can Get 59 MPG in a Plain Old Accord. Beat That, Punk." *Mother Jones*, January–February 2007. https://www.motherjones.com/politics/2007/01/guy-can-get-59-mpg-plain-old-accord-beat-punk/.

Garber, Jonathan. "A Company Called Zoom Technologies Is Surging Because People Think It's Zoom Video Communications (ZOOM, ZM)." *Markets Insider*, April 18, 2019. https://markets.businessinsider.com/news/stocks/publicly-listed-zoom-video-communications-traders-buying-zoom-technologies-2019-4-1028122561?op=1.

Giovanelli, Justin, and Emily Curran. "Efforts to Support Consumer Enrollment Decisions Using Total Cost Estimators: Lessons from the Affordable Care Act's Marketplaces." Commonwealth Fund, 2017. https://www.commonwealthfund.org/publications/issue-briefs/2017/feb/efforts-support-consumer-enrollment-decisions-using-total-cost.

Glazerman, Steven, Ira Nichols-Barrer, Jon Valant, Jesse Chandler, and Alyson Burnett. "The Choice Architecture of School Choice Websites." *Journal of Research on Educational Effectiveness* 13, no. 2 (2020): 1–29. doi:10.1080/19345747.2020.1716905.

Glazier, Alexandra, and Thomas Mone. "Success of Opt-In Organ Donation Policy in the United States." *JAMA* 322, no. 8 (August 8, 2019): 719–20. doi:10.1001/jama.2019.9187.

Goldstein, Daniel G., Eric J. Johnson, Andreas Herrmann, and Mark Heitmann. "Nudge Your Customers Toward Better Choices." *Harvard Business Review* 86, no. 12 (December 1, 2008).

Goldstein, Daniel G, Eric J. Johnson, and William F. Sharpe. "Choosing Outcomes versus Choosing Products: Consumer-Focused Retirement Investment Advice." *Journal of Consumer Research* 35, no. 3 (2008): 440–56. doi:10.1086/589562.

Goldstein, Daniel G., and David Rothschild. "Lay Understanding of Probability Distributions." *Judgment and Decision Making* 9, no. 1 (January 1, 2014): 1–14. http://journal.sjdm.org/13/131029/jdm131029.pdf.

Gomez-Uribe, Carlos A. and Neil Hunt. "The Netflix Recommender System: Algorithms, Business Value, and Innovation." *ACM Transactions on Management Information* Systems 6, no. 4 (December 2015): 1–19.

Grant, Darren. "The Ballot Order Effect Is Huge: Evidence from Texas." *Public Choice* 172, no. 3–4 (May 18, 2017): 421–42. doi:10.1007/s11127-017-0454-8.

Green, Adam. "How Derren Brown Remade Mind Reading for Skeptics." *New Yorker*, September 30, 2019. https://www.newyorker.com/magazine/2019/10/07/how-derren-brown-remade-mind-reading-for-skeptics.

Greenleaf, Eric A., Eric J. Johnson, Vicki G. Morwitz, and Edith Shalev. "The Price Does Not Include Additional Taxes, Fees, and Surcharges: A Review of Research on Partitioned Pricing." *Journal of Consumer Psychology* 26, no. 1 (2016): 105–24. doi:10.1016/j.jcps.2015.04.006.

Hafner, Katie. "AT&T's Overstuffed iPhone Bills Annoy Customers." *New York Times*, August 23, 2007. https://www.nytimes.com/2007/08/23/business/23bill.html?em&ex=1188014400&en=de1fe8dde56cab98&ei=5087%0A.

Haggag, Kareem, and Giovanni Paci. "Default Tips." *American Economic Journal: Applied Economics* 6, no. 3 (2014): 1–19. doi:10.1257/app.6.3.1.

Halpern, Scott D., George Loewenstein, Kevin G. Volpp, Elizabeth Cooney, Kelly Vranas, Caroline M. Quill, Mary S. McKenzie et al. "Default Options in Advance Directives Influence How Patients Set Goals for End-Of-Life Care." *Health Affairs* 32, no. 2 (February 1, 2013): 408–17. doi:10.1377/hlthaff.2012.0895.

Halpern, Scott D., Dylan S. Small, Andrea B. Troxel, Elizabeth Cooney, Brian Bayes, Marzana Chowdhury, Heather E. Tomko et al. "Effect of Default Options in Advance Directives on Hospital-Free Days and Care Choices among Seriously Ill Patients." *JAMA Network Open* 3, no. 3 (March 2, 2020): e201742. doi:10.1001/jamanetworkopen.2020.1742.

Hamilton, Lawrence C., and Mary D. Stampone. "Blowin' in the Wind: Short-Term Weather and Belief in Anthropogenic Climate Change." *Weather, Climate, and Society* 5, no. 2 (February 23, 2013): 130123150419007–119. doi:10.1175/wcas-d-12-00048.1.

Hardisty, David J., Eric J. Johnson, and Elke U. Weber. "A Dirty Word or a Dirty World?" *Psychological Science* 21, no. 1 (January 13, 2010): 86–92. doi:10.1177/0956797609355572.

Hardwick, Joshua. "Top 100 Most Visited Websites by Search Traffic (as of 2020)." *Ahrefsblog*, 2020. https://ahrefs.com/blog/most-visited-websites/.

Haskin, David. "Technology's 10 Most Mortifying Moments." *Computerworld*, October 17, 2007. https://www.computerworld.com/article/2539067/technology-s-10-most-mortifying-moments.html?page=2.

Heath, Chip, Richard P. Larrick, and George Wu. "Goals as Reference Points." *Cognitive Psychology* 38 (1999): 79–109.

Hedlin, Simon, and Cass R. Sunstein. "Does Active Choosing Promote Green Energy Use: Experimental Evidence." *Ecology Law Quarterly* 43, no. 1 (2016). doi:http://dx.doi.org/10.2139/ssrn.2624359.

Helman, Ruth, Craig Copeland, and Jack VanDerhei. "The 2015 Retirement Confidence Survey: Having a Retirement Savings Plan a Key Factor in Americans' Retirement Confidence." Employee Benefit Research Institute, April 21, 2015. https://www.ebri.org/content/the-2015-retirement-confidence-survey-having-a-retirement-savings-plan-a-key-factor-in-americans-retirement-confidence-5513.

Henrich, Joseph, Robert Boyd, Samuel Bowles, Colin Camerer, Ernst Fehr, and Herbert Gintis. *Foundations of Human Sociality: Economic Experiments and Ethnographic Evidence from Fifteen Small-Scale Societies*. Oxford University Press, 2004. doi:10.1093/0199262055.001.0001.

Ho, Daniel E., and Kosuke Imai. "Estimating Causal Effects of Ballot Order from a Randomized Natural Experiment: The California Alphabet Lottery, 1978–2002." *Public Opinion Quarterly* 72, no. 2 (May 21, 2008): 216–40. doi:10.1093/poq/nfn018.

Hofman, Jake M., Daniel G. Goldstein, and Jessica Hullman. "How Visualizing Inferential Uncertainty Can Mislead Readers about Treatment Effects in Scientific Results." Proceedings of the 2020 CHI Conference on Human Factors in Computing Systems, April 1, 2020, 1–12. doi:10.1145/3313831.3376454.

Holladay, Becca. "Alexander Kearns Remembered by UNL Community as Positive, Always Willing to Help." *Daily Nebraskan*, June 23, 2020. http://www.dailynebraskan.com/news/alexander-kearns-remem bered-by-unl-community-as-positive-always-willing-to-help/article _774332ec-b575-11ea-80de-6f15d51a3087.html.

Hoover, Hanna. "Default Tip Suggestions in NYC Taxi Cabs." *SSRN Electronic Journal*, March 15, 2019. doi:10.2139/ssrn.3333460.

"House of Commons Rebuilding: HC Deb 28 October 1943 Vol 393 Cc403-73." *Hansard 1803–2005*, October 28, 1943. https://api.par liament.uk/historic-hansard/commons/1943/oct/28/house-of -commons-rebuilding.

House of Lords, Science and Technology Select Committee. "Behavior Change (Second Report)." London, United Kingdom: Authority of the House of Lords, July 19, 2011.

"How the Retirement Estimator Works." Social Security Administration. https://www.ssa.gov/benefits/retirement/estimator.html. Accessed March 24, 2016.

Hulgaard, Kasper, Emilia Herrick, Thomas Køster Madsen, Johannes Schuldt-Jensen, Mia Maltesen, and Pelle Guldborg Hansen. "Nudging Passenger Flow in CPH Airports." INudgeYou.com, June 17, 2016. https://inudgeyou.com/wp-content/uploads/2017/08/OP-ENG -Passenger_Flow.pdf.

Hullman, Jessica, Paul Resnick, and Eytan Adar. "Hypothetical Outcome Plots Outperform Error Bars and Violin Plots for Inferences about Reliability of Variable Ordering." *PLoS One* 10, no. 11 (2015): e0142444. doi:10.1371/journal.pone.0142444.

Irwin, Neil. "How Economists Can Be Just as Irrational as the Rest of Us." *New York Times*, September 4, 2015. http://nyti.ms/1N7iyXZ.

Jachimowicz, Jon M., Shannon Duncan, Elke U. Weber, and Eric J. Johnson. "When and Why Defaults Influence Decisions: A Meta-Analysis of Default Effects." *Behavioural Public Policy* 3, no. 2 (2019): 159–86. doi:10.1017/bpp.2018.43.

Jena, Anupam B., Michael Barnett, and Dana Goldman. "How Health Care Providers Can Help End the Overprescription of Opioids." *Harvard Business Review*, October 24, 2017. https://hbr.org/2017/10/how-health-care-providers-can-help-end-the-overprescription-of-opioids.

Johnson, Eric J., and Daniel G. Goldstein. "Decisions by Default." In *The Behavioral Foundations of Public Policy*, edited by Eldar Shafir. (Princeton, NJ: Princeton University Press, 2012), 417–27.

———. "Do Defaults Save Lives?" *Science* 302, no. 5649 (November 21, 2003): 1338–39. doi:10.1126/science.1091721.

Johnson, Eric J., Ran Hassin, Tom Baker, Allison T. Bajger, and Galen Treuer. "Can Consumers Make Affordable Care Affordable? The Value of Choice Architecture," edited by Thomas Boraud. *PLoS One* 8, no. 12 (2013): e81521. doi:10.1371/journal.pone.0081521.

Johnson, Eric J., Gerald Häubl, and Anat Keinan. "Aspects of Endowment: A Query Theory of Value Construction." *Journal of Experimental Psychology: Learning, Memory, and Cognition* 33, no. 3 (2007): 461–74. doi:10.1037/0278-7393.33.3.461.

Johnson, Eric J., John Hershey, Jacqueline Meszaros, and Howard Kunreuther. "Framing, Probability Distortions, and Insurance Decisions." *Journal of Risk and Uncertainty* 7, no. 1 (January 1, 1993): 35–51. doi:10.1007/BF01065313.

Johnson, Eric J., and John W. Payne. "Effort and Accuracy in Choice." *Management Science* 31, no. 4 (April 1985): 395–414. doi:10.1287/mnsc.31.4.395.

Johnson, Eric J., Suzanne B. Shu, Benedict G. C. Dellaert, Craig Fox, Daniel G. Goldstein, Gerald Häubl, Richard P. Larrick et al. "Beyond Nudges: Tools of a Choice Architecture." *Marketing Letters* 23, no. 2 (May 25, 2012): 487–504. doi:10.1007/s11002-012-9186-1.

Johnson, Steve. "Apple, AT&T Shares Fall on Fewer-than-Expected iPhone Subscriptions." *Mercury News*, July 24, 2007. https://www.mercurynews.com/2007/07/24/apple-att-shares-fall-on-fewer-than-expected-iphone-subscriptions/.

Jung, Minah H., Chengyao Sun, and Leif D. Nelson. "People Can Recognize, Learn, and Apply Default Effects in Social Influence." *Proceedings of the National Academy of Sciences* 115, no. 35 (August 14, 2018). doi:10.1073/pnas.1810986115.

Kahneman, Daniel, Jack L. Knetsch, and Richard H. Thaler. "Experimental Tests of the Endowment Effect and the Coase Theorem." *Journal of Political Economy* 98, no. 6 (December 1990): 1325–48. http://www.jstor.org/stable/2937761.

Kaiser, Micha, Manuela Bernauer, Cass R. Sunstein, and Lucia A. Reisch. "The Power of Green Defaults: The Impact of Regional Variation of Opt-Out Tariffs on Green Energy Demand in Germany." *Ecological Economics* 174 (August 1, 2020): 106685. doi:10.1016/j.ecolecon .2020.106685.

Kam, Dara. "No, Donald Trump's Name Will Not Appear Automatically at the Top of Your Ballot." *Orlando Weekly*, November 18, 2019. https://www.orlandoweekly.com/Blogs/archives/2019/11/18/no -donald-trumps-name-will-not-appear-automatically-at-the -top-of-your-ballot-ending-a-70-year-old-state-law.

Karchmer, Michael A., and Eugene Winograd. "The John Brown Effect." *Psychonomic Science* 25, no. 4 (1971): 224–25. doi:10.3758/bf033 29100.

Kaufmann, Christine, Martin Weber, and Emily Haisley. "The Role of Experience Sampling and Graphical Displays on One's Investment Risk Appetite." *Management Science* 59, no. 2 (2013): 323–40. doi:10.1287/mnsc.1120.1607.

Kaye, Kate. "Use of Limit Ad Tracking Drops as Ad Blocking Grows." *AdAge*, May 9, 2016. https://adage.com/article/privacy-and-regulation /limit-ad-tracking-drops-ad-blocking-grows/303911.

Keh, Andrew. "Eliud Kipchoge Breaks Two-Hour Marathon Barrier." *New York Times*, October 12, 2019. https://www.nytimes.com/2019 /10/12/sports/eliud-kipchoge-marathon-record.html.

Kim, Jungkeun, Euejung Hwang, Jooyoung Park, Jacob C. Lee, and Jong-won Park. "Position Effects of Menu Item Displays in Consumer Choices: Comparisons of Horizontal Versus Vertical Displays." *Cornell Hospitality Quarterly* 60, no. 2 (July 17, 2018): 116–24. doi:10.1177/1938965518778234.

Kim, Nuri, Jon Krosnick, and Daniel Casasanto. "Moderators of Candidate Name-Order Effects in Elections: An Experiment." *Political Psychology* 36, no. 5 (March 13, 2014): 525–42. doi:10.1111/pops.12178.

Kincaid, Clark S., and David L. Corsun. "Are Consultants Blowing Smoke? An Empirical Test of the Impact of Menu Layout on Item Sales." *International Journal of Contemporary Hospitality Management* 15, no. 4 (2003): 226–31. https://doi.org/10.1108/09596110310475685.

King, Amy, and Andrew Leigh. "Are Ballot Order Effects Heterogeneous?" *Social Science Quarterly* 90, no. 1 (March 1, 2009): 71–87. doi:10.1111/j.1540-6237.2009.00603.x.

Knoll, Melissa A. Z., Kirstin C. Appelt, Eric J. Johnson, and Jonathan E. Westfall. "Time to Retire: Why Americans Claim Benefits Early and

How to Encourage Delay." *Behavioral Science and Policy* 1, no. 1 (2015): 53–62.

Koppell, J. G. S., and J. A. Steen. "The Effects of Ballot Position on Election Outcomes." *Journal of Politics* 66, no. 1 (February 1, 2004): 267–81. doi:10.1046/j.1468-2508.2004.00151.x.

Kristensen, Emil. "8 E-Commerce A/B Testing Examples You Can Learn From." *Sleeknote*, March 7, 2019. https://sleeknote.com/blog/a-b -testing-examples.

Krosnick, J. A., J. M. Miller, and M. P. Tichy. "An Unrecognized Need for Ballot Reform: The Effects of Candidate Name Order on Election Outcome." In *Rethinking the Vote: The Politics and Prospects of American Election Reform*, edited by Ann N. Crigler, Marion R. Just, and Edward J. McCaffer. Oxford University Press, 2003: 51–74.

Laberee, Leonard W., and Whitfield J. Bell, eds. *Mr. Franklin: A Selection from His Personal Letters.* New Haven, CT: Yale University Press, 1956.

Langewiesche, William. "Anatomy of a Miracle." *Vanity Fair*, June 2009.

Larrick, Richard P., and Jack B. Soll. "The MPG Illusion." *Science* 320, no. 5883 (June 20, 2008): 1593–94. doi:10.1126/science.1154983.

Leswig, Kif. "Apple Makes Billions from Google's Dominance in Search— and It's a Bigger Business than iCloud or Apple Music." *Business Insider*, September 29, 2018. https://www.businessinsider.com/aapl -share-price-google-pays-apple-9-billion-annually-tac-goldman- 2018-9.

Levin, Irwin P., and Richard D. Johnson. "Estimating Price-Quality Tradeoffs Using Comparative Judgments." *Journal of Consumer Research* 11, no. 1 (1984): 593–600. doi:10.2307/2489146.

Li, Ye, and Nicholas Epley. "When the Best Appears to Be Saved for Last: Serial Position Effects on Choice." *Journal of Behavioral Decision Making* 22, no. 4 (October 2009): 378–89. doi:10.1002/bdm.638.

Lichtenstein, Sarah, and Paul Slovic. *The Construction of Preference.* Cambridge, UK: Cambridge University Press, 2006.

Loewenstein, George, Cindy Bryce, David Hagmann, and Sachin Rajpal. "Warning: You Are about to Be Nudged." *Behavioral Science and Policy* 1, no. 1 (2015): 35–42. doi:10.1353/bsp.2015.0000.

LoGiurato, Brett. "Meet the 16-Year-Old Kid Who Got to Introduce President Obama In Brooklyn." *Business Insider*, October 27, 2013. https://www.businessinsider.com/radcliffe-saddler-obama-brooklyn -speech-p-tech-2013-10.

Long, Michael W., Deirdre K. Tobias, Angie L. Cradock, Holly Batchelder, and Steven L. Gortmaker. "Systematic Review and Meta-Analysis of the Impact of Restaurant Menu Calorie Labeling." *American Journal of Public Health* 105, no. 5 (2015): e11–24. doi:10.2105/ajph .2015.302570.

Lopez, German. "Purdue Pharma Pleads Guilty to Criminal Charges in $8 Billion Settlement with the Justice Department." *Vox*, October 21, 2020. https://www.vox.com/2020/10/21/21526868/purdue-pharma -oxycontin-opioid-epidemic-department-of-justice.

Low, How-Cheng, Maureen Da Costa, Krishnan Prabhakaran, Manjit Kaur, Aileen Wee, Seng-Gee Lim, and Chun-Tao Wai. "Impact of New Legislation on Presumed Consent on Organ Donation on Liver Transplant in Singapore: A Preliminary Analysis." *Transplantation* 82, no. 9 (November 15, 2006): 1234–37. doi:10.1097/01.tp.000023 6720.66204.16.

Lynch, John G., and Dan Ariely. "Wine Online: Search Costs Affect Competition on Price, Quality, and Distribution." *Marketing Science* 19, no. 1 (December 1, 2000): 83–103. doi:10.1287/mksc.19.1.83.15183.

MacDonald, John. "How Long Do Workers Consider Retirement Decision?" Employee Benefit Research Institute, July 16, 2008. https:// www.ebri.org/crawler/view/how-long-do-workers-consider -retirement-decision.

Malhotra, Sameer, Adam D. Cheriff, J. Travis Gossey, Curtis L. Cole, Rainu Kaushal, and Jessica S. Ancker. "Effects of an E-Prescribing Interface Redesign on Rates of Generic Drug Prescribing: Exploiting Default Options." *Journal of the American Medical Informatics Association* 23, no. 5 (February 17, 2016): ocv192-9. doi:10.1093/jamia/ ocv192.

Mandel, Naomi, and Eric J. Johnson. "When Web Pages Influence Choice: Effects of Visual Primes on Experts and Novices." *Journal of Consumer Research* 29, no. 2 (February 1, 2002): 235–45. doi:10.1086/ 341573.

Mantonakis, Antonia, Pauline Rodero, Isabelle Lesschaeve, and Reid Hastie. "Order in Choice: Effects of Serial Position on Preferences." *Psychological Science* 20, no. 11 (2009): 1309–12. doi:10.1111/j.1467 -9280.2009.02453.x.

Marewski, Julian N., and Lael J. Schooler. "Cognitive Niches: An Ecological Model of Strategy Selection." *Psychological Review* 118, no. 3 (2011): 393–437. doi:10.1037/a0024143.

Matesanz, Rafael. "Factors Influencing the Adaptation of the Spanish Model of Organ Donation." *Transplant International* 16, no. 10 (2003): 736–41. doi:10.1007/s00147-003-0623-1.

Mathur, Arunesh, Gunes Acar, Michael J. Friedman, Elena Lucherini, Jonathan Mayer, Marshini Chetty, and Arvind Narayanan. "Dark

Patterns at Scale: Findings from a Crawl of 11K Shopping Websites."
Proceedings of the ACM on Human-Computer Interaction 3, no.
CSCW (November 2019): 1–32. doi:https://doi.org/10.1145/3359183.

May, Channing. "Transnational Crime and the Developing World."
Global Financial Integrity, March 2017. http://www.gfintegrity.org
/wp-content/uploads/2017/03/Transnational_Crime-final.pdf.

McAlone, Nathan. "The Exec Who Replaced Netflix's 5-Star Rating System with 'Thumbs Up, Thumbs Down' Explains Why." *Business Insider*, April 5, 2017. https://www.businessinsider.com/why-netflix
-replaced-its-5-star-rating-system-2017-4?op=1.

McKenzie, Craig R. M., Lim M. Leong, and Shlomi Sher. "Default Sensitivity in Attempts at Social Influence." *Psychonomic Bulletin and
Review* 28, no. 2 (November 2, 2020): 695–702. doi:10.3758/s13423
-020-01834-4.

McKenzie, Craig R. M., and Michael J. Liersch. "Misunderstanding Savings Growth: Implications for Retirement Savings Behavior." *Journal
of Marketing Research* 48 (February 1, 2011): S1–13. doi:10.1509/
jmkr.48.spl.s1.

McKenzie, Craig R. M., Michael J. Liersch, and Stacey R. Finkelstein.
"Recommendations Implicit in Policy Defaults." *Psychological Science* 17, no. 5 (May 1, 2006): 414–20. doi:https://doi.org/10.1111
/j.1467-9280.2006.01721.x.

Meeker, Daniella, Jeffrey A. Linder, Craig R. Fox, Mark W. Friedberg,
Stephen D. Persell, Noah J. Goldstein, Tara K. Knight, Joel W. Hay,
and Jason N. Doctor. "Effect of Behavioral Interventions on Inappropriate Antibiotic Prescribing among Primary Care Practices: A Randomized Clinical Trial." *JAMA* 315, no. 6 (2016): 562. doi:10.1001/
jama.2016.0275.

Menni, Cristina, Ana M. Valdes, Maxim B. Freidin, Carole H. Sudre, Long
H. Nguyen, David A. Drew, Sajaysurya Ganesh et al. "Real-Time
Tracking of Self-Reported Symptoms to Predict Potential COVID-19."
Nature Medicine 26 (2020): 1037–40. doi:10.1038/s41591-020-0916-2.

Meredith, Marc, and Yuval Salant. "On the Causes and Consequences of
Ballot Order Effects." *Political Behavior* 35, no. 1 (January 6, 2012):
175–97. doi:10.1007/s11109-011-9189-2.

Meyer, Robert J., Jay Baker, Kenneth Broad, Jeff Czajkowski, and Ben
Orlove. "The Dynamics of Hurricane Risk Perception: Real-Time
Evidence from the 2012 Atlantic Hurricane Season." *Bulletin of the
American Meteorological Society* 95, no. 9 (2014): 1389–1404.
doi:10.1175/bams-d-12-00218.1.

Meyer, Robert, Kenneth Broad, Ben Orlove, and Nada Petrovic. "Dynamic Simulation as an Approach to Understanding Hurricane Risk

Response: Insights from the Stormview Lab." *Risk Analysis* 33, no. 8 (2013): 1532–52. doi:10.1111/j.1539-6924.2012.01935.x.

Meyer, Robert, and Eric J. Johnson. "Empirical Generalizations in the Modeling of Consumer Choice." *Marketing Science* 14, no. 3 (1995): G180–89. http://www.jstor.org/stable/184160.

Miller, Joanne M., and Jon A. Krosnick. "The Impact of Candidate Name Order on Election Outcomes." *Public Opinion Quarterly* 62, no. 3 (November 1, 1998): 291–330. doi:10.1086/297848.

Morwitz, Vicki G., E. A. Greenleaf, and Eric J. Johnson. "Divide and Prosper: Consumers' Reactions to Partitioned Prices." *Journal of Marketing Research* 35 (November 1998): 453–63.

Moskowitz, Clara. "Hypermiling: Driving Tricks Stretch Miles Per Gallon." *Live Science*, July 24, 2008. Accessed August 16, 2020. https://www.livescience.com/5031-hypermiling-driving-tricks-stretch-miles-gallon.html.

Mrkva, Kellen, Nathaniel Posner, Crystal Reeck, and Eric Johnson. "Do Nudges Reduce Disparities? Choice Architecture Compensates for Low Consumer Knowledge." *Journal of Marketing*, working paper, Columbia Business School, 2020.

Muldoon, Dan, and Richard W. Kopcke. "Are People Claiming Social Security Benefits Later?" *Center for Retirement Research at Boston College*, May 1, 2008. https://crr.bc.edu/briefs/are-people-claiming-social-security-benefits-later.

Mullainathan, Sendhil, Markus Noeth, and Antoinette Schoar. "The Market for Financial Advice: An Audit Study." National Bureau of Economic Research, working paper, March 2012. doi:10.3386/w17929.

Musicus, Aviva A., Alyssa J. Moran, Hannah G. Lawman, and Christina A. Roberto. "Online Randomized Controlled Trials of Restaurant Sodium Warning Labels." *American Journal of Preventive Medicine* 57, no. 6 (December 1, 2019): e181–93. doi:10.1016/j.amepre.2019.06.024.

Nathanson, Lori, Sean P. Corcoran, and Christine Baker-Smith. "High School Choice in New York City: A Report on the School Choices and Placements of Low-Achieving Students." Research Alliance for New York City Schools, April 25, 2013.

National Transportation Safety Board. "Loss of Thrust in Both Engines After Encountering a Flock of Birds and Subsequent Ditching on the Hudson River, US Airways Flight 1549 Airbus A320–214, N106US Weehawken, New Jersey, January 15, 2009" (2010): 1–213.

Netflix. "Netflix Quick Guide: How Does Netflix Decide What's on Netflix." YouTube, June 6, 2013. https://www.youtube.com/watch?v=VvpoUh9gx58.

Nguyen, Thanh Cong, Jackie Robinson, Shinji Kaneko, and Nguyen The Chinh. "Examining Ordering Effects in Discrete Choice Experiments: A Case Study in Vietnam." *Economic Analysis and Policy* 45 (March 1, 2015): 39–57. doi:10.1016/j.eap.2015.01.003.

Nichols, Shaun. "Experimental Philosophy and the Problem of Free Will." *Science* 331, no. 6023 (2011): 1401–3. doi:10.1126/science.1192931.

Nichols, Shaun, and Joshua Knobe. "Moral Responsibility and Determinism: The Cognitive Science of Folk Intuitions." *Noûs* 41, no. 4 (2007): 663–85. doi:10.1111/j.1468-0068.2007.00666.x.

Novemsky, Nathan. "Preference Fluency in Choice." *Journal of Marketing Research* 44, no. 3 (August 1, 2007): 347–56. doi:10.1509/jmkr.44.3.347.

Obar, Jonathan A., and Anne Oeldorf-Hirsch. "The Biggest Lie on the Internet: Ignoring the Privacy Policies and Terms of Service Policies of Social Networking Services." *SSRN Electronic Journal*, 2018. doi:10.2139/ssrn.2757465.

O'Donovan, Caroline. "An Invisible Rating System at Your Favorite Chain Restaurant Is Costing Your Server." *BuzzFeed News*, June 21, 2018. https://www.buzzfeednews.com/article/carolineodonovan/ziosk-presto-tabletop-tablet-restaurant-rating-servers#.ygDPa9EW2.

O'Malley, A. James, Richard G. Frank, Atheer Kaddis, Barbara M. Rothenberg, and Barbara J. McNeil. "Impact of Alternative Interventions on Changes in Generic Dispensing Rates." *Health Services Research* 41, no. 5 (October 1, 2006): 1876–94. doi:10.1111/j.1475-6773.2006.00579.x.

Oppenheimer, Daniel M. "The Secret Life of Fluency." *Trends in Cognitive Sciences* 12, no. 6 (June 2008): 237–41. doi:10.1016/j.tics.2008.02.014.

"Organ Trafficking: The Unseen Form of Human Trafficking." *ACAMS Today*, June 26, 2018. https://www.acamstoday.org/organ-trafficking-the-unseen-form-of-human-trafficking.

Pailhès, Alice. "Mental Priming Force." *OSF*, April 9, 2020. osf.io/2z6rw.

Pailhès, Alice, and Gustav Kuhn. "Influencing Choices with Conversational Primes: How a Magic Trick Unconsciously Influences Card Choices." *Proceedings of the National Academy of Sciences of the United States of America* 117, no. 30 (2020): 17675–79. doi:10.1073/pnas.2000682117.

Panitz, B. "Does Your Menu Attract or Repel Diners?" *Restaurant USA Magazine* 8 (August 2000): 81–87.

Partners Advantage. "Getting Your Prospect to Think About Longevity, and Longevity Calculators." *Partners Advantage,* January 30, 2018.

https://blog.partnersadvantage.com/getting-your-prospect-to-think-about-longevity-and-longevity-calculators.

Payne, John W., James. R. Bettman, and Eric. J. Johnson. *The Adaptive Decision Maker.* Cambridge University Press, 1993.

Payne, John W., Namika Sagara, Suzanne B. Shu, Kirstin C. Appelt, and Eric J. Johnson. "Life Expectancy as a Constructed Belief: Evidence of a Live-to or Die-by Framing Effect." *Journal of Risk and Uncertainty* 46, no. 1 (December 29, 2012): 27–50. doi:10.1007/s11166-012-9158-0.

Perenson, Melissa J. "The 300-Page iPhone Bill to Disappear." *Network-World,* August 23, 2007. http://web.archive.org/web/2007090320 5536/http://www.networkworld.com/news/2007/082307-the-300-page-iphone-bill-to.html.

Peters, Ellen. *Innumeracy in the Wild: Misunderstanding and Misusing Numbers.* Oxford University Press, 2020.

Peters, Ellen, Daniel Västfjäll, Paul Slovic, C. K. Mertz, Ketti Mazzocco, and Stephan Dickert. "Numeracy and Decision Making." *Psychological Science* 17 (February 1, 2006): 407–13.

Peters, Jay. "Zoom Adds New Security and Privacy Measures to Prevent Zoombombing." *Verge,* April 3, 2020. https://www.theverge.com/2020/4/3/21207643/zoom-security-privacy-zoombombing-passwords-waiting-rooms-default.

Pichert, Daniel, and Konstantinos V. Katsikopoulos. "Green Defaults: Information Presentation and Pro-environmental Behaviour." *Journal of Environmental Psychology* 28, no. 1 (March 2008): 63–73. doi:10.1016/j.jenvp.2007.09.004.

"Picwell." Picwell, Inc., 2020. https://www.picwell.com.

Pope, Devin, and Uri Simonsohn. "Round Numbers as Goals." *Psychological Science* 22, no. 1 (January 2011): 71–79. doi:10.1177/0956797610391098.

Popper, Nathaniel. "Robinhood Has Lured Young Traders, Sometimes with Devastating Results." *New York Times,* July 8, 2020. https://www.nytimes.com/2020/07/08/technology/robinhood-risky-trading.html.

Popper, Nathaniel, and Michael J. de la Merced. "Robinhood Pays $65 Million Fine to Settle Charges of Misleading Customers." *New York Times,* December 17, 2020. https://www.nytimes.com/2020/12/17/business/robinhood-sec-charges.html.

Posner, Michael I., and C. R. R. Snyder. "Attention and Cognitive Control." In *Cognitive Psychology: Key Readings,* edited by David A. Balota and Elizabeth J. Marsh. Psychology Press, 2004: 205–23.

"President—Forecasting the US 2020 Elections." *Economist*. Accessed January 21, 2021. https://projects.economist.com/us-2020-forecast /president.

"President Trump's Energy Independence Policy," December 17, 2007. https://www.whitehouse.gov/briefings-statements/president-trumps -energy-independence-policy.

"Quiz and Video." The MPG Illusion. Accessed December 8, 2020. http:// www.mpgillusion.com/p/quiz-and-bideo.html.

Raghubir, Priya, and Ana Valenzuela. "Center-of-Inattention: Position Biases in Decision-Making." *Organizational Behavior and Human Decision Processes* 99, no. 1 (January 2006): 66–80. doi:10.1016/j .obhdp.2005.06.001.

Read, Daniel, Shane Frederick, and Marc Scholten. "DRIFT: An Analysis of Outcome Framing in Intertemporal Choice." *Journal of Experimental Psychology: Learning, Memory, and Cognition* 39, no. 2 (2012): 573–88. doi:10.1037/a0029177.

Read, Daniel, George Loewenstein, and Matthew Rabin. "Choice Bracketing." *Journal of Risk and Uncertainty* 19 (December 1999): 171–97.

Reber, Rolf, Pascal Wurtz, and Thomas D. Zimmermann. "Exploring 'Fringe' Consciousness: The Subjective Experience of Perceptual Fluency and Its Objective Bases." *Consciousness and Cognition* 13, no. 1 (March 2004): 47–60. doi:10.1016/s1053-8100(03)00049-7.

Reisch, Lucia A., and Cass R. Sunstein. "Do Europeans Like Nudges?" *Judgment and Decision Making* 11, no. 4 (July 4, 2016): 310–25. doi:10.2139/ssrn.2739118.

"Retirement Benefits." Social Security Administration. Accessed 2020. https://www.ssa.gov/benefits/retirement/learn.html.

Reyes, Marcela, María Luisa Garmendia, Sonia Olivares, Claudio Aqueveque, Isabel Zacarías, and Camila Corvalán. "Development of the Chilean Front-of-Package Food Warning Label." *BMC Public Health* 19, no. 1 (2019): 906. doi:10.1186/s12889-019-7118-1.

Reynolds, Dennis, Edward A. Merritt, and Sarah Pinckney. "Understanding Menu Psychology." *International Journal of Hospitality and Tourism Administration* 6, no. 1 (2005): 1–9. doi:10.1300/j149v06n01_01.

Risen, Jane L., and Clayton R. Critcher. "Visceral Fit: While in a Visceral State, Associated States of the World Seem More Likely." *Journal of Personality and Social Psychology* 100, no. 5 (2011): 777–93. doi:10 .1037/a0022460.

Rithalia, Amber, Catriona McDaid, Sara Suekarran, Lindsey Myers, and Amanda Sowden. "Impact of Presumed Consent for Organ Donation on Donation Rates: A Systematic Review." *BMJ* 338 (January 15, 2009): a3162. doi:10.1136/bmj.a3162.

Robbins, Liz. "Lost in the School Choice Maze." *New York Times*, August 11, 2019. https://www.nytimes.com/2011/05/08/nyregion/in-applying-for-high-school-some-8th-graders-find-a-maze.html.

Robinson, Carly D., Gonzalo A. Pons, Angela A. Duckworth, and Todd Rogers. "Some Middle School Students Want Behavior Commitment Devices (but Take-Up Does Not Affect Their Behavior)." *Frontiers in Psychology* 9, no. 206 (February 28, 2018). doi:10.3389/fpsyg.2018.00206.

Rogers, Stuart. "How a Publicity Blitz Caused the Myth of Subliminal Advertising." *Public Relations Quarterly* 37, no. 4 (1992): 12–17. http://www.repiev.ru/doc/subliminal.pdf.

Rosenblatt, Seth. "Ad Tracking 'Blocker' Comes to iOS6." *CNET*, September 14, 2012. https://www.cnet.com/news/ad-tracking-blocker-comes-to-ios-6/.

Rosenfeld, Michael J., Reuben J. Thomas, and Sonia Hausen. "Disintermediating Your Friends: How Online Dating in the United States Displaces Other Ways of Meeting." *Proceedings of the National Academy of Sciences of the United States of America* 116, no. 36 (September 3, 2019): 17753–58. doi.org/10.1073/pnas.1908630116.

Rozin, P., S. Scott, M. Dingley, and J. K. Urbanek. "Nudge to Nobesity I: Minor Changes in Accessibility Decrease Food Intake." *Judgment and Decision Making* 6, no. 4 (June 2011): 323–32.

Ruginski, Ian T., Alexander P. Boone, Lace M. Padilla, Le Liu, Nahal Heydari, Heidi S. Kramer, Mary Hegarty et al. "Non-expert Interpretations of Hurricane Forecast Uncertainty Visualizations." *Spatial Cognition and Computation* 16, no. 2 (2016): 154–72. doi:10.1080/13875868.2015.1137577.

Russo, J. Edward, Kurt A. Carlson, and Margaret G. Meloy. "Choosing an Inferior Alternative." *Psychological Science* 17 (October 2006): 899–904.

Saddler, Radcliffe. "The Day I Introduced Barack Obama." WNYC, November 12, 2013. https://www.wnyc.org/story/day-i-introduced-barack-obama.

Salsa, Reuben. "Subliminal Advertising Doesn't Exist." *Medium*, March 12, 2020. https://medium.com/better-marketing/subliminal-advertising-doesnt-exist-d67c0249d646.

Samuelson, William, and Richard Zeckhauser. "Status Quo Bias in Decision Making." *Journal of Risk and Uncertainty* 1 (1988): 7–59.

Santistevan, Jamie R., Brian R. Sharp, Azita G. Hamedani, Scott Fruhan, Andrew W. Lee, and Brian W. Patterson. "By Default: The Effect of Prepopulated Prescription Quantities on Opioid Prescribing in the Emergency Department." *Western Journal of Emergency Medicine: Integrating Emergency Care with Population Health* 19, no. 2 (2018): 392–97. doi:10.5811/westjem.2017.10.33798.

Saunders, Jim. "Court Refuses to Reconsider Ballot Order Ruling." WPEC CBS12 News, October 29, 2020. https://cbs12.com/news/local/court-refuses-to-reconsider-ballot-order-ruling.

Scheibehenne, Benjamin, Rainer Greifeneder, and Peter M. Todd. "Can There Ever Be Too Many Options? A Meta-Analytic Review of Choice Overload." *Journal of Consumer Research* 37, no. 3 (October 2010): 409–25. doi:10.1086/651235.

Scheibehenne, Benjamin, Peter M. Todd, and Rainer Greifeneder. "What Moderates the Too-Much-Choice Effect?" *Psychology and Marketing* 26, no. 3 (April 2009): 229–53. doi:10.1002/mar.20271.

Schwartz, Barry. *The Paradox of Choice: Why More Is Less*. HarperCollins, 2004.

Shaban, Hamza. "Uber Will Ban Passengers with Low Ratings." *Washington Post*, May 29, 2019. https://www.washingtonpost.com/technology/2019/05/29/uber-will-ban-passengers-with-low-ratings.

Sharpe, William F., Daniel G. Goldstein, and Philip W. Blythe. "The Distribution Builder: A Tool for Inferring Investor Preferences." October 10, 2000. http://web.stanford.edu/~wfsharpe/art/qpaper/qpaper.pdf.

Shealy, Tripp, Leidy Klotz, Elke U. Weber, Eric J. Johnson, and Ruth Greenspan Bell. "Using Framing Effects to Inform More Sustainable Infrastructure Design Decisions." *Journal of Construction Engineering and Management* 142, no. 9 (September 2016). doi:10.1061/(asce)co.1943-7862.0001152.

Shepherd, Lee, Ronan E. O'Carroll, and Eamonn Ferguson. "An International Comparison of Deceased and Living Organ Donation/Transplant Rates in Opt-In and Opt-Out Systems: A Panel Study." *BMC Medicine* 12, no. 1 (September 24, 2014): 1338–14. doi:10.1186/s12916-014-0131-4.

Shi, Savannah Wei, Michel Wedel, and F. G. M. Rik Pieters. "Information Acquisition During Online Decision Making: A Model-Based Exploration Using Eye-Tracking Data." *Management Science* 59, no. 5 (May 2013): 1009–26. doi:10.1287/mnsc.1120.1625.

Shrank, William H., Tuyen Hoang, Susan L. Ettner, Peter A. Glassman, Kavita Nair, Dee DeLapp, June Dirstine, Jerry Avorn, and Steven M. Asch. "The Implications of Choice: Prescribing Generic or Preferred

Pharmaceuticals Improves Medication Adherence for Chronic Conditions." *Archives of Internal Medicine* 166, no. 3 (2006): 332–37. doi:10.1001/archinte.166.3.332.

Simon, Dan, and Keith J. Holyoak. "Structural Dynamics of Cognition: From Consistency Theories to Constraint Satisfaction." *Personality and Social Psychology Review* 6 (February 1, 2002): 283–94.

Simon, Dan, Daniel C. Krawczyk, and Keith J. Holyoak. "Construction of Preferences by Constraint Satisfaction." *Psychological Science* 15, no. 5 (May 1, 2004): 331–36. doi:10.1111/j.0956-7976.2004.00678.x.

Simon, Dan, Lien B. Pham, Quang A. Lee, and Keith J. Holyoak. "The Emergence of Coherence over the Course of Decision Making." *Journal of Experimental Psychology: Learning, Memory, and Cognition* 27, no. 5 (February 1, 2001): 1250–60. doi:10.1037//0278-7393.27.5.1250.

Small World of Words. Accessed December 30, 2020. https://smallworld ofwords.org/en/project.

Smith, N. Craig, Daniel G. Goldstein, and Eric J. Johnson. "Choice Without Awareness: Ethical and Policy Implications of Defaults." *Journal of Public Policy and Marketing* 32, no. 2 (September 1, 2013): 159–72. doi:10.1509/0743-9156-32.2.159.

Soll, Jack B., Ralph L. Keeney, and Richard P. Larrick. "Consumer Misunderstanding of Credit Card Use, Payments, and Debt: Causes and Solutions." *Journal of Public Policy and Marketing* 32, no. 1 (May 29, 2013): 66–81. doi:10.1509/jppm.11.061.

Song, Changcheng. "Financial Illiteracy and Pension Contributions: A Field Experiment on Compound Interest in China." *Review of Financial Studies* 33, no. 2 (February 2020): 916–49. doi:10.1093/rfs/hhz074.

Song, Jae, and Joyce Manchester. "Have People Delayed Claiming Retirement Benefits? Responses to Changes in Social Security Rules." *Social Security Bulletin* 67, no. 2 (2007): 1–23. https://pubmed.ncbi.nlm.nih .gov/18457082.

Stango, Victor, and Jonathan Zinman. "Exponential Growth Bias and Household Finance." *Journal of Finance* 64, no. 6 (2009): 2807–49. doi:10.1111/j.1540-6261.2009.01518.x.

Steffel, Mary, Elanor F. Williams, and David Tannenbaum. "Does Changing Defaults Save Lives? Effects of Presumed Consent Organ Donation Policies." *Behavioral Science and Policy* 5, no. 1 (2019): 68–88. doi:10.1353/bsp.2019.0005.

Sunstein, Cass R., and Lucia A. Reisch. "Automatically Green: Behavioral Economics and Environmental Protection." *Harvard Environmental Law Review* 38, no. 1 (2014). doi:http://dx.doi.org/10.2139/ssrn .2245657.

―――. "Green by Default." *Kyklos* 66, no. 3 (August 1, 2013): 398–402. doi:10.1111/kykl.12028.

Sunstein, Cass R., Lucia A. Reisch, and Julius Rauber. "A World-Wide Consensus on Nudging? Not Quite, but Almost." *Regulation and Governance* 12 (March 2018): 3–22. doi: https://doi.org/10.1111/rego.12161.

Taillie, Lindsey Smith, Marcela Reyes, M. Arantxa Colchero, Barry Popkin, and Camila Corvalán. "An Evaluation of Chile's Law of Food Labeling and Advertising on Sugar-Sweetened Beverage Purchases from 2015 to 2017: A Before-and-After Study." *PLOS Medicine* 17, no. 2 (2020): e1003015. doi:10.1371/journal.pmed.1003015.

Thaler, Richard H., and Eric J. Johnson. "Gambling with the House Money and Trying to Break Even—The Effects of Prior Outcomes on Risky Choice." *Management Science* 36, no. 6 (June 1990): 643–60.

Thaler, Richard H., and Cass R. Sunstein. *Nudge.* Penguin Books, 2009.

"300-Page iPhone Bill." *Wikipedia*, December 20, 2020. https://en.wikipedia.org/wiki/300-page_iPhone_bill.

"2016 Election Forecast." FiveThirtyEight.com. Accessed January 21, 2021. https://projects.fivethirtyeight.com/2016-election-forecast/.

"2019 National Survey of Organ Donation Attitudes and Practices: Report of Findings." Health Resources and Services Administration, February 2020. https://www.organdonor.gov/about-dot/grants/research-reports.

"The Tyranny of Choice: You Choose." *Economist*, December 16, 2010. https://www.economist.com/christmas-specials/2010/12/16/you-Choose.

Undorf, Monika, and Malte F. Zimdahl. "Metamemory and Memory for a Wide Range of Font Sizes: What Is the Contribution of Perceptual Fluency?" *Journal of Experimental Psychology: Learning, Memory, and Cognition* 45, no. 1 (January 2019): 97–109. doi:10.1037/xlm0000571.

Ungemach, Christoph, Adrian R. Camilleri, Eric J. Johnson, Richard P. Larrick, and Elke U. Weber. "Translated Attributes: Aligning Consumers' Choices and Goals Through Signposts." *Management Science* (June 9, 2014), 1–39. doi:https://doi.org/10.1287/mnsc.2016.2703.

United States of America v. Practice Fusion, Inc., No. 2:20-cr-00011 (United States District Court for the District of Vermont, January 27, 2020).

U.S. Department of Energy. "Gas Mileage of 2008 Honda Civic," n.d. https://www.fueleconomy.gov/feg/bymodel/2008_Honda_Civic.shtml.

U.S. Department of Health and Human Services, Centers for Disease Control and Prevention. "Checklist for Prescribing Opioids for

Chronic Pain." February 25, 2016. https://www.cdc.gov/drugoverdose /pdf/pdo_checklist-a.pdf.

Ursu, Raluca M. "The Power of Rankings: Quantifying the Effect of Rankings on Online Consumer Search and Purchase Decisions." *Marketing Science* 37 no. 4 (June 29, 2018): 530–52. https://doi.org /10.1287/mksc.2017.1072.

Valentino-DeVries, Jennifer. "How E-Commerce Sites Manipulate You into Buying Things You May Not Want." *New York Times*, June 24, 2019. https://www.nytimes.com/2019/06/24/technology/e-commerce -dark-patterns-psychology.html.

Wakabayashi, Daisuke, and Jack Nicas. "Apple, Google and a Deal That Controls the Internet." *New York Times*, October 25, 2020. https:// www.nytimes.com/2020/10/25/technology/apple-google-search -antitrust.html.

"Wales' Organ Donation Opt-Out Law Has Not Increased Donors." BBC News, December 4, 2017. http://www.bbc.com/news/uk-wales -42213813.

Wall, Daniel, Raymond D. Crookes, Eric J. Johnson, and Elke U. Weber. "Risky Choice Frames Shift the Structure and Emotional Valence of Internal Arguments: A Query Theory Account of the Unusual Disease Problem." *Judgment and Decision Making* 15, no. 5 (2020): 685–703. doi:http://journal.sjdm.org/20/200604a/jdm200604a.pdf.

Wansink, Brian, and Katie Love. "Slim by Design: Menu Strategies for Promoting High-Margin, Healthy Foods." *International Journal of Hospitality Management* 42 (September 1, 2014): 137–43. doi:10 .1016/j.ijhm.2014.06.006.

Waters, Michael. "Meet the 'Menu Engineers' Helping Restaurants Re- tool During the Pandemic." *Hustle*, August 29, 2020. https://thehustle .co/meet-the-menu-engineers-helping-restaurants-retool-during-the -pandemic/.

Weber, E. U., E. J. Johnson, K. F. Milch, H. Chang, J. C. Brodscholl, and D. G. Goldstein. "Asymmetric Discounting in Intertemporal Choice." *Psychological Science* 18, no. 6 (June 2007): 516–23. doi:10.1111/ j.1467-9280.2007.01932.x.

Wichter, Zach, and Micah Maidenberg. "More Jobs Will Be Cleared for Takeoff. Aspiring Pilots Are Ready." *New York Times*, May 27, 2018. https://www.nytimes.com/2018/05/27/business/airlines-jobs-aspiring -pilots.html.

Wodtke, Carl von. "Sully Speaks Out." HistoryNet.Com, October 18, 2016. https://www.historynet.com/sully-speaks-out.htm.

Wurtz, Pascal, Rolf Reber, and Thomas D. Zimmermann. "The Feeling of Fluent Perception: A Single Experience from Multiple Asynchronous

Sources." *Consciousness and Cognition* 17, no. 1 (March 2008): 171–84. doi:10.1016/j.concog.2007.07.001.

Yadav, Kuldeep N., Nicole B. Gabler, Elizabeth Cooney, Saida Kent, Jennifer Kim, Nicole Herbst, Adjoa Mante, Scott D. Halpern, and Katherine R. Courtright. "Approximately One in Three US Adults Completes Any Type of Advance Directive for End-Of-Life Care." *Health Affairs* 36, no. 7 (2017): 1244–51. doi:10.1377/hlthaff.2017.0175.

Yang, Sybil S. "Eye Movements on Restaurant Menus: A Revisitation on Gaze Motion and Consumer Scanpaths." *International Journal of Hospitality Management* 31, no. 3 (September 2012): 1021–29. doi:10.1016/j.ijhm.2011.12.008.

Zaval, Lisa, Elizabeth A. Keenan, Eric J. Johnson, and Elke U. Weber. "How Warm Days Increase Belief in Global Warming." *Nature Climate Change* 4, no. 2 (January 12, 2014): 143–47. doi:10.1038/nclimate2093.

Zazulia, Nicholas. "Early College High School a Strong Path for IBM's Radcliffe Saddler." *U.S. News*, May 6, 2016. https://www.usnews.com/news/stem-solutions/articles/2016-05-06/early-college-high-school-a-strong-path-for-ibms-radcliffe-saddler.

Zink, Sheldon, and Stacey Wertlieb. "A Study of the Presumptive Approach to Consent for Organ Donation." *Critical Care Nurse* 26, no. 2 (2006): 129–36. https://doi.org/10.4037/ccn2006.26.2.129.

Zlatev, Julian J., David P. Daniels, Hajin Kim, and Margaret A. Neale. "Default Neglect in Attempts at Social Influence." *Proceedings of the National Academy of Sciences of the United States of America* 114, no. 52 (December 26, 2017): 13643–48. doi:10.1073/pnas.1712757114.

Zúñiga-Fajuri, Alejandra. "Increasing Organ Donation by Presumed Consent and Allocation Priority: Chile." *Bulletin of the World Health Organization* 93, no. 3 (March 1, 2015): 199–202. doi:10.2471/blt.14.139535.

Zwank, Michael D., Shaun M. Kennedy, Logan H. Stuck, and Bradley D. Gordon. "Removing Default Dispense Quantity from Opioid Prescriptions in the Electronic Medical Record." *American Journal of Emergency Medicine* 35, no. 10 (October 2017): 1567–69. doi:10.1016/j.ajem.2017.04.002.

Index